International Joint Ventures

Pearson Education

In an increasingly competitive world, it is quality of thinking that gives an edge. An idea that opens new doors, a technique that solves a problem, or an insight that simply helps make sense of it all.

We work with leading authors in the fields of management and finance to bring cutting-edge thinking and best learning practice to a global market.

Under a range of leading imprints, including *Financial Times Prentice Hall*, we create world-class print publications and electronic products giving readers knowledge and understanding which can be applied, whether studying or at work.

To find out more about our business and professional products, you can visit us at www.business-minds.com.

For other Pearson Education publications, visit www.pearsoned-ema.com.

MANAGEMENT BRIEFINGS
EXECUTIVE BRIEFINGS

International Joint Ventures

A Practical Guide

SIMON BERGER

FINANCIAL TIMES
Prentice Hall

London   New York   San Francisco   Toronto   Sydney
Tokyo   Singapore   Hong Kong   Cape Town Madrid
Paris   Milan   Munich   Amsterdam

PEARSON EDUCATION LIMITED

Head Office:
Edinburgh Gate
Harlow CM20 2JE
Tel: +44 (0)1279 623623
Fax: +44 (0)1279 431059

London Office:
128 Long Acre, London WC2E 9AN
Tel: +44 (0)207 447 2000
Fax: +44 (0)207 240 5771
Website: www.business-minds.com

First published in Great Britain 1999

The article 'Keeping Cool in China' is reproduced by kind permission of *The Economist*. The two cartoon illustrations are reproduced by kind permission of David Simonds.

ISBN 0 273 64508 0

British Library Cataloguing in Publication Data
A CIP catalogue record for this book can be obtained from the British Library.

10 9 8 7 6 5 4 3 2 1

Typeset by Boyd Elliott Typesetting
Printed and bound in Great Britain

The Publishers' policy is to use paper manufactured from sustainable forests.

About the author

Simon Berger is a commercial lawyer with wide practical experience of joint ventures and international commercial transactions. He currently works in private practice as a partner at a London commercial law firm, specialising in acquisitions and joint ventures, venture capital and MBO projects, IP/IT issues and general commercial transactions.

He has also practised as a corporate attorney at an international law firm in Chicago, USA, where he worked on international business acquisitions, joint ventures and trade agreements and has served as international legal counsel to a quoted UK electronics group, where he was responsible for structuring and negotiating the group's joint venture projects in the fields of engineering, electronics and telecoms.

Simon Berger is admitted as a solicitor in England and as an attorney in the United States of America. He is a member of various professional associations including the American Bar Association and the International Bar Association. He has an MA from Balliol College, Oxford and a JD from IIT College of Law, Chicago. Simon may be contacted at:

E-mail: simonberger2000@hotmail.com
or: simonberger2000@yahoo.co.uk
Address: PO Box 27003, London N2 9WN

Contents

Foreword and acknowledgements

Certain types of project can best be achieved by a cooperation of labour and resources, and this is what joint ventures essentially entail. What applied to pyramids and cathedrals in earlier times applies now to power stations or the assembly of jet engines. For this reason joint ventures will continue to be resorted to regardless of changing international trading conditions or corporate law regimes. The flexibility and business logic which they can offer make them an important option for any organisation with genuine overseas ambitions.

I would like to thank Hilary Prescod for her enthusiastic help in typing the early drafts of the manuscript and for her encouragement at the outset of this project. I am grateful also to Colin Musgrave and Simon Boyle of GEC-Marconi for their helpful suggestions, and to Bill Houston of Elsworth & Associates and Jon Morley of Venture Associates for some excellent technical and business insights.

My thanks also to Andrew Mould, Martin Drewe, Elizabeth Teague, Kate Lodge and all the staff at Pearson Education, who provided words of encouragement and much practical guidance in bringing the final version of the book into print.

Finally, thanks to my family for their encouragement and support.

Terms and abbreviations

CIS	Commonwealth of Independent States
director	A director of the JV company
EEIG	European Economic Interest Grouping
EU	European Union
EU Treaty	The European Economic Community Treaty (or Treaty of Rome) 1957 (as amended)
foreign party	The overseas investor or one of them
IP	Intellectual property
JV business	The agreed scope of business activities to be carried on by the joint venture
JV company	An incorporated JV company formed by two or more persons or entities
JV parties	One or more parties to the joint venture
JV territory	The national jurisdiction in which the business of the joint venture is based
joint venture	The jointly undertaken project or business, in its commercial context
Joint Venture Agreement	The written agreement constituting the legally agreed terms for the joint venture
local party	The resident investor in the JV territory or one of them
R&D	Research and development
shareholder	A shareholder in the JV company
UK	United Kingdom
US	United States

List of figures

General issues

What is a joint venture?

1 INTRODUCTION

A joint venture exists where two or more enterprises combine resources to create a new business venture, either in a corporate form or by means of one or more mutual agreements. Joint ventures have existed in commerce and industry for a long time. More recently, and especially in the 1980s and 1990s, the joint venture has become a popular device in the business world as a sound and flexible means of developing new business activities and, in the context of a cultural trend of decentralisation, an alternative to the strategy of corporate acquisition. Joint ventures are also part of the movement toward geographical expansion into the developing world and its growing economies. They are used as a means to provide wider access to international markets, to execute complex projects or to form strategic alliances between corporations from different territories having common economic or business interests.

The term 'joint venture' is not a legally defined term under English companies law, although in essence it resembles the legal concept of 'partnership', in which a number of partners come together to form a common business enterprise with a view to sharing the profits and the financial risks of the venture. Many kinds of commercial activities, including manufacturing, sales and distribution and research and development, can sometimes be structured in such a manner that all parties participate in the operating business. However, these arrangements are not usually structured as partnerships in the strict sense, importing all the legal and statutory implications which follow, including joint and several liability. The parties should carefully consider the nature of their co-operative activities, and the written agreements which govern them, in order to avoid the automatic implication that they are jointly and severally liable for all the activities of the new enterprise.

2 STRUCTURAL OPTIONS FOR TRADING

In many business sectors there will be a number of alternative structural options for obtaining market access (see Fig. 1.1), which may include the following:

2.1 Distribution agreements

In some cases a manufacturer wishing to expand its sales in an overseas territory will prefer to maintain an arm's-length sales arrangement with its overseas distributors whereby products are ordered and paid for on an independent arm's-length basis. This policy may be more profitable and can help to avoid some of the legal problems which may result from legal or physical presence in the sales territory.

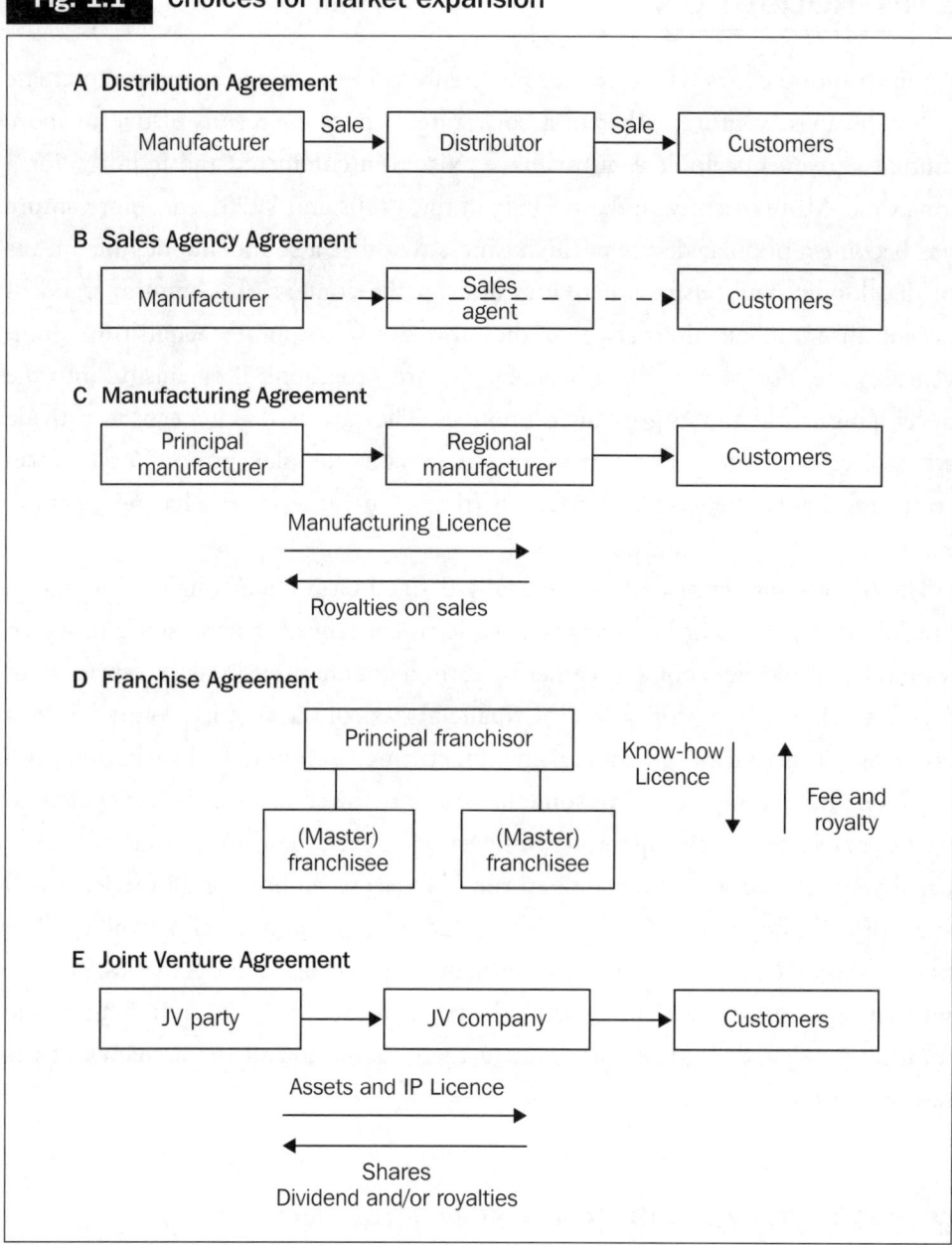

Fig. 1.1 Choices for market expansion

A **Distribution Agreement**

Manufacturer —Sale→ Distributor —Sale→ Customers

B **Sales Agency Agreement**

Manufacturer – –→ Sales agent – –→ Customers

C **Manufacturing Agreement**

Principal manufacturer → Regional manufacturer → Customers

Manufacturing Licence →

← Royalties on sales

D **Franchise Agreement**

Principal franchisor

(Master) franchisee   (Master) franchisee

Know-how Licence ↓   ↑ Fee and royalty

E **Joint Venture Agreement**

JV party → JV company → Customers

Assets and IP Licence →

← Shares
Dividend and/or royalties

2.2 Sales agency agreements

Under these agreements the sales agent has power to contract on the principal's behalf. This may result in undesirable legal or tax implications for the principal.

2.3 Manufacturing agreements

The principal manufacturer may seek to license the know-how for its product to a number of regional manufacturers in return for a royalty payment, in order to benefit from product sales without incurring any direct costs of production or sales, including the logistical issue of setting up new manufacturing facilities.

2.4 Franchise agreements

The principal's business intellectual property (IP) and know-how can be licensed as a package, in return for a fixed fee and/or a commission on sales. It should be noted that royalty payments relating to the exploitation of intellectual property will often attract more favourable tax treatment than payment of dividends, since they are usually paid free of withholding tax.

In any of the above arrangements, the principal's independence and its ownership of the underlying commercial assets may be affected by the chosen structure, and this could have an impact on its operations in other territories where it operates.

2.5 The joint venture option

In deciding whether to establish a joint venture the parties should make sure at the outset of the proposal that:

(a)   their principal business activities as parent are not adversely impacted by the business of the joint venture;

(b)   the joint venture will not be a directly competitive force with the business of either parent company;

(c)   the party will not be required to underwrite losses incurred by the joint venture in the event of unforeseen events or an economic downturn in the business.

The joint venture parties may each have different objectives and approaches to the joint venture project according to their own business imperatives. For example:

(a)   Sometimes one of the participants will contribute its entire business while the other is contributing only a minor portion of its business.

(b)   The participant may wish to conduct essentially the same business as its own domestic business by means of the joint venture.

(c)   The participant may be obliged to use the joint venture to pursue its regional expansion plans. Many developing countries have enacted laws which require a foreign investor to enter into a joint venture with a local investor, and sometimes it is expected to take a minority interest.

(d)   The participant may have established the joint venture with a particular intention to limit the degree of its financial exposure. Consequently, one of the most important protections contained in a joint venture agreement will be a clause limiting financial recourse to the parties, whether under share issues, guarantees or other devices, otherwise than by mutual consent.

This work deals mainly with joint ventures in an international context. Accordingly we will frequently refer to the parties respectively as the 'foreign party' and the 'local party' in highlighting their different perspectives. In the case of corporate joint ventures we will refer to the 'JV company'; for all types of joint venture we will refer to the 'Joint Venture Agreement' which constitutes the principal agreement governing the project, and the geographical area of activity will be referred to as the 'JV territory'.

Checklist 1 Is a joint venture appropriate?

1   Could an independent distributor sell our products and services?

2   Would the JV compete with or hinder our principal business?

3   Would the JV be self-financing?

4   Would the JV impose a financial risk?

Why set up a joint venture?

The principal reasons why a company may seek to set up a joint venture project may include one or more of the following:

1 MARKET EXPANSION

In the competitive global environment corporations will survive and prosper by their ability to refine their range of products and to sell the products in wider markets. If they fail to do so their competitors will exploit the advantage.

An effective method of penetrating overseas markets is by means of an alliance or a joint venture with a local party which can provide the resources, knowledge and reputation to promote the products or make contracts. The joint venture can help to diffuse linguistic and cultural differences and promote brand loyalty.

The joint venture also represents an appropriate structure for the establishment of a regional manufacturing base for sales and exports. The foreign party can take advantage of special enterprise zones in an overseas territory, and help to lower its regional labour and transportation costs.

2 LIMITING THE RISK EXPOSURE OF THE PARENTS

Conducting business in emerging markets can offer the prospect of high returns, but may give rise to contingency risks due to political and economic instability. The proper division of commercial risk can greatly increase the viability of a joint venture project. Fig. 2.1 illustrates the manner in which risk and funding may be allocated between two parties to a Joint Venture Agreement.

The parties can seek to limit recourse to them as parents, whether under guarantees or indemnities, and they should seek to develop a mutually beneficial strategy to deal with the potential risks and liabilities which impact upon the parent companies.

It is also important to consider the timing of the operating risk and its impact over the longer term of the proposed project. Capital development projects will involve long-term risks, and an investor should keep this in mind when choosing a joint venture partner likely to demonstrate permanence and durability in the marketplace.

This issue of risk has special relevance to international joint ventures. Many developing countries have laws which impose sanctions on foreign investors, such as shareholding limits or share divestment provisions. Before granting necessary approvals their foreign investment authorities will assess the activities of the foreign investor and the potential benefits offered to the local economy.

Fig. 2.1 Allocation of risk and funding

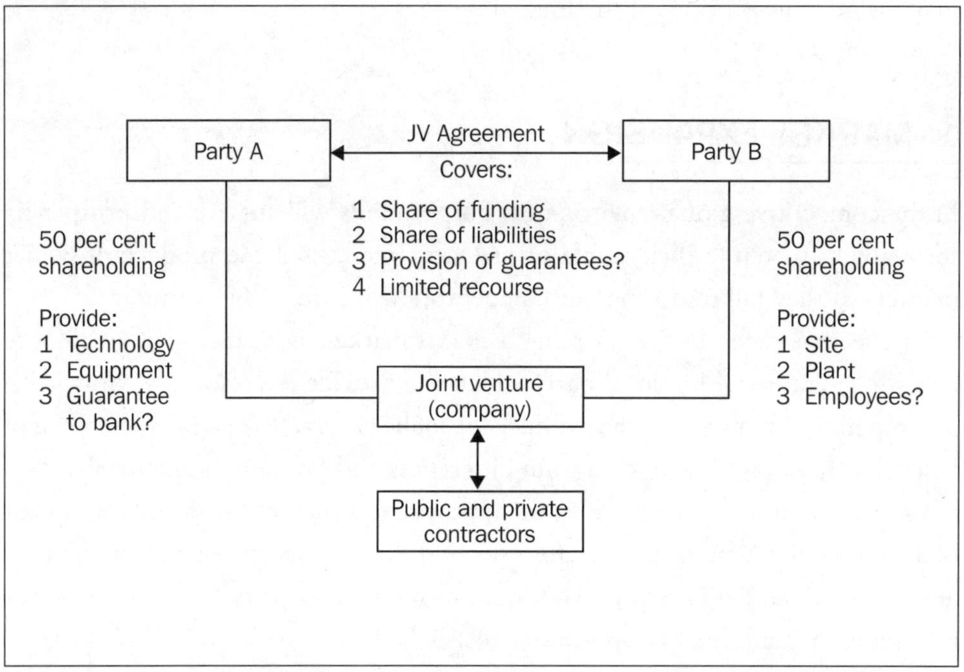

```
                    JV Agreement
  ┌──────────┐      Covers:          ┌──────────┐
  │ Party A  │◄────────────────────►│ Party B  │
  └──────────┘   1 Share of funding  └──────────┘
                 2 Share of liabilities
  50 per cent    3 Provision of guarantees?   50 per cent
  shareholding   4 Limited recourse           shareholding

  Provide:                                    Provide:
  1 Technology        ┌──────────────┐        1 Site
  2 Equipment         │ Joint venture │        2 Plant
  3 Guarantee         │  (company)    │        3 Employees?
    to bank?          └──────────────┘
                            ▲
                            ▼
                   ┌──────────────────┐
                   │ Public and private│
                   │   contractors     │
                   └──────────────────┘
```

The foreign party should therefore ensure that it understands the requirements of local laws or government agencies, takes legal advice on these and develops a strategy to limit the risks. The party should consider the following factors:

(a) How much share capital is required to be paid into the joint venture?

(b) Will the share capital be refundable in full if any required approvals are not forthcoming or if sanctions are invoked?

(c) Will the party be able to convert and withdraw profits made in local currency, and to recover capital paid in by way of loans?

(d) Will the foreign party be able to sell or transfer its shares or other interests in the joint venture?

All the elements of risk limitation will need to be considered carefully by each party, and the joint venture mechanism offers some useful methods for limiting risk. This degree of financial insulation will be especially important in territories where the political situation is not stable.

3 SHARING THE COSTS AND OVERHEADS OF A LONG-TERM DEVELOPMENT

Sharing costs and overheads is generally a good reason to set up a new business in the form of a joint venture, particularly in the form of project joint ventures.

3.1 Venture capital projects

These types of projects will generally involve high research and development (R&D) costs and are likely to provide low initial returns. Sometimes the projected returns will be some years into the future. Parties to an R&D joint venture can limit their overheads by sharing development costs amongst a number of participants. Collaborative R&D joint ventures may sometimes include a dozen or more partners with arrangements to apportion among them the benefits of the R&D.

In structuring such joint ventures, due consideration should be given to competition laws and regulations which apply to R&D projects (see Chapters 9 and 19).

3.2 Capital developments – project finance

Capital projects for major industrial developments often require long-term financing, and their characteristic feature is a syndicate of banks or commercial lenders who advance funds on a limited recourse basis. The lenders will impose financial restrictions and may take security interests over the assets of the project.

For an industrial corporation sponsoring such a project, the aim will be to retain a degree of management control and to limit the extent of leverage imposed by the lenders. The sponsor should also ensure that interest payments will not damage the project's viability.

4 SHARING RESOURCES, INCLUDING TECHNOLOGY, KNOW-HOW, SKILLS AND TECHNIQUES

The sharing of technical resources and know-how is often a good reason to set up a joint venture. For such co-operation to work effectively the parties need a high level of mutual understanding. It is advisable for this purpose that the parties should not be direct competitors in the relevant market. In addition to any competition law considerations (see Chapter 9 below), such an overlap of activity may lead to a fear of co-operating and sharing commercial information, which in turn could hamstring the successful operation of the joint venture. The Joint Venture Agreement should contain restrictions on either party misusing confidential information or IP rights provided exclusively for use by the joint venture (see Chapter 21).

5 MINORITY SHAREHOLDER PERSPECTIVE ON THE JOINT VENTURE

In some situations the participant wishes to be a passive investor, with some rights to veto basic changes in the joint venture, but otherwise leaves major business decisions to the management team appointed by the majority shareholder. Alternatively, there may be a number of minority participants who will take decisions by consensus voting procedures. A minority investor will wish to have a shareholding sufficient to enable it to receive beneficial tax treatment, including withholding tax relief where possible (see Chapter 11).

6 INTERNATIONAL ASPECTS

Forming a joint venture with an influential local party may provide the foreign participant with a level of protection against the economic restrictions which could be encountered. It is useful if the local party has a strategic presence in the relevant industry and in related industrial sectors.

The foreign party may be able to take advantage of specific local joint venture laws (or other regulations) which grant benefits and concessions to foreign companies doing business by means of a JV company. These may include taxation benefits such as a 'tax holiday' for a period of several years or more, during which period normal profits taxes on the JV company will not be assessed. These may also include the rights to have patent, copyright and other intellectual property registrations in the JV territory, which are sometimes denied to foreign-owned companies directly.

In addition to the specific laws relating to joint ventures in the territory, the foreign party may seek to negotiate certain specific assurances or undertakings from the foreign investment agency or other government department. However, if such benefits are negotiated, they should be formally granted in writing and the conduct of the matter should be kept entirely on the record.

Checklist 2 What are our objectives in the JV?

1 Set up a manufacturing base.

2 Increase sales into the region.

3 Maintain market presence

4 Exchange IP and know-how.

5 Allocate contractual tasks and combine skills.

6 Allocate development costs and financial risk.

3

Planning the joint venture

1 STRUCTURING THE JOINT VENTURE

In choosing the operating structure of the joint venture project the principals will have a number of choices. The choice of structure will be dictated by the business objectives and the nature of the project. However, a consideration of taxation and accounting treatment, competition law and other legal matters will have a role to play, especially where the JV territory offers incentives to encourage use of a particular structure.

1.1 Contractual joint venture

This is a term generally given to projects where the parties enter into binding commercial agreements to establish a co-operative business enterprise, without transferring the resources of the parties into a separate JV company. In such cases the parties often intend that each of them will independently carry on a different part of the business, possibly in their home territory. These arrangements are commonly established for the purpose of co-operative marketing or research activities. Other examples include production or sales joint ventures by means of cross-funding arrangements, for example where one party contributes to the costs of production in return for product supply, or where the parties agree to grant or exchange shareholding interests.

Such contractual joint venture arrangements may be suitable where:

(a) the parties view the project as temporary and do not wish to create a new economic force which will compete with the parent organisations;

(b) the joint venture involves research activities or is experimental in nature;

(c) the parties are better able to carry on the activities within their own organisation, and it will be more efficient to do so.

(d) a party is reluctant to transfer valuable IP.

One significant problem with the contractual structure is that each party will be fully responsible for the activities of the joint venture, unless the agreement re-allocates such liabilities to the other party or parties.

The disadvantages of contractual joint ventures can be seen in Section 1.2 below which summarises the advantages of corporate joint ventures.

Contractual joint ventures have the additional disadvantage of some special problems in the area of competition or anti-trust law:

(a) The complex nature of contractual joint venture arrangements will attract more detailed scrutiny from competition authorities.

(b) Within the EU area significant contractual joint ventures will almost always be treated as 'co-operative joint ventures' regulated under Articles 81 or 82 of the EU Treaty (see Chapter 9 below).

1.2 Corporate joint venture

The majority of joint ventures in the international context take the form of corporate joint ventures. The formation of an independent limited liability company to conduct the new business activities will in most circumstances be advantageous for all parties because:

(a) the limited liability company will insulate each party from the direct legal and financial risks of operating in a new territory and provides each party with a measure of protection for liabilities above its capital contribution;

(b) it facilitates clearer agreements between the JV parties and the proposed JV company which should be more readily understood and approved by the investment authorities of the JV territory; and

(c) it generally facilitates beneficial tax planning and prudent accounting treatment, and especially enables the principals to obtain reliefs under local taxation laws or double tax treaties. Profits and other benefits will not automatically be deemed to be taxable in the hands of the JV parties.

However, a disadvantage of using a corporate joint venture can be the need to transfer sensitive IP or assets which in a contractual joint venture would remain vested in the parent.

1.3 'Partnership' joint venture

A joint venture has some of the characteristics of a partnership between commercial enterprises. It is generally established with a view to making profits, and the parties will also share losses, although they may choose to re-adjust their liabilities in a mutually beneficial manner. However, joint ventures are not usually intended to be partnerships in the strict sense, and the parties will invariably wish to limit the application of general partnership law to the joint venture.

There are, it is suggested, few commercial situations where operation as a full partnership will be advisable. A partnership will have numerous implications under taxation laws and accounting rules in the principals' territories and the JV territory. The Joint Venture Agreement will always contain a 'no partnership' clause where this is the intention, but of course this is not conclusive and the issue is determined by the substance of the arrangements.

The three main types of joint venture structure described above are illustrated in Fig. 3.1.

Fig. 3.1 Three types of joint venture

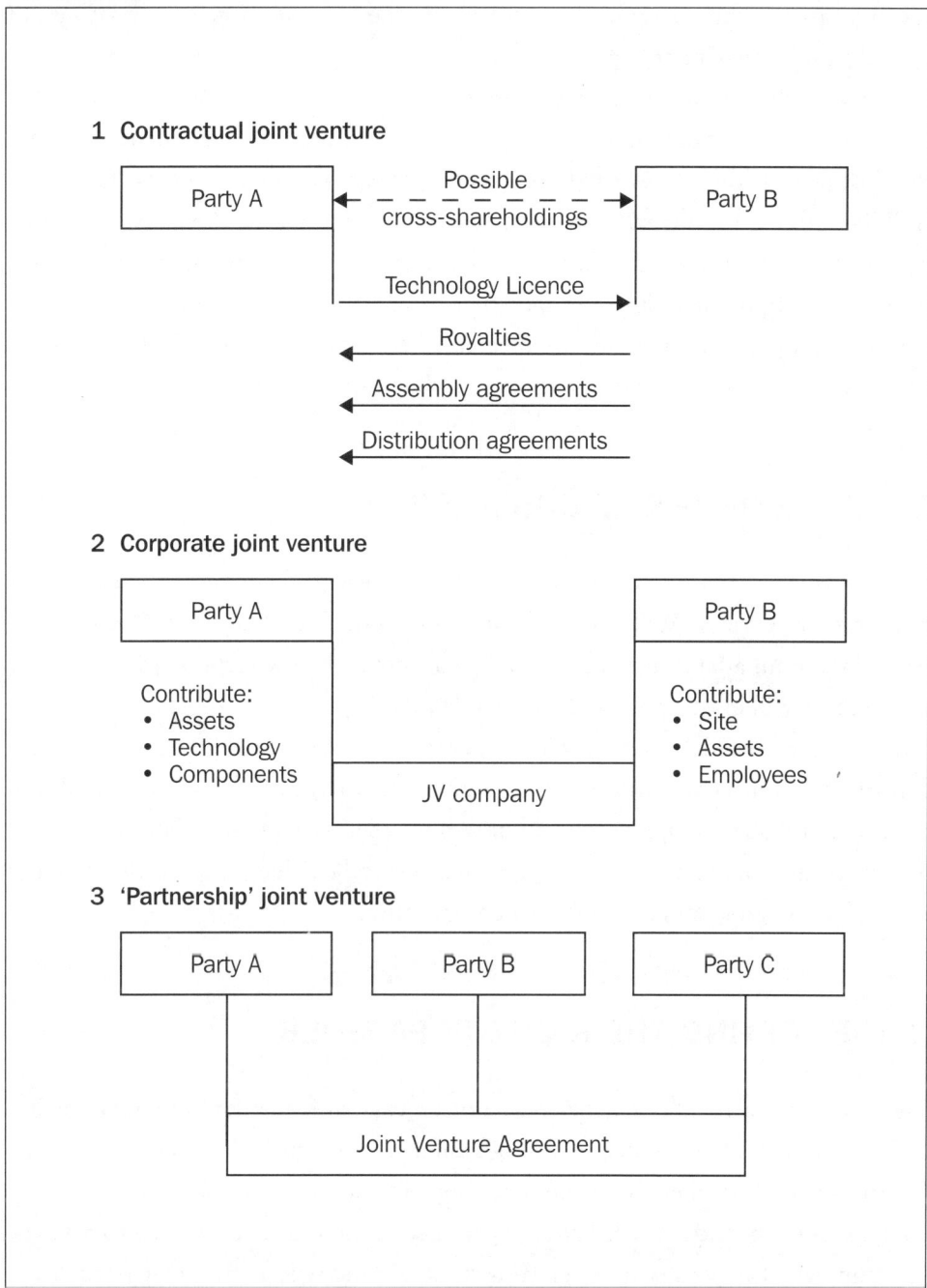

1 Contractual joint venture

| Party A | Possible cross-shareholdings | Party B |

Technology Licence

Royalties

Assembly agreements

Distribution agreements

2 Corporate joint venture

Party A

Contribute:
• Assets
• Technology
• Components

Party B

Contribute:
• Site
• Assets
• Employees

JV company

3 'Partnership' joint venture

Party A   Party B   Party C

Joint Venture Agreement

1.4 Strategic alliances and European Economic Interest Groupings

Companies may enter into strategic alliances in order to create a stronger market presence or co-operate in joint marketing and/or sales activities. These may include commercial activities or may be limited to co-operation in technical matters. Where they extend to production and sales, they may constitute forms of specialisation agreement, and if the parties have each agreed to market and sell in specific areas, they should be aware of the competition implications of specialisation (see Chapter 9).

Strategic alliances are often structured as flexible organisations, without high capitalisation or the creation of a corporate vehicle. For strategic alliances within the European Economic Area (EEA), the European Economic Interest Grouping (EEIG) can be a useful structure for a trade grouping where the activity is to be non-profit-making and ancillary to the parties' principal business. Certain restrictions apply, including the fact that no party is able to exercise majority control, and the grouping is not expected to employ more than 500 employees. Liability for the debts of the enterprise will be joint and several.

2 SCOPE OF THE JV BUSINESS

In planning the structure of the joint venture, much depends on the nature of its products or services. Will the new business produce the same products as the principals or an adaptation for the local market? Will new technology need to be acquired or will existing know-how be adequate?

Each party should undertake a management review of its own business line to confirm that the joint venture will be a good fit between the parties. In addition to combining plant, employees and know-how, there are the so-called 'synergetic' aspects of the combination including reductions to be achieved in production and research costs and similar benefits of co-operation.

3 IDENTIFYING THE RIGHT JV PARTNER

The search for a reliable partner may not be easy in some developing countries, and the use of contacts made through international organisations such as the International Chamber of Commerce or similar bodies may help to find companies or individuals who have experience of international business activities.

A number of factors will be relevant to determine who is the right partner for an overseas investor, including the nature of the commercial activity and the intended shareholding structure. If the local party is to be a majority shareholder, its status in the JV territory will be more important since it will have effective management control and the success of the joint venture may depend upon its organisational strengths. Its good standing with the government and regulatory authorities will also be crucial.

The most important factors will be as follows:

(a) The local party's strategic and commercial status in the market.

(b) The local party's political and financial good standing in the JV territory.

(c) The local party's track record and overall business reliability.

(d) It is important that the foreign party is able to perceive a cultural affinity with the proposed local party, and any evident language or communication difficulties should be given due attention.

4 TERRITORIAL COVERAGE OF THE JOINT VENTURE

The initial market coverage of the joint venture should be established at the outset. The area of market coverage can be increased or redrawn at a later time should the parties believe this to be worthwhile.

Where substantial sales are to be made by the joint venture outside the JV territory by employees or sales agents, there is a risk that tax resident status will be incurred in the other territories, and potential exposure to value added tax or other indirect taxation (see Chapter 11 dealing with taxation issues).

From the legal viewpoint, it is important for the parties to avoid any implicit commitment to move the activities of the joint venture into adjacent countries which may not be conducive to trading, or where one partner may have political difficulties. To ensure that this is reflected in the agreement, it is prudent to define the JV business strictly and include the restriction in the reserved matters requiring shareholders' approval (see Chapter 16 below and Appendix E).

Checklist 3 What structure should we adopt?

1 Will the business activities of the JV be separate from the parent activities?

2 Will the JV business involve financial risks?

3 Will the JV develop new IP or know-how?

4 Will the JV's products compete with either parent?

4

Memorandum of Understanding

1 PURPOSES

A company proposing to enter into a joint venture should consider at the early stages, before any sensitive commercial information is exchanged:

(a) signing a Memorandum of Understanding; and/or

(b) signing a Confidentiality Agreement with the intended joint venture partner in good time to protect its trade secrets and prevent their misuse.

A foreign party will not usually succeed in negotiating or obtaining commercial information from its proposed partner without indicating a degree of commitment. This will be done by signing a Memorandum of Understanding or similar document, which will usually be subject to further due diligence enquiries on the conduct of the business. There may be pressure to make this a legally binding document, but this should be resisted. It is therefore suggested that the use of titles such as 'Letter of Intent' and 'Heads of Agreement' should be avoided and the 'Memorandum of Understanding' formula preferred.

The Memorandum of Understanding will help to establish the framework for the transaction, and will help to establish agreement on the basic approach to the proposed JV business. Without a Memorandum of Understanding there is a possibility that the joint venture may become mired in financial and legal argument without a clear understanding of the premises which have been agreed.

2 CONTENTS

A sample Memorandum of Understanding is included as Appendix A to this study. The main characteristics of a properly drafted Memorandum of Understanding are:

(a) It should not be a legally binding document (except in so far as it may contain confidentiality or similar provisions). The Memorandum can, however, make reference to what system of law will govern the definitive agreements.

(b) It will usually make conclusion of a definitive agreement subject to conditions.

(c) It will adequately describe the scope and objectives of the joint venture.

(d) It may contain provisions granting exclusivity of the joint venture opportunity.

(e) It will include guidelines as to the intended structure for the board of directors and the management board.

(f) It will specify very precisely the intended shareholding structure of the JV company, including reference to vetoes on shareholder resolutions.

(g) It will identify the assets to be brought into the joint venture.

(h) It will describe the framework for intellectual property rights being used by the joint venture.

(i) It will outline the proposals for financing the joint venture, including the principles for payment of dividends.

(j) It will contain provisions governing the confidentiality of the information exchanged between the parties.

(k) The terms for duration or termination of the joint venture should be addressed.

(l) The timing of the proposed transaction will be addressed in the Memorandum of Understanding, and the framework for conducting due diligence enquiries and concluding a definitive Joint Venture Agreement. Usually a long-stop date of up to six months ahead will be the deadline for concluding the documentation.

Appendix B is a sample Confidentiality Agreement important especially if (for any reason) a Memorandum of Understanding is not entered into, in order to clarify the understanding relating to information exchange.

Checklist 4   Why sign a Memorandum of Understanding?

1 Establish good faith of each party.

2 Establish mutual exclusivity in the JV.

3 Enable confidential information review to proceed.

4 Determine basic objectives and structure.

Due diligence enquiries

The term 'due diligence' is usually applied to the investigations which a purchaser will carry out upon acquiring a business. However, a similar set of enquiries will generally be appropriate for a company proposing to enter a joint venture.

It will invariably be necessary to review the proposed partner's business and financial situation. For a foreign party, a review will be more important in those cases where the JV business is synonymous with that of the local party. Furthermore, the local party is usually required to assume control of the 'domestic' aspects of the JV business (including operating the factory, supervising employees, dealing with suppliers and customers and liaising with governmental authorities).

The foreign party will therefore wish to assure itself about the economic strength and business procedures of the local party. In addition, the reviews should look at the commercial prospects of the joint venture, including matters such as plant and equipment, employees, production methods and overheads, distribution networks and the existence of hidden contractual liabilities. Many industrial joint ventures involve taking over an existing factory and plant, in which event the condition of the facilities and their compatibility with new technology will always be crucial considerations. The foreign party should approach these matters as if it were buying the plant outright.

The due diligence process can be divided into two sections.

1 OVERVIEW OF LEGAL AND FINANCIAL CONCERNS

A good strategy for conducting a due diligence review is to begin in general terms:

(a) Ask the local party for its basic documents, including its corporate charter, statutory accounts and any trading information considered relevant.

(b) Ask the legal advisers to perform a company search and any legal or public searches which they consider necessary in the jurisdiction. Search appropriate registers for the property of the partner and its trade marks or patents.

(c) Ask the joint venture partner for permission to review relevant financial records of the business transferring to the joint venture. Asking an affiliated accountancy firm to conduct a financial review is often the most diplomatic method of obtaining detailed information. If the accountants conduct such a review, they must be asked to prepare a full report on the business.

(d) It may be prudent to instruct property surveyors (and in some cases also an environmental audit firm) to carry out a physical inspection and survey of the factory site.

(e) A bank reference should be requested from the local party's regular bankers.

Then have the information internally reviewed by all relevant personnel, and a confidential reference report compiled with appropriate speed. As the JV party gathers sufficient information to proceed with the negotiations, it can frame more detailed questions on specific matters of concern. However, it should be kept in mind that due diligence can be a double-edged sword, and it is not advisable to prepare an unduly burdensome list of questions as this may invite a similar level of enquiry in response, and can also create bad feelings within the joint venture.

The various categories of expert advice which may be required while undertaking due diligence are outlined in Fig. 5.1.

Fig. 5.1 Due diligence enquiries – expert advice

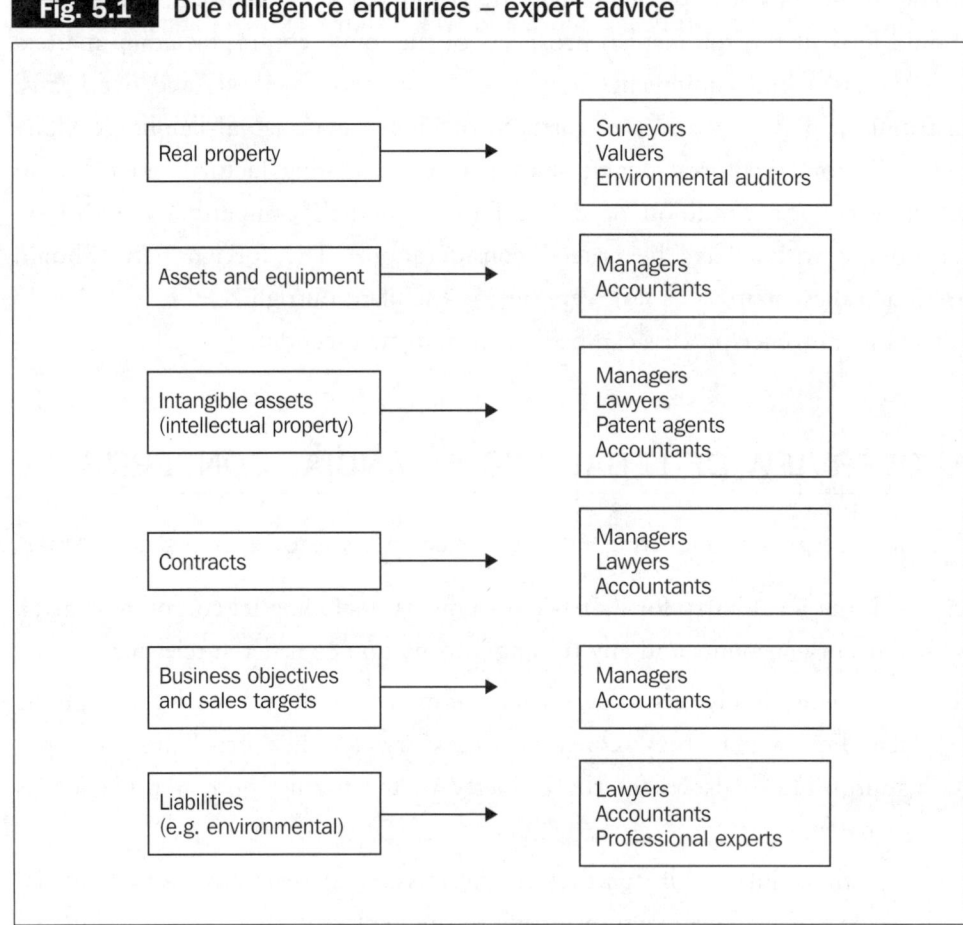

2 DETAILED INVESTIGATIONS

The foreign party should assemble a mixed team of staff and, where appropriate, advisers, to review the following matters:

(a) The condition of the manufacturing site and of important items of plant and equipment. The assets registers of the business provided to the party may not record the current condition of the plant, as the accounts may not duly reflect depreciation. The machinery may not be compatible with equipment to be provided by the foreign party.

(b) The rights and obligations under the trading contracts of the business which are intended to be transferred to the joint venture and the commercial viability of these contracts.

(c) The status of relevant employment contracts to be transferred, including whether the joint venture will incur hidden employee-related liabilities, and the need for additional staff.

(d) The status of patents, know-how and design rights required for the production and marketing of products, and world-wide validity of these rights.

(e) The existence of hidden environmental problems or liabilities which could attach to the existing manufacturing site or the JV business.

Appendix G contains an article from *The Economist* (6 April 1996) which discusses the practical experience of a United States air conditioning manufacturer in seeking a joint venture partner in China. One thing that comes across is the political point that a balance needs to be struck between, on the one hand, seeking important information from the joint venture partner and, on the other hand, not appearing unduly suspicious and threatening the establishment of a good working relationship.

If one party needs to obtain information about the finances, assets and contracts of its joint venture partner, there are ways of doing so diplomatically. Because of the need to understand their business thoroughly, it is a good idea to send a standard information request list to the prospective partner at an early stage. A basic sample Due diligence information checklist is included as Appendix C.

Checklist 5 **Main issues for due diligence review**

1 Premises and principal assets.

2 Contracts of the JV.

3 Status of the JV partner(s).

4 Economic strength of the JV.

6

Legal advice in the JV territory

The need to obtain sound legal advice in a foreign territory on the application of local laws to the joint venture will arise before the definitive Joint Venture Agreement is negotiated and before government approvals are applied for.

1 WHEN SHOULD LEGAL ADVICE BE SOUGHT?

Initial legal advice in the JV territory should be sought at an early stage to assist in planning or structuring the transaction. When to seek advice may depend on the extent to which the business personnel possess recent commercial experience in the jurisdiction of the joint venture.

If the structure of the joint venture remains open for negotiation, it will be wasteful to submit the proposals to lawyers for detailed advice only to find that the advice needs to be thoroughly redrafted to deal with the revised proposals. A balance should be sought between obtaining advice which is strategic in nature while providing sufficient information to the advisers for their advice on legal and tax planning to be reliable.

2 INITIAL PROPOSALS AND SELECTION OF ADVISERS

Because joint venture projects commonly involve a number of ancillary commercial arrangements, including technology licensing, asset transfers, distribution agreements and similar issues, it is important to draw up a coherent set of proposals dealing with the commercial transactions before instructing the local lawyers and financial advisers to give detailed legal and tax advice relating to the arrangements.

The approach to selecting appropriate legal advisers in the JV territory should be given very careful consideration, taking into account factors such as:

(a)   the competence of the legal firm in corporate matters, joint ventures and any ancillary matters to be dealt with;

(b)   their experience in the particular field of production or commercial activity;

(c)   their speed and responsiveness to overseas clients; and

(d)   their likely costs and expenses based (if possible) on a proven track record.

A company that conducts a lot of overseas business will no doubt build up its own independent record of overseas law firms and professionals, including comments on their competence, reliability, speed and cost-effectiveness. If there is no internal guidance, the views of the company's regular lawyers may produce a reliable recommendation, as may the specialised legal publications of financial publishers, chambers of commerce or similar bodies. However, recommendations as to legal advisers given by any official government organisations should be viewed with scepticism.

Checklist 6 What legal advice is needed?

1 Advice on structural matters – general advisers.

2 Advice on documents – general advisers; vetting by local advisers.

3 Advice on local laws and foreign investment regulation – local advisers.

4 Commercial–legal matters (e.g. IP, employment, tax, property) – general advisers and local advisers as necessary.

7

Preparation of the Joint Venture Agreement

1 DRAFTING THE JOINT VENTURE AGREEMENT

It is advantageous for the foreign party to commence the drafting of the principal agreement (see Fig. 7.1 for the main headings), especially since the local party usually has an interest in keeping a number of legal provisions at a minimal level.

Fig. 7.1 **Joint Venture Agreement – principal issues**

1 Company structure

- Share capital
  (division of shares)
- Capital contributions
  (assets and/or cash)

2 Governance and control

A Board composition
  - appointment of directors
  - voting procedure
B Shareholder rights
  - corporate resolutions
  - voting procedure

3 Financial matters

- Funding (shares, loans, guarantees)
- Accounting matters

4 Commercial matters

- Assets and IP
- Property and environmental matters
- Employment matters
- Non-compete and confidentiality

5 Termination

- Term and termination events
- Disputes; deadlock procedure; share transfer options

Note: headings 1 and 2 are not relevant for a contractual JV.

It is suggested that the foreign party should prepare the initial draft agreement, attempting to summarise therein the major commercial objectives. Appendix E is a suggested draft Joint Venture Agreement which is suitable for use in most territories. The local lawyers will be able to adapt this document or, if necessary, produce an appropriately revised version. In this manner the costs of drafting the Joint Venture Agreement may be kept to a manageable level.

The conclusion of a definitive Joint Venture Agreement may take a period of several months, and the agreement itself is usually negotiated in tandem with the draft Business Plan.

Some cautionary notes on the Joint Venture Agreement:

(a) if legally permissible in the JV territory, the agreement should be titled as a 'Shareholders' Agreement' in order to avoid any implication that there exists an equal partnership, instead of the agreed division of benefits and liabilities.

(b) for a discussion on whether the JV company should be made a party to the Joint Venture Agreement, see Chapter 32, Section 2.

Figure 7.1 summarises the main categories of issue to be addressed in the Joint Venture Agreement.

2 'INTERIM' JOINT VENTURE AGREEMENT?

The timetable for concluding definitive documentation will be affected in some jurisdictions by the fact that the foreign investment authorities will require the parties to prepare and sign a preliminary Joint Venture Agreement summarising the intended structure of the transaction, before they issue approval to proceed with the joint venture. China has a requirement for the parties to lodge such an agreement with its Ministry of Foreign Economic Relations before the identity of the foreign party or any movements of capital can be approved. Malaysia and Indonesia have similar requirements.

3 ARTICLES OF ASSOCIATION

While the important legal and commercial matters affecting the JV parties will be addressed in the Joint Venture Agreement, the Articles of Association or Corporate Charter of the JV company is the document that formally constitutes the company under the local companies law. It is generally a specialised document based on the company law or joint venture statutes of the JV territory. This is the document that formally governs the company, and it will generally be open to public inspection in the JV territory. For this reason the document should be agreed between the legal advisers of each parties.

The Articles of Association will usually be fairly standard in form. However, if they contain provisions not contained in the main Joint Venture Agreement, such as special share rights or voting provisions, they will need to be submitted for early investment approval. There will be danger in leaving certain provisions in the Articles unresolved after signing the main agreement, as this may cause the corporate agreement to become unravelled in some respects.

In some jurisdictions the Corporate Charter or Articles will be an inclusive document of the JV company's constitution. Where this is not the case, there may be a separate Memorandum of Association or Certificate of Incorporation containing details of the incorporating parties and the share capital. Care should also be taken in drafting the Objects Clause of the JV company, especially in those common law or other jurisdictions where the *ultra vires* doctrine is legally active. Without due attention to this, the company may be prevented from branching into new commercial activities not provided for in the Memorandum or Articles and duly approved by the local investment authorities (see Chapter 10 below).

In the English case of *Russell* v. *Northern Bank Development Corporation Ltd* (1992) [3 All ER 161, 1 WLR 588] the House of Lords held that while voting restrictions or similar provisions may be included in a Shareholders' Agreement and duly enforced between the parties, the inclusion of a similar provision in the Articles of Association (that it would not increase its share capital without all shareholders' consent) was invalid. This decision would be followed in most common law jurisdictions.

The position under the *Russell* case may be contrasted with the position in certain territories (such as France and the Czech Republic) where the Shareholders' Agreement is not the appropriate means of imposing restrictions on voting or other shareholder rights, since these rights derive from the Corporate Charter or Statutes (as appropriate) of the JV company.

Many of the purely commercial terms contained in the Joint Venture Agreement or agreed by the JV parties for the management of the JV business will not be appropriate for inclusion in the Articles. The parties should keep in mind in this respect that the Articles or Corporate Charter will be a document available for public inspection at the company's registry or appropriate body, and therefore the confidentiality of any sensitive *business information* of the joint venture must be carefully considered.

The Joint Venture Agreement will always contain a provision to the effect that its own terms and conditions will prevail over the Articles in the event of any conflict between the two documents, at least as regards any dispute between the JV parties. This provision may have limited effect in proceedings in the JV territory, and this highlights the importance of proper legal drafting in the Articles of Association.

4 VARIOUS ANCILLARY AGREEMENTS

The various ancillary agreements which are proposed to be implemented between the JV parties, including technology licensing and distribution arrangements from, to or between the parties, should be considered in principle and draft agreements prepared as schedules to the main Joint Venture Agreement.

The issues relating to ancillary agreements are discussed in greater detail in Part VI.

8

The Business Plan

1 AGREEING THE COMMERCIAL OBJECTIVES

When a joint venture proposal has been prepared, the parties will begin to address the business needs of the joint venture, and a number of commercial matters will be considered in more depth. These include the markets the joint venture seeks to penetrate, whether it is expected to go into profit immediately, or how many years it will take to move into profitable production.

The parties will need to compare their respective commercial objectives to establish whether they are compatible. For example, the foreign party may wish to take products made by the joint venture and distribute them in Europe, and the local party may intend to exploit its own domestic market. However, the parties may not be *ad idem* in this division.

Each partner will need to consider separately its overall objectives in entering into the joint venture before the parties can determine if they have accord.

1 Why is the foreign party entering the territory? It may have a variety of different aims, for example:

   (a) to establish an overseas manufacturing base so that it can take advantage of local manufacturing or trading incentives;

   (b) to develop an overseas sales market so that it can actively participate in direct sales;

   (c) to take advantage of import/export laws (including economic duty-free zones) and regulations which encourage development;

   (d) to take advantage of tax incentives such as withholding tax exemptions, income and capital gain reliefs, or low corporate tax rates.

2 What is the local party seeking from the joint venture? In most cases the local party is, in size, the 'junior' partner, and is seeking to acquire know-how, technology and economic clout to increase its strength and reputation in its own territory.

3 Will the objectives of the two partners be reconcilable?

   (a) The commercial objectives of the joint venture. The local party will seek to exploit its own domestic market. The overseas partner will usually have better international contacts. The foreign party may wish to advance the technical and innovation side of production more than the other party.

   (b) The business philosophy of the joint venture. Will the parties share the same overall business approaches to achieving the agreed objectives? One area of potential dispute may be whether profits should be re-invested in plant or research activities or paid out in dividends.

2 STRATEGIC PLANNING ISSUES

The major strategic objectives of the joint venture should be agreed at an early stage and explained in the introductory section of the Business Plan (see Fig. 8.1). These will include the basic framework for projected growth and sales. In planning the strategic growth of the joint venture during the medium term (five years) a useful analytical tool is the 'SWOT' analysis, which attempts to summarise the following matters:

(a) Strengths. What do the main strengths of the business consist of? Do they lie in the product itself, the technology, the staff or the managers?

(b) Weaknesses. In reverse, what are the weak points? For example, is there a deficiency of training in the workforce? The parties should identify where work or expenditure is needed.

(c) Opportunities. Do certain markets provide great potential for sales? Will the business benefit from certain areas of technology in transition? It may be worth incurring additional expense to maximise the opportunities.

(d) Threats. Which areas of activity or sales should the business avoid? Which business competitors should the joint venture be prepared to trade against?

Fig. 8.1 Business Plan – the basic format

Overall objectives

- low-cost manufacture
- expand regional sales
- obtain prime contract
- tax planning
- R&D aspects?

Strategic issues

- product analysis/market analysis
- production and sales targets
- competitors
- 'SWOT' analysis

Commercial issues

- management structure
- factory
- assets – equipment and IP
- employees

Financial strength of JV

- opening balance sheet
- projected profit and loss account
- lending – gearing ratio
- additional shareholder funds

The following are some of the principal commercial issues which will need to be examined in more detail in preparing the Business Plan.

2.1 Production and sales

When the JV parties have identified which products are to be produced and sold, they should draw up a realistic growth plan for the increase of sales in the regional market, usually over a medium-term period of five to ten years. They should seek to establish who the initial customers will be, what penetration of the regional market can be achieved in the initial years of the joint venture and attempt to analyse the barriers to market entry which may affect the venture, or alternatively its competitors.

It is important to define correctly the nature and extent of the joint venture's regional market. The market should be analysed from the point of view of its technical sophistication *vis-à-vis* the joint venture's products, and whether there is demand for existing products or newly-designed products. It should also be analysed with a view to its economic fluidity, so as to form an idea of the possible rate of sales penetration. The local party must take a responsible role in defining the marketing objectives of the joint venture, including a review of its own distributor network.

Finally, pricing will be a key factor in assessing market penetration in regional markets. The parties need to consider the possibility of low-priced pirated goods, and whether their pricing policy will have competition law consequences.

2.2 Factory and premises

The most important asset of a manufacturing joint venture is the factory or production site. The principal matter to be addressed will be the physical condition and the production capabilities of the factory site, what further investment will be required and what other sites may be needed in order to service the production and sales targets of the joint venture.

2.3 Machinery, plant and equipment

An inventory of the machinery, plant and equipment may be appended to the plan. This will greatly assist the technical analysts to ascertain whether the factory is able to achieve critical production capacity without any further expenditure. The parties must consider the potential obsolescence of the machinery and plant, and whether new investment will be required.

2.4 Employees and manpower

The issue of whose employees are needed to fulfil the production and other requirements of the joint venture needs to be addressed in the Business Plan. It is suggested that an appendix to the plan should attempt to summarise the initial position of the JV company, including a list of employees divided into their various categories, to be agreed by the JV parties.

Where the existing business of the local party is being transferred into the joint venture, the staffing requirements will be mainly supplied by the local party from its existing business operation. The foreign party may be expected to contribute senior employees or consultants, often in connection with technology or support activities. These persons will usually be seconded to the joint venture and destined to return to the parent organisation.

3 FINANCIAL AUDITING

The first step is to itemise what assets the joint venture will have available to commence business. Consideration will be given to the following:

(a) Initial assets and capital contributions. What will the opening balance sheet look like?

(b) Will the assets include working capital to begin initial operations? What additional asset contributions or capital will be called upon to get the existing factory or plant up to full production capacity?

Assuming both partners have provided sufficient information about their own contributions, they will need to co-operate to produce agreed reconciliations on which to base the Business Plan. In doing this the parties should form a Joint Audit Committee to report to the boards of each company.

For significant joint ventures the parties should instruct independent accountants so that the management of the JV company can be provided with detailed and reliable financial information to begin their business operations. The process will also need input from management and the following points should be kept in mind:

(a) The auditors may prove to be expensive if their instructions as to scope of financial review are not clear.

(b) The auditors may have a conflict of interest if their firm has also acted for a JV party in its due diligence or other work.

4 FORMAT OF THE BUSINESS PLAN

(a) Summarise the basic objectives of the joint venture. This can help resolve disputes about ancillary activities of the venture.

(b) Survey the markets which the JV company is expected to be involved in, the nature of the products and the geographical extent of markets. Identify existing and potential customers, and significant competitors actual or forseen.

(c) Summarise the intended shareholding, control and management structures of the JV company, the site and other assets available to the joint venture.

(d) Analyse the opening financial position of the joint venture and provide rational forecasts for the opening years of trading.

See Fig. 8.1 for the basic format of a Business Plan, and Appendix D for a summary of matters to be included in the Business Plan.

Checklist 8 Main aims of the Business Plan

1 Summarise overall business objectives.

2 Outline production and sales and development strategies.

3 Assess property and assets of the JV.

4 Assess financial position and trading prospects.

Contractual JV between UK and French engineering companies

Contractual JV between UK and French engineering companies

GIS Systems PLC (GIS) is a UK heavy engineering company specialising in construction of oil-field and mining equipment; Dumanche Ingenieurs SA (Dumanche) is a French company making hydraulic and drilling equipment for the oil and gas industries. The companies propose to set up a joint venture for the purpose of jointly tendering for the construction of six new well-heads in a field on the Black Sea coast of Russia. They intend to contract jointly to furnish fully operational well-heads, with several local companies subcontracting additional components and labour.

The parties decide that they do not wish to set up an independent joint venture company, but that they prefer to receive their respective contract profits directly, taking advantage of certain tax concessions applicable to the region. Under the contract arrangements discussed with the State Oil Company, each party will receive its share of the contract profits partly in hard currency and partly in roubles.

GIS proposes to Dumanche that they sign a Memorandum of Understanding in order to agree the basic structure of the venture, the agreed shares of work and profits and the obligations each will bear in contributing finance for the contractual overheads. The MOU which the parties eventually sign contains the following points:

- The parties are to be joint contractors with the state for the provision of well-heads and profits are to be shared equally.

- GIS is responsible for the well-head structure, and Dumanche for the drilling and extraction; other work to be subcontracted as required.

- GIS will indemnify Dumanche against liabilities on well-heads and will be similarly indemnified against liability on the drilling side.

- Subject to the above, all liabilities of the JV, including any guarantee liabilities, will be split equally with each party severally liable for its half-share.

- The parties agree to license relevant IP to each other for the duration of the JV.

- The parties agree to second employees to each other to work on designated areas of interface activity, their salaries and expenses to be paid by the original employer.

- The parties to establish a joint supervisory board to be responsible for the preparation, approval and execution of the contract.

- The contracts to be governed by English Law. Arbitration to be conducted in Stockholm under the Swedish Chamber of Commerce.

- Each party to be allowed to do due diligence on the other party to confirm that it is capable of satisfying the contractual requirements of the project.

- The joint venture to be conditional on necessary investment approvals, both parties to be fully satisfied with the State Oil Company's contractual terms and the parties to conclude the joint contract within three months of the MOU.

The parties then designate individual managers within their respective organisations to conduct both technical and financial due diligence enquiries in order to ascertain their respective abilities to co-operate in performing the principal project contract. They agree to designate specified categories of plant, equipment and components to the needs of the joint venture, and to be equally responsible for arranging the finance and for providing the working capital for the project.

Problem: You are a member of the due diligence team set up by GIS to investigate. Consider the types of concerns which you will raise as to:

■ the financial strength of Dumanche to support its contract and JV obligations;

■ the legal status of Dumanche as a JV partner, its ability to enter the contracts, and the enforceability of its contractual obligations;

■ the equipment and assets which Dumanche is dedicating to the JV contract;

■ the patents and know-how which Dumanche is contributing to the JV;

■ the technicians and other employees whom each party is to transfer or second.

Corporate JV between UK and Russian engineering companies

Corporate JV between UK and Russian engineering companies

Atlantic Pipelines Group PLC (APG) is a UK company which manufactures valves for land and sea pipelines in the oil industry. It is entering into a joint venture with a privatised Russian company called Norskei whereby an outdated factory operated by that company will be transferred to a new joint venture company, and improved by reinvestment. The joint venture will then manufacture improved versions of pipeline equipment for use in the Caspian Sea oil-fields.

While the parties intend that both of them will have an influence in management and business strategy, APG is insistent that it must retain ultimate management control of the joint venture, and therefore wishes to have at all times in the life of the joint venture a shareholding of at least 51 per cent of issued share capital. Furthermore, APG wishes to have in the Joint Venture Agreement an option to purchase all the shares of Norskei at a specified fair price in the event of breach of contract by Norskei or certain other events (such as events of *force majeure* interrupting business or the event of Norskei becoming wholly owned by a Russian state company).

The main features of the MOU which the parties have signed are:

■ The company is to be capitalised at a value of £10 000 000, of which £5 100 000 (51 per cent) is to be the contribution of APG and £4 900 000 (49 per cent) is to be the contribution of Norskei.

■ APG will provide £500 000 working capital, in hard currency, to be used for purchase of vital capital assets, and its remaining capital is to be represented by the written-down value of APG's plant and equipment, machinery and tooling from its existing production lines in Coventry and Nottingham.

■ Both parties will license important patents and know-how to the joint venture.

■ Norskei is to contribute the existing site, the plant and production lines which by agreement of the parties remain commercially operable, and the agreed employees who work on those product lines.

■ Other employees are to be transferred within Norskei's business group, and Norskei will negotiate with the appropriate trade unions to relocate these employees and minimise redundancies.

■ Norskei agrees to be fully responsible for the environmental condition of the site, for which it is agreed that past malpractices in waste disposal will expose the JV to potential state liability, and to this end has commissioned a full-scale environmental survey and cost review.

■ Norskei agrees fully to indemnify APG in respect of all employment and environmental liabilities in connection with the factory.

■ The Russian government undertakes in certain stated circumstances to guarantee the Norskei indemnity in respect of employment and environmental liabilities.

■ The parties propose to enter an ancillary Contribution Agreement to provide for revaluation of the asset contributions if it becomes apparent that some of the existing plant of either party is obsolescent, in which case either APG will receive shares to compensate for Norskei shortfall, or APG will contribute more case to compensate for an APG shortfall.

The joint venture will be conditional on the grant by the Russian investment authorities of all requisite approvals. Under Russia's Law of Foreign Investment, the investment proposal contained in the draft MOU will need to be approved and registered by Russia's GosComStat (State Committee on Statistics) and the relevant municipal investment authority, and the arrangements for payment of some of the profits in hard currency will require approval by the Central Bank of Russia and the state taxation authorities. Special sector approvals are required for activities and imports in the oil and gas industry.

Following the signing of the MOU the parties start to carry out extensive due diligence on each other's asset and contractual contributions to the JV. The due diligence investigations by APG include review of the following matters in respect of:

- Norskei's constitutional position as the JV partner and the role of the government;
- the status of the site, including all relevant planning authorities and approvals;
- the environmental history of the site and any potential liabilities arising from this;
- the technical expertise of the employees to be seconded to the JV.

Problem: You are a member of the due diligence team set up by APG to investigate. Consider the types of concerns which you will raise as to:

- the legal status of Norskei as a JV partner, its ability to enter the contracts, and the enforceability of its contractual obligations;
- the operational capability of the site, and its related environmental problems;
- the equipment and assets which Norskei is dedicating to the JV contract;
- the patents and know-how which Norskei is contributing to the JV;
- the technicians and other employees which Norskei is to transfer or second.

Part II

Regulatory issues

9

Competition laws and regulations

1 EUROPEAN UNION COMPETITION LAWS

1.1 Concentrative joint ventures

A corporation may need to comply with various competition law systems in respect of its participation in a joint venture. The European Union laws and regulations on competition establish a general distinction between concentrative joint ventures which create an autonomous new entity and those which do not.

The EU Regulation on Control of Concentrations (Regulation 4064/89) (the 'Merger Regulation') provides that a specific *clearance* from the EU Commission must be obtained in the case of significant 'concentrations' which have a 'Community dimension' within the EU. The clearance procedure is intended to permit significant mergers and joint ventures to proceed on a faster track while leaving 'co-operative joint ventures' to remain within the scope of Article 81 of the EU Treaty.

A joint venture will be held under the Merger Regulation to be a concentration where:

(i)   it performs on a lasting basis all the functions of an autonomous economic entity; and

(ii) it does not give rise to co-ordination of the competitive behaviour of the parties amongst themselves or between them and the joint venture.

(Merger Regulation, Article 3(2))

The condition of autonomy requires an analysis of the capacity of the joint venture to operate independently, including a review of its capital structure and asset base. The condition relating to co-ordination may take some joint venture companies outside the regulation. However, this condition has been relaxed, with effect from January 1998, in the case of what are termed 'full-function joint ventures' which carry on a full range of commercial operations independently and without reliance on preferential support from the parent organisations. The EU Commission (the 'Commission'), which is charged with responsibility for competition law administration, has issued guidance notices to the effect that co-ordination is most likely to arise out of the various arrangements between the joint venture itself and its respective parents. See Section 1.2 below.

It should be noted that the turnover threshold for application of the Merger Regulation will normally apply only to significant mergers or concentrations, since transactions will not be deemed to have a 'Community dimension' unless:

(a) the combined aggregate world-wide turnover of all the undertakings involved exceeds ECU 5000 million;

(b) at least two of the concerned undertakings have an aggregate community-wide turnover in excess of ECU 250 million; and

(c) any one of the concerned undertakings does not achieve more than two-thirds of its aggregate community-wide turnover within one single member state.

(Merger Regulation, Article 1(2))

The Commission is also permitted to review mergers where (a) world-wide turnover exceeds ECU 250 million; (b) the combined turnover in three or more EU states exceeds ECU 100 million; and (c) in each such state two or more concerned undertakings have an individual turnover above ECU 25 million.

For the above purposes turnover is to be measured by taking the aggregate group-wide turnover of the relevant company's group. This means that less sizeable transactions concluded by large corporate entities are brought within the Merger Regulation.

Any proposed concentration is required to be notified to the Commission on Form CO at least three weeks prior to the signing of the agreements for its implementation, and the clearance must be given within one month of notification unless the Commission intends to conduct a detailed investigation. If so, a period of four additional months is permitted for the Commission's investigation before clearance must either be denied or granted.

1.2 Co-operative joint ventures

Co-operative joint ventures are regulated as before by Articles 81 and 82 of the EU Treaty (formerly Articles 85 and 86 respectively, now renumbered under the Amsterdam Treaty). Article 81(1) prohibits all agreements or arrangements which have on their effect the prevention, restriction or distortion of competition in any part of the European Community, in such manner as to affect trade between member states.

Article 82 prohibits agreements or arrangements which constitute the abuse of a dominant position within any part of the European Community, and will be a concern for corporations entering a joint venture where they have a strong market share.

In general, the Commission is prepared to take a favourable view of co-operative joint ventures where they are intended to further R&D or to increase the range of products on the market.

1.2.1 The EU guidelines on joint co-operative ventures

A set of guidelines issued by the EU Commission in relation to co-operative joint ventures offers some assistance in determining the criteria to be applied under Article 81. The Commission will consider whether the joint venture arrangements, both in their corporate structure and in the details of their commercial activity, are likely to have 'an appreciable effect' on competition within the common market, when assessed in the economic context of the relevant national markets. Of particular concern will be the risk that the joint venture arrangements may restrict actual competitive activity between the parties themselves, or between one party and the JV company.

In examining these issues, the Commission will consider whether the arrangements do in fact confer 'joint control' on both (or all) the parties, including giving minority shareholders a say in economic decisions. It will examine the activities of the joint venture in relation to those of the JV parties, including any convergence of their product markets and access to those markets, and the incidence of exclusive supply or distribution arrangements. It will also determine if the parties use similar technologies.

In addition, the Commission reviews the effect of the joint venture sales on other product markets in which the parties are involved (commonly referred to as 'spillover'), and the possibility of third parties being 'foreclosed' from effective competition (especially in the case of R&D joint ventures) will be considered.

The guidelines will apply only to full joint venture agreements and not to teaming or other co-operative arrangements of more limited commercial effect. Furthermore, they are silent as to the assessment of breaches under Article 82, which may have an impact if either joint venture party has a dominant position in part of the EU territory, and due regard should be given to a number of cases under Article 82.

1.2.2 Clearance for co-operative joint ventures

Where there is risk of breach of Articles 81 or 82, a negative clearance can be sought which will confirm either that there is no breach or that the terms of the guidelines mentioned above, including the interests of consumers, have been complied with.

Alternatively, a specific exemption can be applied for from the Commission under Article 81(3) on the basis that, on a balance of the economic factors, the interests of consumers will be served by the arrangements. The application may be made in the alternative so as to request consideration for exemption if clearance is not granted.

A full exemption or a negative clearance pursuant to Article 81 may each take up to two years to obtain. However, since 1993 a more amenable 'fast-track' procedure has been implemented for obtaining an informal clearance from the

Commission. A full application must still be made on the revised form A/B (March 1995 format including detailed market information). A preliminary notice is published in the EU's *Official Journal* (OJ), and within two months following this the Commission is expected to issue a preliminary ruling as to whether it has any serious doubts in relation to the proposals. Following such ruling, the parties may either request a comfort letter to this effect or decide to await the Commission's formal decision on the application.

1.3 Cases on co-operative joint ventures

The leading case on Article 81(1) restrictions applicable to joint ventures is Elopak/Metal Box/Odin; OJ (1990) L209/15, which involved a joint venture to develop a carton-type container for foods. It was held that a possible product overlap between the joint venture's products and those of its parent, Metal Box, did not amount in itself to implicit market co-ordination, if competition between the parties and the joint venture was not adversely affected.

The earlier case of Mitchell Cotts/Sofiltra; OJ (1987) L41/31 had adopted similar reasoning in respect of a UK venture for air filtration devices into which Sofiltra licensed its unique technology. The Commission held that the parties could not have been actual competitors in manufacturing the product.

Another leading case is GEC/Weir; OJ (1977) L327/26 in relation to a joint project for the development and production of sodium circulators for high-pressure nuclear reactors. The parties' separate production activities were under a joint management arrangement in respect of development and sales, and a non-compete covenant. The Commission held that the joint venture was *prima facie* a breach of Article 81(1) because it prevented competition between the parties, especially as the parents' technology and personnel were tied into the venture. However, the Commission was prepared to grant an exemption under Article 81(3) because it was held that the collaboration was necessary in order for the product to be successfully developed.

It is useful to contrast the GEC/Weir analysis with two other cases:

(a) Ford/Volkswagen: the Commission granted exemption on grounds that the joint development (of the prototype MPV 'people carrier' vehicle) would improve the underlying technology, with consumers in particular being expected to benefit;

(b) Eurosport, where the Commission refused to grant the Article 81(3) exemption to a transnational consortium to combine the sports satellite broadcasting activities of Sky and Eurosport. The Commission ruled that advantages to consumers were outweighed by the distortion of competition in a 'young and developing industry'.

1.4 Notice on co-operation agreements

This notice exempts joint ventures intended exclusively to perform R&D activities at the pre-production phase, joint sales and advertising, and certain internal administrative functions carried on for either parent which are not expected to have an impact upon competition.

1.5 Notice on minor agreements

Sometimes referred to as the '*de minimis*' notice, this now exempts joint ventures where:

(a) the joint venture parties' combined share of the total relevant market in goods or services does not exceed five per cent; and

(b) their combined aggregate annual turnover does not exceed ECU 300 million.

It is important not to overlook the minor agreements exemption. However, note that again the application of this limit will depend on whether the JV party is a member of a larger corporate group with the prescribed turnover level. Certain arrangements which are otherwise deemed to be co-operative may fall within the scope of an applicable block exemption. See Section 1.6 below.

1.6 The EU block exemptions

Where any of the proposed joint venture arrangements involve granting exclusive technology rights, distribution or sales rights, franchises or other benefits, the parties must consider the provisions of the relevant EU 'block exemptions':

(a) R&D joint ventures which comply with the conditions of the R&D agreement block exemption (Regulation 418/85) will permit joint R&D activities involving mutual licensing, joint funding and (within certain parameters) joint exploitation and sales.

(b) The EU block exemption applicable to technology and know-how licences or transfers (Regulation 240/96) will permit exclusive licensing of technology (principally unregistrable know-how and similar rights) to the JV company or either JV party, to permit the recouping of funds spent on research.

(c) If the joint venture will involve the grant of exclusive distribution or supply rights to sell products in any EU territory the agreement should comply with the appropriate EU block exemptions (Regulations 1983/83 and 1984/83). Care should be taken to avoid imposing (under any agreements) any other restrictions on competition other than those permitted in respect of the exclusive arrangements.

1.7 Specialisation agreements

As an additional concern in some proposed joint ventures, care should be taken where the joint venture arrangements (and in particular contractual joint ventures) will involve a reorganisation or cessation of the parents' respective manufacturing capabilities, in which case the arrangements might contravene Article 81(1), and would need to comply with the block exemption on specialisation agreements (Regulation 417/85).

This regulation exempts agreements relating to specialisation arrangements whereby the parties accept reciprocal undertakings:

(a) not to manufacture certain products or to have them manufactured, but to leave it to other parties (such as the other JV party or the JV company) to manufacture or commission those products; or

(b) not to manufacture certain products or have them manufactured jointly.

The reciprocal arrangements will often involve express or implied undertakings not to manufacture certain goods or components, but to order them from the other party. Since the purpose of specialisation is generally for each party to confine itself to those areas of production where it is most efficient, it can help to rationalise production with resulting benefits for all intermediate users.

The Commission has therefore adopted the approach that joint venture specialisations may be permitted if they are not unduly restrictive or intended to divide the EU market territorially. Regulation 151/93 on specialisation arrangements therefore applies this view to cases where the specialisation joint venture has a market share exceeding 20 per cent in the EU territory (or a substantial part of it), where the aggregate turnover for all the participating undertakings (JV parties and joint venture) does not exceed ECU 1000 million.

1.8 Conclusion

All joint venture arrangements will need to be examined for compliance with EU regulations by analysing their constituent elements independently. Similar principles will apply in other territories where competition law regimes are in place.

As a general comment, EU laws and regulations generally impose community-wide restrictions in most areas which are covered under domestic laws in an EU territory. However, certain territories may impose tighter restrictions in limited areas, for example vertical restrictions or resale price maintenance, which may need to be examined in light of the joint venture proposals, and the competition authorities of these territories will almost certainly take a narrower view of any transaction based on their conception of national interest.

An analysis of the inter-action of European competition law issues arising on a joint venture is given in Fig. 9.1 (and see Case Study 4).

Fig. 9.1 Competition law issues

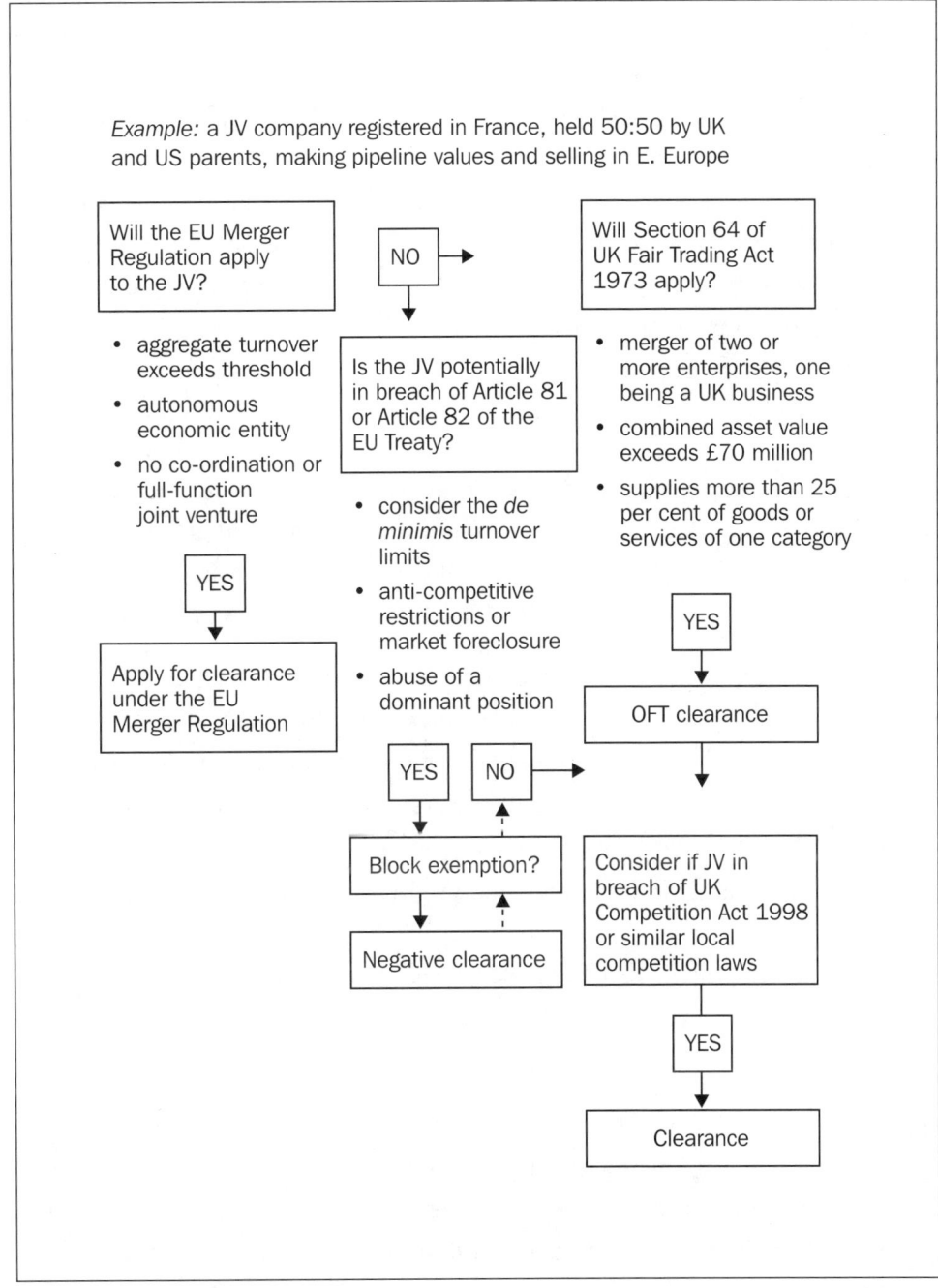

Example: a JV company registered in France, held 50:50 by UK and US parents, making pipeline values and selling in E. Europe

2 UNITED KINGDOM COMPETITION LAWS

Most countries have their own laws to deal with monopolies or other anti-competitive restrictions on trade. It is the laws governing mergers and concentrations that have an immediate impact on a joint venture formation. However, other laws relating to pricing, sharing of information and similar matters may affect the joint venture.

The UK has an additional tier of competition regulations which, with recent changes, has become more like the EU provisions. Some proposals will need to be cleared by the UK's Department of Trade or the Office of Fair Trading as well as the EU Commission's investigations under Article 81 of the EU Treaty.

The following enactments contain the UK's principal monopolies and merger laws applicable to joint ventures.

2.1 The Fair Trading Act 1973

Under the Fair Trading Act (FTA) certain mergers are prohibited and subject to an investigation by the Competition Commission ('Commission') based on an analysis of the benefits to consumers and the resultant public interest involved.

Of primary importance is Section 64 of the Act which provides in Sub-section (1):

(1) A merger reference may be made to the Commission by the Secretary of State (for Trade) where ... two or more enterprises (of which at least one was carried on in the United Kingdom or by or under the control of a body corporate incorporated in the United Kingdom) have ... ceased to be distinct enterprises, and that either –

   (a) as a result, at least one quarter of all the goods of the relevant description which are supplied in the United Kingdom (or in a substantial part thereof) are supplied by or to the same person; and

   (b) the value of the assets taken over exceeds £70 million.

The provision has survived a recent legal review, and means that if the merger results in a market share of 25 per cent or more of the relevant product group, the Secretary of State can investigate with a view to reference to the Commission. If the merger is referred, the Commission will report as to whether the merger would operate against the public interest, based upon its effect on competition and the interests of consumers (Section 84, FTA).

Under Section 65 it is clear that the requirement that two enterprises cease to be distinct is met in any case where they are 'brought under common ownership or control'. Thus it applies to any corporate joint venture involving one or more UK companies, or a merger between non-UK corporations if one of them carried on a relevant enterprise in the United Kingdom.

Certain joint ventures may fall within the FTA pursuant to Section 6, applicable to monopoly situations as opposed to mergers. This has effect if a market share of 25 per cent or more exists as a result of the joint venture arrangements.

2.2 The Competition Act 1998

The newly enacted UK Competition Act repeals the anti-competition provisions of both the Restrictive Trade Practices Act and the Resale Prices Act and replaces it with simplified legislation which is more akin to the European Community model, being essentially based on the Article 81 restriction. The Competition Act also introduces mechanisms for consultation and guidance in relation to potentially anti-competitive agreements or proposals.

Section 2 of the Competition Act prohibits the following agreements:

Agreements between undertakings, decisions of associations of undertakings or concerted practices which:

(a) may affect trade within the United Kingdom, and

(b) have as their object or effect the prevention, restriction or distortion of competition within the United Kingdom

subject to those agreements or practices being otherwise exempted under the Act.

It should be kept in mind that mergers regulated under Section 64 of the FTA will continue to be so regulated and do not fall within the ambit of the new Act. The larger mergers will be regulated under the EU Merger Regulation (see Section 1.1 above). The Department of Trade and Industry has been accorded the power to implement new rules which may exempt from Section 2 certain classes of vertical agreements, property agreements and (possibly) certain joint ventures also.

The Act allows for direct consultation with the Office of Fair Trading (OFT) over proposed agreements, and positive guidance will prevent the OFT taking further action to investigate the case or to terminate the agreement. The OFT also has a power to issue *post facto* negative clearances or exemptions under the Act in respect of an agreement submitted for formal clearance, in which event such an agreement will be valid and enforceable for the purposes of Section 2.

The new Competition Commission has been constituted under the Act to supervise its implementation and to act as the appellate body for decisions of the OFT.

Checklist 9 Principal concerns under competition laws

1   Will the JV be an autonomous economic entity, and will the turnover level bring the JV within the EU Merger Regulation? Consider fast-track merger clearance.

2   Will the JV and either parent be operating in any overlapping product or service markets? If so, there is a risk of the agreement being anti-competitive.

3   Does the JV possess other anti-competitive or restrictive aspects, such that it could infringe Article 81 of EU Treaty or UK Competition Act?

4   Will any block exemptions to Article 81 apply? Consider negative clearance.

10

Government investment approvals

1 FOREIGN INVESTMENT APPROVALS

The controls and regulations that are imposed by overseas governments on inward foreign investments and joint ventures may be encountered by joint venture parties at a variety of levels.

Some territories such as Hong Kong and Singapore have sought to attract investment by foreign corporations with a liberal system of foreign investment and foreign exchange regulations which, compounded with tax benefits, have helped to give these territories a competitive advantage.

However, a few developing countries have implemented trade regulations intended to protect significant sectors of their domestic industries from foreign investment. This has been done by devices such as 'negative investment lists' or limitations on share ownership by non-resident persons, notably in Malaysia, where foreign ownership may be limited to 30 per cent of equity in a JV company which is not predominantly exporting its production.

Some developing countries such as Indonesia are currently relaxing their share divestment requirements. Such restrictions take different forms in various countries, although they are not so common in developed economies outside the spheres of national security and defence. Government regulations may in some instances take a more indirect form; for example, in the Philippines government contracts are generally awarded to Philippine corporations or to joint venture companies with foreign holdings of 40 per cent or less. Some other territories will put different acceptance conditions on bids by foreign-controlled companies or joint ventures.

Most states will require foreign-owned joint venture formations to be submitted for approval by the appropriate regulatory body, which is usually either an agency of its national department of trade or a specific foreign investment authority.

Those countries which have legal requirements for foreign investment approvals or consents sometimes have a specific channel of approval for foreign-owned joint venture companies incorporated in the local joint venture laws. This provides a means of obtaining swift investment approval and a mechanism for imposing control on various aspects of the joint venture.

In particular, payments of money to and from the JV company's accounts, in the form of share capital or parent company loans, can be effectively monitored by the government. The ownership of property, including patents and other intellectual property, can also be regulated under the joint venture laws. The application of legal provisions governing receiverships and liquidations can also be a powerful control. These potential pitfalls require that care must be taken at the outset in incorporating the JV company, in providing correct information to the government authorities and in drafting the Joint Venture Agreement.

In complying with any legal regulations, perhaps the most important requirement is to comply in good faith with requests for information from the regulatory authority, and to provide accurate replies to their questions. If it is necessary to withhold relevant but commercially sensitive information, this should be explained clearly. As in any legal review process, the supply of incorrect information can operate to vitiate any investment consent. The consequences will be both economic, in terms of lost capital, and more indirect, in terms of the loss of goodwill in the territory or the region.

Obtaining foreign investment approvals will usually take a period of six months and possibly more, depending on the territory. The period may be determined by the level of investigation and enquiry which the investment authority wishes to carry out. In some countries, such as Indonesia, a further approval from the Ministry of Justice or comparable authority is required before incorporation of the JV company is officially sanctioned, and the form of the Articles of Association approved.

A summary of the issues relating to government approvals for joint ventures is provided in Fig. 10.1.

Fig. 10.1 **Issues relating to government investment approvals**

Shareholders/participants

- identity
- good standing
- financial adequacy

Share capital/finance

- capital adequacy
- sufficient collateral
  (e.g. banking, financial services)

Ownership of property or IP

- title/right to hold land
- ability to register title
  (esp. patents and IP)

Payment of dividends

- currency/exchange controls
- taxation/withholding

Business activities

- market activity permitted?
  (esp. for foreign-held companies)
- special business licences (e.g. telecoms)
  or permits (e.g. environment/health)

2 FOREIGN EXCHANGE CONTROLS

With the increasing liberalisation of world trade, a number of foreign exchange restrictions are being widely relaxed, but the issue remains of significance for most overseas joint ventures. It may not be possible to return, during the life of the joint venture, capital which has been invested, and in any event such capital will not in general be freely transferable out of the JV territory. Specific concessions will frequently allow the repatriation of profits earned in local or foreign currency, but may not provide for a conversion procedure.

The lack of convertibility of currency remains a problem in most developing countries, and will often have a large impact on projected profits. Many developed countries such as Japan maintain a strict foreign exchange regulation, in Japan's case through its widely empowered Ministry of Trade and Investment (MITI), whose Committee on Foreign Exchange is empowered to recommend modification or cancellation of certain foreign investment proposals, based on an analysis of their impact on the Japanese economy.

China is sometimes prepared to facilitate conversion of investment capital through special government-sponsored loans of Chinese currency which can be reconverted at specified times. China has introduced regulations permitting foreign exchange earnings by a Chinese joint venture to be held in a designated Foreign Investment Enterprise (FIE) bank account (formerly they had to be converted into Renminbi) and remitted out of China in certain situations, including termination of the joint venture. Malaysia, by contrast, has a fully convertible currency and will freely permit debits out of non-resident Malaysian currency accounts, although an exchange control form must be completed if a sum above Ringgit 10 000 is credited to the account.

In the absence of free convertibility of currency, dividends or other payments must be paid in the domestic currency and retained in an account in the territory (or possibly a specially designated overseas account). More usually the profits will not be distributed but retained in the JV company as retained earnings or reserves. The foreign party may also have the option to convert the earnings into goods or services in the JV territory, or leave the balance outstanding in the JV company as additional share or loan capital.

In general, joint venture parties will need to accept the existing foreign exchange regulations in the territory. Under some investment regimes the contribution of share capital (or loans) in sterling or dollars is permitted, although usually in the context of an investment for a fixed duration. Some investment authorities will permit the parties to negotiate the terms upon which capital contributions may be made in foreign currency (generally US dollars), and the capital paid out again in such currency. The ability to do so on termination of the joint venture will depend on the level of realised losses.

3 CAPITALISATION REQUIREMENTS

The joint venture laws of many of the developing countries specify a minimum share capital requirement for starting an approved joint venture. This will often be related to the size of the parents (usually combined) and the intended activities of the joint venture. Joint ventures which are to be involved in capital-intensive activities such as infrastructure or power generation will frequently be subject to higher capital adequacy requirements.

In the CIS territories, China and many other territories attention also needs to be paid to the laws governing the social fund requirements. These rules often require a separate capital reserve to be applied to employee, pension and related social obligations of the company. The JV company may be required to set up a social fund upon its incorporation, though in a number of CIS territories it is usually given a period of two to five years in which to consolidate the social fund at the required level. In general the requirements will call for the fund to be at least 15 to 20 per cent of accumulated capital and reserves, which serves at least to ensure that the fund, when established, will remain at the relevant percentage of the minimum capital requirement.

Another issue relating to capitalisation is the choice of the JV company's debt-to-equity ratio, or gearing status. If the gearing is excessive, the JV territory may deem some of the interest payments due to the foreign party to be in effect distributions and subject to withholding tax, and at the same time any deductibility of interest payments against realised profits will be forfeited. The United States tax authorities may impose such treatment on a 50 per cent plus subsidiary, where the ratio of debt to equity share capital exceeds one-third. The United Kingdom tax authorities may do so in the case of any paying company which is a 75 per cent subsidiary or affiliate of the receiving company, if the loan is deemed not to be on reasonable arm's-length terms, or otherwise an arrangement which would have been made in the absence of an affiliate relationship.

Checklist 10 **What type of restrictions may apply to the JV?**

1 Restrictions on market sector, e.g. defence, construction.

2 Restrictions on size of shareholding participation.

3 Restriction on movement of currency.

4 Restrictions on ownership of IP, property or other assets.

11

Taxation issues in joint ventures

1 INTRODUCTION

The taxation of joint ventures is a complex topic and any attempt to survey the alternatives facing the joint venture parties cannot properly serve as more than a set of guidelines. Taxation issues will need to be given due consideration at the planning phase of the joint venture, and in particular when considering the territory in which the JV company is to be incorporated and the shareholding structure to be adopted between the principals and the JV company.

In the case of contractual joint ventures and partnerships, each participant will in general be taxed on its own respective income and benefits. A key consideration will be the need to avoid having the arrangements automatically treated as a partnership for taxation purposes. Thus the parties should seek to avoid any implication that property is to be jointly owned, or any imputed agreement that they intend to share their respective expenses and operating costs of their respective contractual activities. Therefore separate records and accounts should be maintained at all times.

Due to the multinational nature of many joint venture projects, taxation aspects always require detailed analysis and professional advice in the operative territory and in other relevant territories, including each principal's domestic territory. It has been necessary to deal here with taxation issues principally from a UK-based viewpoint. While the principles underlying profits taxation and dividends taxation have common elements throughout the world, their relative prominence will vary from one taxation system to another.

2 TAXATION OF JOINT VENTURE CORPORATE PROFITS

2.1 General

The first issue to consider is the taxation of profits made within the joint venture, and under which tax system they fall to be assessed. In the case of a regional joint venture the parties may have a choice as to the territory in which the JV company will be resident for tax purposes. The following factors will need to be taken into account:

(a) the effective rate of corporate profits tax;

(b) the availability of a tax credit or similar relief;

(c) the incidence of withholding taxes on dividends paid out;

(d) the availability of tax losses to the shareholders; and

(e) any other tax incentives or investment benefits available.

Taxation structures for the main forms of joint venture are shown in Fig. 11.1.

Fig. 11.1 Taxation structures of joint ventures

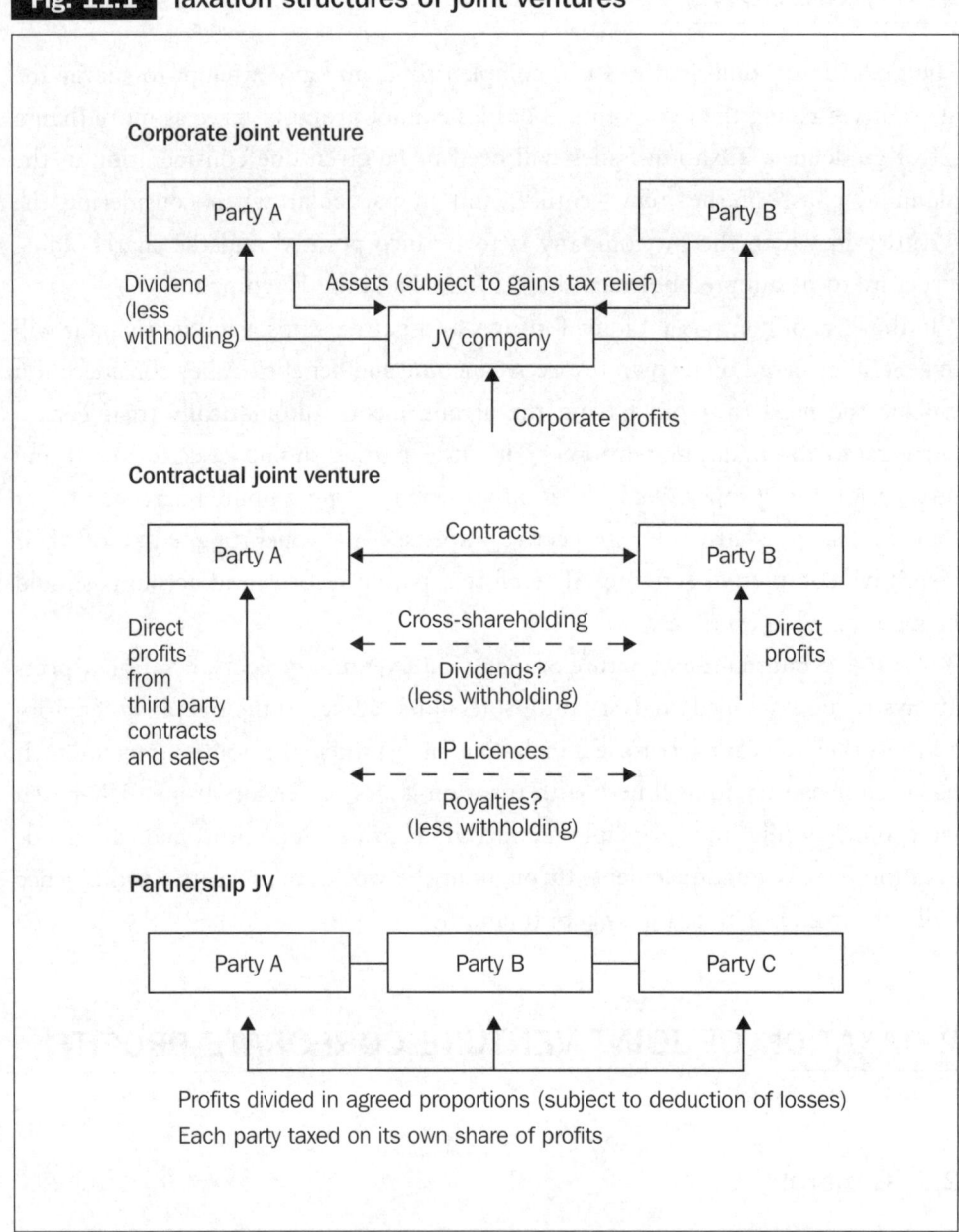

2.2 Corporate residency for tax purposes

The imposition of profits taxation on a corporation is based on its corporate residence. The term 'domicile' is sometimes used. As there are conflicting rules to determine tax residency, instances of dual or multiple residency may be encountered.

Under English law a company is resident where its 'central management and control' is exercised, usually where the board of directors regularly meet to conduct business.

Other territories have adopted different residency tests. Corporate residency can be based on an analysis of where the substance of the corporation's activity is carried on. However, the manner of defining such substance has been subject to various approaches, often including the full range of a company's commercial activities.

2.3 Permanent establishment

Where a corporation resident in one country establishes an agency or a branch operation (but not a subsidiary) in another country, or conducts commercial activities involving, for example, the maintenance of a factory or a sales depot, it may become liable for income or profits taxation.

Many double taxation treaties now have standard provisions that where:

(a) the corporation is conducting trading activity by means of a branch office, or has certain assets or stocks located in the territory; or

(b) sales are transacted by agents who are not independent contractors,

the corporation will be deemed to have a 'permanent establishment' in the territory, and liable for profits taxation based on the 'attributable proportion' of its taxable profits, which is the portion derived from the activities in the territory. In this event the taxation authority in some countries may agree to assess the relevant tax on a 'cost plus percentage' basis if reasonable evidence can be provided for this.

The risk of permanent establishment may apply in relation to activities or services undertaken by the parties in relation to the joint venture, such as secondment of employees or leasing of equipment. The potential exposure may be limited by drafting services agreements or limited 'agency' agreements which exclude the right to conclude contracts on behalf of the company.

2.4 Rates of profit tax

Where a regional joint venture is active in various countries it can seek a low-tax base from which to operate. Many countries are keen to encourage foreign companies to incorporate and base their operation in the territory. Some countries have introduced rules whereby a 'tax holiday' is available to foreign investors for the purposes of profits taxation. The corporation may be wholly or partly exempt from profits tax, dividend withholdings or similar impositions for a certain period.

2.5 Loss relief and capital allowances

Tax losses cannot generally be surrendered between different tax jurisdictions in such a manner as to offset profits in another jurisdiction. However, two or more UK resident companies which together own more than 75 per cent of a JV company's equity shares (and thus form a 'consortium' pursuant to Section 413 of the Income and Corporation Tax Act (ICTA) 1993) will be able to agree the surrender of tax losses incurred by the JV company, except if one shareholder holds 75 per cent or more of the voting rights in the JV company, or if one holds less than five per cent. The Inland Revenue has by concession extended the practice to apply where one company is UK resident and the other(s) all resident in an EU territory.

2.6 Value added tax and indirect taxation

It is not possible to provide general advice on the wide variety of sales, use and indirect tax systems, except to note that decisions at the planning stage of a joint venture should take into account the incidence of indirect taxes and the applicability of reliefs relating to the joint venture's products and services.

The parties should always consider the effect of value added taxes on any proposed transactions between themselves or with the JV company. In relation to the exchange of goods or services which are chargeable, it may be possible in certain circumstances to treat the JV company as being within the party's VAT group if its shareholding exceeds 50 per cent.

3 TAXATION OF DIVIDENDS PAID BY THE JV COMPANY

3.1 Dividends paid by a UK company – in general

Effective from 6 April 1999, the payment of Advance Corporation Tax (ACT) on all dividends paid in the UK has been abolished, and the full pre-distribution profits of the paying company are subject to corporation tax for each fiscal year. Prior to 6 April 1999, a UK-resident company paying a dividend was liable to make a payment, latterly at 20/80, on the grossed-up amount of the dividend, which was then offset against the company's 'mainstream' corporation tax liability.

An individual shareholder who is a UK resident will still receive a tax credit equal to 10 per cent of the amount of the dividend payment when paid and, if a higher-rate taxpayer, will obtain marginal relief at 32.5 per cent. Where the dividend has been paid to a non-UK-resident shareholder, the tax credit is not given under the UK system. However, a number of double tax treaties to which the UK is party provide for a limited tax credit to be applied.

3.2 Taxation on dividends remitted out of the JV territory

3.2.1 General comments

Distributions paid to non-resident shareholders will in general be taxable in the hands of the recipient shareholder, but may be first subject to a withholding tax in the paying jurisdiction. The shareholder may be afforded a credit under a double tax treaty.

A mechanism often used to mitigate withholding tax is the 'income access' share structure, whereby each shareholder holds equity shares in the JV company, and also takes a specific class of non-voting, income-yielding shares in a separate company resident in its own state. This company will be a subsidiary of the JV company, which retains the equity shares and control (see Fig. 16.1, p. 130). A part of the business may then be hived off into the subsidiary, which pays dividends directly to the shareholder free of withholding tax.

The European Union Parent/Subsidiary Companies Directive, 1990 (90/435/EEC) provides that all distributions paid to shareholders resident in an EU state which own 25 per cent or more of the voting shares of a company resident in an EU state are to be exempt from withholding tax, and afford the shareholder a tax credit at the basic rate. The UK's double tax treaties provide in many cases for a limited rate of dividend withholding, or alternatively for payment of tax credit in the hands of the recipient which can be offset against their outstanding taxation liability.

3.2.2 Dividends paid by a UK-resident company to non-EU resident shareholders

In the case of dividends paid by a UK-resident company to a non-EU resident shareholder, withholding tax is no longer payable on the dividend. Accordingly, the dividend payment will have the following implications:

(a) no withholding is imposed on the divided;

(b) the paying company will account for UK corporation tax liability in respect of the dividend;

(c) a voucher will be issued to the recipient in respect of the tax accounted for at the rate of 10 per cent;

(d) a tax credit may be available to the recipient shareholder under the relevant double taxation treaty, or under the tax laws of its own state.

3.2.3 Dividends paid by a non-UK-resident company to UK residents

Any dividend received by a shareholder resident in the UK, whether individual or corporate by nature, is *prima facie* taxable in the UK as an income receipt of the recipient. There may be a withholding in the paying jurisdiction on the amount to be remitted as dividend. Many double taxation agreements allow the recipients tax credits, reliefs or exemptions.

4 ASSET TRANSFERS TO THE JOINT VENTURE

4.1 Permanent establishment risks

There is potential risk that a UK-resident company which transfers capital assets and equipment to an overseas JV company could be deemed to have created a permanent establishment in the JV territory. If local tax advisers believe that a risk of permanent establishment exists, the asset transfers to the JV company should be made so far as possible by subsidiary or affiliate companies which are specifically involved in overseas sales or activities.

4.2 Transfers at an under-value

One significant difficulty which will arise in the case of asset transfers (at book or similar low value) by a UK company to the JV company is presented by the case of *Aveling Barford* v. *Perion* (1989) BCLC 626, in which it was held that the proceeds of a sale of assets by a company at an under-value may be treated as a distribution to the shareholders and taxable accordingly. The UK Inland Revenue could assess such a transaction as an under-value sale between associated persons under Section 770, ICTA 1988.

   The price at which the assets pass from the UK party to the joint venture should be compatible with a transfer on arm's-length terms and between connected persons. If the proposed price does not meet these criteria the Inland Revenue may deem the disposal to have been made at market value.

4.3 Tax on chargeable gains

When a UK-resident company makes a transfer of assets to a JV company, it will be liable *prima facie* to corporation tax on chargeable gains. This may be subject to loss relief and deductions. When the transferor and the transferee are both UK-resident and are also both 75 per cent affiliates, the group exemption will apply, and no corporation tax will be payable until the event of a disposal of the assets by the joint venture, or the liquidation of the JV company.

Various reliefs may be available under UK taxation statutes to reduce the chargeable gain realised on the disposal of assets to the joint venture.

4.3.1 Rollover relief – Section 152 Taxation of Chargeable Gains Act 1992 (TCGA)

This relief is available when the consideration received for business assets is applied in the acquisition of replacement assets for use in the same division of the principal's business. The Inland Revenue has confirmed in a concession statement that the relief should be available where the consideration has been satisfied by an issue of shares in the transferee company, i.e. the JV company, provided that an equivalent amount of cash has been applied to the repurchase of business assets.

4.3.2 Transfer of a trade – Section 140 TCGA

(a) The tax on chargeable gains may be postponed where the UK-resident transferor company already has a branch business in the JV territory and now wishes to transfer such assets situated in the JV territory to a non-UK-resident company (in this case the JV company). In this event the consideration for the transfer should be, wholly or partly, shares or loan stock in the JV company amounting to 25 per cent or more of the share capital of the issuing company.

(b) Section 140A of TCGA provides an exemption for gains tax purposes in any case where the transferor company, being resident in the EU, transfers to another (non-UK) EU-resident company the whole or part of a trade carried on by it in the UK, and the transfer is made wholly in consideration of the issue of securities in the transferee company directly to the transferor.

(c) Section 140C of TCGA provides gains tax relief in the case where the UK-resident company transfers to a (non-UK) EU-resident company the whole or part of a trade which is carried on in any non-UK territory of the EU through a branch or agency. The transfer must include all the assets used in the trade which are owned by the transferor company, and the consideration must consist wholly or partly of securities in the transferee issued directly to the transferor.

4.3.3 Loss relief

Any capital or income losses which are available to the transferor may be applied to relieve the chargeable gain arising from the asset transfer, in the same manner as for other taxable income.

4.4 Value added taxes and stamp duty on transfers

4.4.1 Value added tax

Value added tax (VAT) would be chargeable *prima facie* where the JV party is transferring assets to the joint venture, where the transferor is registrable for VAT in the UK and the transfer itself is not exempt. The seller is accountable for the VAT, and if the parties intend that the transferee is to pay the tax, they should specify that the price is exclusive of VAT.

However, pursuant to Article 5(1) VAT (Special Provisions) Under 1995, VAT will not be chargeable on the transfer of a business as a going concern, provided that the JV company uses the transferred assets in carrying on the same kind of business as that carried on by the transferor, and certain other conditions are satisfied.

Where the transfer does not amount to the transfer of a business as a going concern, the transferring JV party may, where it holds more than 50 per cent of the company's shares, be able to treat the JV company as being in the same VAT group as itself. Where the transferor and the transferee are 50 per cent affiliates for the purpose of the VAT regulations, the VAT charge should not apply to the transfer.

4.4.2 Stamp duties

The incidence of stamp duty on asset transfers in the UK and in other jurisdictions should always be kept in mind. Certain jurisdictions may also levy a documentary transfer duty. It may be possible to minimise the incidence of such duties by providing for the title to the assets to pass by delivery, or by means of a special agreement. All appropriate legal and tax advice should be taken in the jurisdiction.

5 INTEREST AND ROYALTIES

5.1 Tax treatment of interest and royalties

The receipt of interest or royalty payments from the JV company can also be an efficient method of extracting benefits from the joint venture. A UK-resident JV company will be able to obtain income tax deductibility on sums paid by way of interest or royalty, provided that the payment is not otherwise held to constitute a distribution. A UK-resident JV party will be able to treat its received interest or royalties as part of its notional income stream, unless it is a 75 per cent plus affiliate and the sums are held by the Inland Revenue to constitute a distribution.

5.2 Double taxation relief

In order to protect their own residents and comply with international conventions, many countries adopt standard tax provisions relating to interest and royalty payments. The common forms of double taxation treaty reflect this policy trend. Interest and royalties are usually taxable in the state where the recipient is resident and not in the state where the payment is made or the profits arise, provided that the recipient is the beneficial owner of the payments.

Accordingly, for the JV company making payments in respect of interest or royalties to the JV parties, if the territories have the appropriate double taxation agreement, no withholding tax is payable.

The situation may be different if the JV party otherwise carries on business in the JV territory, and the tax-free element of the interest or royalty payment may be reduced by the local tax authorities if the payments are held to be 'excessive' by reason of any special relationship between payor and payee, or because they do not reflect the value of the underlying property.

Checklist 11 Questions for tax planning

1   Where will JV profits mainly be taxed? that is, where is corporate residence or presence?

2   What is the prevailing profits tax rate?

3   How will dividend and royalty income be taxed?

4   What indirect taxation will the JV incur?

5   What is the party's position on contributing assets?

12

Accounting issues in joint ventures

1 ACCOUNTING ISSUES AFFECTING THE JOINT VENTURE

The accounting treatment of the joint venture will be approached from differing perspectives by each party. A corporate joint venture will be required to comply with the local accounting laws and regulations of the JV territory. In addition, the JV company will need to comply with generally accepted international accounting practice. A foreign party may want to impose compliance with its own domestic accounting practice so as to enable it to incorporate the JV company's trading results with its own accounts. If the JV territory is a developing country with minimal accounting laws and regulations, the foreign investor will want to guarantee that acceptable standards will be followed in the preparation of all accounting records, and especially the annual (statutory) accounts of the JV company.

The requirement that the annual audit and accounts should be performed in a manner consistent with internationally accepted accounting practice will help to provide a reasonable degree of assurance against accounting abuse. The foreign party may also wish to impose compliance with the schedule of its own accounting principles required to be followed in the company's annual audit. However, any such list of principles should be expressed as not exclusive, and it is important that the list be scrutinised by the party's local accounting advisers in order to minimise the possibility of conflict between the agreed principles and the domestic regulations of the JV territory. Such a conflict would cause problems for the auditors of the company, who must comply with local requirements in order to certify the accounts.

With the growth of international trade and affiliated accountancy firms, a reference to international generally accepted accounting principles (GAAP) is becoming more definite and understood, although there remains the possibility of insoluble conflict with domestic practices in certain areas. Goodwill is a particular example, where local practice may not allow for incremental value to attach to the company's assets or shares in respect of trading goodwill. Some countries do not allow for straight-line or accelerated depreciation of fixed assets. If the JV territory is regarded as being somewhat unusual, the parties should consider setting up some further protection in the Joint Venture Agreement, such as:

(a) providing for international (or UK) GAAP to apply, so far as they are not inconsistent with the JV territory domestic laws;

(b) providing that an additional non-statutory audit will be done in accordance with international (or UK) GAAP for the benefit of the parties (probably before the conduct of the statutory audit).

The choice of auditors to act for the JV company can be a political issue in many joint ventures, as clearly the right auditors will be a crucial protection for the foreign party. From this viewpoint, the auditors must be both reputable and reliable, and the foreign party will be well advised to impose the choice of a substantial firm of accountants with a multinational presence, or the official (duly appointed) local affiliate firm to such a practice, for the following reasons:

(a)　a multinational firm is the best guarantee of professional competence and the production of impartial financial statements;

(b)　a multinational firm will be better able to handle the cross-border financial issues affecting the joint venture parties, including the valuation of assets located outside the JV territory and the payment of dividends. They can therefore liaise with the foreign party's own accounting advisers;

(c)　a multinational firm will be more experienced in joint venture work, and usually more efficient and cost-effective in its performance.

Both parties will want to be certain that the auditors are genuinely independent, as there are many possibilities for conflict of interest. It is worth questioning if one party, having had substantial preparatory work performed by accountants acting as its own advisers, should recommend the same accountants to act as auditors to the JV company. Evidently the foreign party will want to satisfy itself that there is no prior relationship or other conflict of interest involving the auditors and the local party.

Each party will also need to have provisions included in the Joint Venture Agreement to the effect that all necessary financial and accounting information will be regularly provided to enable it properly to scrutinise the joint venture and to incorporate financial information into its own results. The local party will in many cases be exercising 'hands-on' day-to-day management of the JV business, and accordingly a stipulation to require the joint venture to provide agreed *pro forma* monthly or quarterly management accounts (in a form prescribed or otherwise agreed) will be of considerable importance to the foreign party. See the suggested clauses in Appendix E relating to financial information and management accounts.

It should be noted that auditors may need to be appointed and annual financial statements prepared in the case of various types of unincorporated joint ventures, and similar assurances will be necessary as regards the provision of information.

2　ACCOUNTING ISSUES AFFECTING THE PARTIES

Traditionally under UK accounting practice, interests held in a partnership or joint venture are required to be accounted in the books and financial statements of the shareholder as either:

(a) an interest in an associated company, in respect of any shareholding between 20 and 50 per cent, in which event the interest should be 'equity-accounted' and the relevant share of net profits (after taxation and similar deductions) included in the participant's consolidated accounts; or

(b) a subsidiary company, in respect of any shareholding exceeding 50 per cent or where the participant had control of the management or board of directors, in which event the full results of the subsidiary should be included in the consolidated financial statements of the parent.

Since the 1980s, with the evolution of accounting standards addressing the problems of consortia and joint ventures, a new approach has developed in the UK to examining the consolidation of joint venture interests, based on a review of the level of control or influence exercised by the participant company. Some of this new approach is reflected in recent changes to UK companies law in the Companies Act 1989, and in the EU's Seventh Directive on Company Law dealing with statutory accounting requirements.

With the growing tendency to look at the degree of influence or management control exercised by a shareholder, certain countries (such as France) have moved to a different basis of accounting for joint ventures, consolidating into the participants' accounts all the joint venture's assets, in an appropriate proportion based on the level of shareholding. The assets and liabilities will accordingly be proportionately consolidated in the manner of a subsidiary company. The trend to proportional consolidation is becoming more widespread, and is frequently favoured by large companies which seek to include gross income receipts in their consolidated annual financial statements.

Proportional consolidation is permitted for UK companies in respect of their interests in certain unincorporated joint ventures which have the nature of a partnership. However, the UK legislation does not permit proportionate consolidation to be applied to corporate joint ventures, except where the JV company falls within the definition of a subsidiary undertaking, when full consolidation of accounts is required. This is the case where the participant holds a majority of the voting shares, has the right to appoint a majority of the directors, or where it otherwise exercises a 'dominant influence' over the affairs of the company.

In those cases where the joint venture interest represents a share in an 'associated company', the more limited 'equity method' of accounting for the party's share of the joint ventures is prescribed. Pursuant to the equity method of accounting, only the participant's fractional share of the net profits and the net assets are included in its consolidated group financial statements after taxation, extraordinary items, interest and other statutory deductions. Under Statement of Standard Accounting Practice 1 (SSAP 1), in the case of equity accounting a separate note to the accounts is required to disclose the shareholder's share of pre-tax profits less losses of the JV company.

The definition of an 'associated undertaking' under the Companies Act (CA) is expressed as a company in which the participant has a 'significant influence' over the operating and financial policy of the company, but falling short of the majority or 'dominant' holding required for subsidiary company status under SSAP 1. A significant influence is presumed to exist in the case of a shareholding of 20 per cent or more, subject to it being demonstrated otherwise, for instance where other large corporate shareholders prevent the participant from having such influence, or there are restrictions in the Shareholders' Agreement. Conversely, a shareholding of less than 20 per cent may in certain conditions amount to the exercise of a significant influence, if the facts or the nature of the agreement clearly demonstrate this to be the case. Regard may be had here to 'golden' or similar preferential share arrangements.

In most 50:50 joint ventures or where overall control is not accorded to either party by virtue of weighted voting rights or similar restrictions, the equity method of accounting will be appropriate and should accurately reflect the absence of any 'dominant' influence being exercised by either shareholder. However, where the terms of the agreements or the Articles of the JV company grant the participant a right to exercise a dominant influence, or where a dominant influence is actually exercised by it, any UK shareholder is required to account for the JV company's results as a subsidiary company and to include a full consolidation in its group accounts (Section 238, CA 1985).

Fig. 12.1 summarises the contrasting accounting systems applicable to joint ventures.

Checklist 12　Questions on accounting treatment

1　What is the party's shareholding?

2　What accounting treatment follows under the party's domestic laws?

3　How will the JV company's accounts be prepared under law?

4　What accounting policies and treatment should be imposed on the JV?

Fig. 12.1 Accounting treatment

A Subsidiary co. accounting (60% interest)

Profit and loss a/c	JV's P & L		Party's P & L
Turnover	100 000	⟶	200 000
Less expenses	70 000	⟶	140 000
Pre-tax profit	30 000	⟶	60 000
Post-tax profit	20 000	⟶	40 000
			To balance sheet

B Equity accounting (40% interest)

Profit and loss a/c	JV's P & L		Party's P & L
Turnover	100 000	‖	100 000
Less expenses	70 000	‖	70 000
Pre-tax profit	30 000	‖	30 000
Post-tax profit	20 000	‖	20 000
	(×40% to balance sheet)		To balance sheet

Balance sheet of party

Current assets	From P & L (of party)	20 000
	Add share of JV interest	8 000
	(i.e. 40% × 20 000).	

C Proportional consolidation (40% interest)

Profit and loss a/c	JV's P & L		Party's P & L
Turnover	100 000	× 40% ⟶	140 000
Less expenses	70 000	× 40% ⟶	98 000
Pre-tax profit	30 000	× 40% ⟶	42 000
Post-tax profit	20 000	× 40% ⟶	28 000
			To balance sheet

Note: the above examples assume that both the JV and the Party have identical figures in their P & L accounts.

Media services JV between US and Chinese cable companies

Media services JV between US and Chinese cable companies

Illinois Telecom Corporation Inc. (ITC) is a US corporation that manufactures systems and equipment for the provision of cable broadcasting. Shanghai Communications Networks (SCN) is the largest telecommunication company in the Shanghai region. The two companies are proposing to establish a joint venture to set up a new TV cable system exclusively aimed at the leisure and hotel industry in the region, to construct the operational centre and the infrastructure for the system, to obtain appropriate licences for the JV from the state authorities and to run the broadcasting system.

From initial discussions on the project with the State Administration of Industry and Commerce, the parties have an indication that the authorities will be prepared to approve the JV in principle on the basis of a shareholding of 60 per cent held by ITC and a shareholding of 40 per cent held by SCN. A condition of approval is likely to be undertakings to partner other Chinese companies in joint ventures in the Special Economic Zones within a period of about five years.

The parties have already signed an MOU setting out the basic corporate structure and business proposals for the JV, in a similar form to the suggested clauses in Chapter 4, and have commenced the preparation of a contract to be entered into with the Shanghai state broadcasting authority for construction of the infrastructure and the provision of broadcasting services. Completion of the joint venture will be made conditional on the contract being negotiated in a form satisfactory to both parties. Under the JV arrangements as stated in the MOU, notwithstanding the 60:40 corporate structure the Chinese party SCN is to have a veto on all matters directly concerning applications for state broadcasting licences and continuing regulatory matters.

Following the signing of the MOU the parties start to carry out extensive due diligence on each other's asset and contractual contributions to the JV, and in particular the suitability of the proposed cable operations centre provided by SCN, which must be adaptable to the US-type broadcasting technology to be provided by ITC.

The due diligence investigations by the US party include review of the following matters:

- the status of the site, including all relevant planning authorities and approvals;
- the environmental history of the site and any potential liabilities arising from this;
- the technical expertise of the employees to be seconded to the JV.

The parties then agree to move on to the more substantive phases of preparation for the JV, instructing legal and financial advisers who begin to prepare regulatory applications and draft the Joint Venture Agreement and the governing documents for the JV. At this stage the senior managers of each party responsible for the JV decide to co-operate to put together the Business Plan. The task of preparing the first draft of the Business Plan is allotted to the Senior Contract Manager of ITC.

Problem: You are the Senior Contract Manager of ITC. What should you state in the Business Plan to be:

(a)   the principal objectives of the joint venture?

(b)   the sales and marketing strategy to be adopted?

(c)   two future business opportunities for the JV company to exploit?

(d)   two future threats to the JV business for which contingency should be made?

Manufacturing JV between UK, Italian and Israeli companies

Case study 4

Manufacturing JV between UK, Italian and Israeli companies

Southern Domestic Appliances Limited (Southern) is a small UK manufacturer of domestic heating and ventilator appliances, with special expertise in the area of energy-saving devices. In order to increase its penetration of the European market and to combine its product knowledge, it is proposing to enter a manufacturing joint venture with an Italian company, Toscana Electric Spa (Toscana) to produce a new domestic air conditioning unit for overseas markets. In addition to the two principal parties, who will each take a 40 per cent shareholding in the joint venture company, it is proposed that a 20 per cent share will be taken by an Israeli company, whose factory will sub-contract the assembly of some of the components, and who will also take a role in promoting sales in Israel and the Far East.

Toscana is to be responsible for establishing the JV operation on a new site at Brindisi. Both the principal parties will furnish the factory with production line and assembly equipment. They will also each contribute patents and other intellectual property to the making of the new appliances, and the Israeli company will contribute certain electronic design know-how. Southern will provide three valuable patents including that for the new air conditioner, and various designs and other know-how, mainly in connection with the energy-saving devices. Toscana will provide a patent to make the devices compatible with the electrical voltage systems in Israel and the Far East countries, and other aspects of know-how, as well as most of the technical staff at the JV's main factory site.

The factory will initially be engaged exclusively on development and manufacture of the new air conditioner. The product will compete in Western and Central Europe with existing appliances sold by both the parties, but at a lower price level. However, a version of the product will be targeted specifically at the Israeli and Far East markets, and each party is willing to confirm their good faith in this by entering into non-compete undertakings to be contained in the main Joint Venture Agreement, which will foreclose direct selling of their own competing products in those markets.

In addition, the parties agree to mutually review their existing product sales in Central and Eastern Europe regarding sales of competing products. Each party will be given an exclusive distribution agreement to sell the appliances in its own country.

In reviewing the regulatory aspects of the JV the parties are aware that they may face problems under EU competition law. The new entity will not meet the size and turnover thresholds for the Merger Regulation to apply to the transaction. However, the combined turnover of the participant groups will exceed the Article 81 threshold, as combined turnover will exceed ECU 300 million, and the parties' combined market share will exceed five per cent of the total relevant market. Therefore the parties need to consider if there is a potential breach of Article 81 of the EU Treaty, and whether the JV is likely to be deemed a co-operative joint venture with anti-competitive aspects.

The parties now have a draft Joint Venture Agreement. In addition to some commercial issues, they need to finalise the competition arrangements secure that they will not face fines from the Commission and possible avoidance of the agreements. Each party therefore takes steps on its own behalf to secure legal advice both on the nature of the JV and its effect on competition, and also on specific aspects such as the effect of their European competition arrangements and the applicability of the technology transfer block exemption to their licensing arrangements to the JV. They are all advised, more or less, as follows.

- If the agreements contain formal non-compete undertakings for Europe, they are more likely to contravene Article 81(1), but may still be exempted (see GEC/Weir).

- Apply immediately, prior to signing the Joint Venture Agreement, to DG IV of the European Commission for negative clearance under Article 81, EU Treaty, and in the alternative for an Article 81(3) exemption.

- State in clearance application that JV is not expected to breach Article 81 because:

  (a) no formal non-compete arrangements are entered for Europe;

  (b) the arrangements will not directly forestall competition in the upstream market as the products are not identical; and

  (c) consumers are expected to benefit from the new energy-saving appliances.

- Under the market share analysis given above, the IP licensing arrangements may not come within the permitted scope of the EU block exemption on technology transfer agreements, so these should also be the subject of the negative clearance application.

- The exclusive distribution agreements should be capable of being drafted to gain exemption under the EU block exemption relating thereto.

Problem: You are one of the team assigned to negotiate the Joint Venture Agreement on behalf of Southern. Consider your team's approach to the questions of:

- entering the proposed non-competition obligations with the other JV parties – see the case of GEC/Weir referred to in Chapter 9, Section 1.3 (*Note:* the party with smaller sales in Europe will be more anxious to have the non-compete clause);

- the IP licensing arrangements; and

- the exclusive distribution arrangements.

Part III

The Joint Venture Agreement – structural issues

13

Concepts and definitions

In drafting the Joint Venture Agreement, certain concepts and terms of reference will be used. Some of these will be technical in nature and relate to the structure of the joint venture or the commercial transactions. Other terms will have general application to the agreement and may need to be defined.

This chapter defines some frequently used terms; in addition, the reader is referred to the draft Shareholders' Agreement in Appendix E.

Affiliate

The term 'affiliate' (sometimes referred to as 'associated company' or 'group company') has application in a number of areas covered by the agreement.

(a) Share transfers. It is common to prohibit transfers of joint venture shares to outsiders (without common consent), but generally the parties seek exceptions for certain intra-group or affiliate transfers.

(b) Issues of new shares. The parties may wish all or part of their initial shares or future issues to be directly issued to a named affiliate.

(c) Technology and intellectual property licensing. Where the parties are to license intellectual property rights to the JV company, it is often intended that some of the rights will be licensed by subsidiaries or other related companies.

Control

A definition of the term 'control' may help to identify the 'affiliates' and the consolidated group of the JV parties. The two principal limbs will be:

(a) the ownership of a majority of the voting rights in the relevant company; and

(b) the right to appoint or nominate a majority of the board of directors.

This second branch will bring in a number of joint venture interests where the party does not own the majority of shares but has *de facto* control of the joint venture.

The Business

Most agreements will have a specific clause dealing with the business objectives of the JV company, defining in broad terms what the business is at the outset and whether the business activity may be expanded. It is important to specify in the agreement that core activities may only be added to by agreement of the parties, except to the extent that certain limited projects may fall within the discretion of the managing director.

Business Plan

The Business Plan will be defined in the Joint Venture Agreement, and a completed (or near complete) draft of the plan should be scheduled to it. The Business Plan will help to bring into definition the agreed trading strategy and to avoid subsequent disputes. Chapter 8 above provides more detail on the Business Plan.

Contract

Some joint ventures centre on a single commercial contract or a series of contracts. In joint ventures intended to discharge one project or to tender for the award of one particular contact, it will be important to precisely define the term. If the contract is subject to tenders the entire joint venture will be conditional, and the principal condition precedent in the Joint Venture Agreement will be the conclusion of the main business contract on terms acceptable to all the parties.

Shares

It is advisable to define the shares for purposes of the capital provisions of the agreement, and in particular to limit the definition to equity voting capital as the term is generally understood (in the UK this is ordinary share capital). Shares may be divided into classes such as 'A' and 'B' shares or similar designations, but this should be done only if it is made clear that the substantive voting and other rights are equal and ranking *pari passu* in all respects as between the shareholders, unless there are special circumstances to distinguish them.

Shareholder

A separate definition of the term 'Shareholder' is also advisable. The parties who are actual signatories of the agreement are usually referred to as the 'Parties', and this term is preferable in respect of the formation stages. The term 'Shareholder' is more applicable for provisions which bind transferees, who will become bound to the main agreement by signing a Deed of Adherence to it or by signing a new Shareholders' Agreement. It is useful to draft the term Shareholder in a wide manner so as to include both the initial Parties and all subsequent holders of shares.

Shareholder proportion

This term clarifies the division of shareholdings between the parties, which is usually the same division as that to be made in respect of liabilities and benefits of the joint venture. In the case of a 50:50 JV company the proportion is obviously 50 per cent. In certain situations the parties' assumption of liabilities or debts may not coincide with their shareholdings. If it is intended that it should in all events, the definition should tie the Shareholder Proportion to the shareholders' fraction of issued capital, leaving the possibility that all new Shareholders would accept the same conditions as to liabilities.

Guarantee

One issue that can cause problems between JV parties is the extent to which they may be required to give parent company guarantees in respect of the joint venture's business or contracts. If the JV business is such that performance guarantees are required to be given by the parties, each party should seek to limit the extent of its liability to the proportion of its respective shareholding. The shareholders may wish to provide that any guarantees will be given only on the basis that several liability applies, in particular where liability is both joint and several (or joint only) the more substantial party may face more risk of pursuit. In any situation where one party is liable to be called upon to settle the guarantee, the issue should be addressed by means of a cross-indemnity by each JV party to the other.

Fair value/net asset value

In a number of Joint Venture Agreements there is a need to establish a fixed mechanism for valuing shareholdings in the company, usually in relation to an intended disposal of shares under option rights contained in the Joint Venture Agreement. There are various alternative formulas for share valuations. They can be based on a minimal 'net asset value' approach (excluding goodwill, the benefit of know-how and intangible assets), or alternatively on a 'fair value' basis, which will reflect the parties' joint efforts in developing the joint venture. The issue of share valuations is discussed in Chapter 16, Section 2, and see also Appendix E, Clause 17.

Reserved Matters/Unanimous Approval

Many Joint Venture Agreements have provisions protecting small shareholders from permanent exclusion on major strategic or business decisions by the majority shareholder. Often termed 'minority protection' provisions, these may in fact sometimes operate to stop several minority shareholders from forming a clique.

These provisions usually stipulate that specified matters ('Reserved Matters') cannot be implemented without the unanimous approval of all the shareholders. As a further layer of control, certain more important commercial and structural matters may also be expressed to require the unanimous approval of all the directors. The Reserved Matters will be listed in the agreement and a mechanism will require that these matters must be approved by a unanimous vote at a board or shareholders' meeting, or by a written resolution of all the directors or shareholders where that is permitted ('Unanimous Approval').

Certain problems should be borne in mind in deciding what will constitute a Unanimous Approval vote, including the following:

(a) It is not desirable to allow for a director's written resolutions to achieve a Unanimous Approval, since any consideration of the Reserved Matters will require full discussion at a board meeting in the light of what is in the company's best interests.

(b) Care should be taken in the definition to require unanimity among all the shareholders who are eligible to vote, regardless of their attendance.

14

Conditions to the Shareholders' Agreement

1 GOVERNMENT APPROVALS

Joint Venture Agreements will frequently be expressed as conditional on the occurrence of certain events, most commonly relating to the attainment of required government or regulatory approvals and consents.

In some cases, joint ventures which involve solely UK-resident parties may require government approvals to be obtained before the parties can proceed to reach agreement. This may be because one of the JV parties is a public company listed on London's International Stock Exchange, which intends to transfer to the JV company a substantial proportion of its assets where the transaction may be a 'Super Class One' transaction involving the acquisition of a 25 per cent or greater share of the assets of the target company, with the result that shareholders' approval must be given for the transaction prior to execution of the Joint Venture Agreement.

The issue of government and regulatory approvals is more significant in the case of investments in overseas joint ventures – see Chapter 10 above. Almost all agreements will need to be made conditional on the obtaining of all requisite government approvals, consent and registrations, both for the transaction as summarised in the Joint Venture Agreement and for the capital structure of the JV company.

Commonly in an overseas joint venture the parties will provide for absolute conditionality, so that the Joint Venture Agreement will not come into effect unless or until the required government consents are given, and will be deemed ineffective if the consents prove invalid. Should consents or approvals be granted subject to any qualifications or conditions imposed by the investment authorities, it is prudent for the parties to reserve the right to approve any such qualifications, and to retain the right to withdraw from the agreement if they affect the party's participation.

The approvals clause should also provide that all parties will co-operate with each other in obtaining the necessary approvals, including providing information and doing whatever is required to ensure that the government approvals will be forthcoming from the authorities. The local party should be obligated actively to pursue the approvals with the government agencies and to forward to them all necessary information on the proposed business. Notwithstanding this, the parties will usually provide that the legal and other costs incurred in obtaining the approvals will be shared between them equally.

In the case of many corporate joint ventures, the Joint Venture Agreement provides that the JV company will be incorporated and the shares issued to the JV parties before the required government approvals are forthcoming. This may be for legal necessity or commercial reasons. In this event the parties will want the Joint Venture Agreement to become operative immediately in respect of all those provisions which relate to the rights attaching to shares, directors, meetings and voting etc.

However, it will be necessary to retain conditionality should the required government approvals not be forthcoming. The best method of achieving this is to provide:

(a) that the completion of the agreement, i.e. the issue of shares to both parties or (if relevant) the transfer of a 50 per cent initial shareholding from the incorporating party to the other party, shall be conditional on the receipt of the required approvals and consents; and

(b) that if the approvals and consents are not forthcoming the parties will promptly pass a resolution voluntarily to wind up the company.

The above provisions will have the effect of unscrambling the joint subscription of shares in the event that the approvals are not given.

2 CONTRACTUAL MATTERS

In certain cases the existence of the joint venture project will be predicated on the award of a significant commercial contract. The joint venture may be the vehicle for a joint bid, tender or similar proposal, or may be seeking the award of a patent or licence agreement in favour of one JV party or the joint venture. If the award of a contract or similar benefit is to be a condition of the joint venture proceeding, the condition clause will make it clear that the contract must be executed by the JV company and the commercial contractor, and that the terms of the contract must be expressly accepted in writing by all parties to the Joint Venture Agreement. The contract will mainly be negotiated in the preliminary phase of the joint venture and may be executed when the Joint Venture Agreement is signed, but the intentions of the JV parties should be clearly expressed.

It may be advisable to include in the agreement the procedures for conducting negotiations concerning the contract, including how certain important matters such as funding and guarantees are to be dealt with, and how the contract is to be approved by the parties. The section of the Joint Venture Agreement dealing with resolutions and corporate decisions should make it clear that the conclusion of the contract and all variations thereto are matters requiring the consent of all the shareholders.

Where the contract itself is not at the execution stage when the Joint Venture Agreement is to be signed, the parties should consider including, as conditions to the Joint Venture Agreement, certain minimum commercial terms for inclusion in the final version of the commercial contract. If it is expected that the commercial contract is likely to follow or resemble an existing form, such a draft could be appended and specified to be the basic and substantial terms of the contract. A condition may be further imposed that the commercial contract shall be substantially in the same form, thus giving the parties effective withdrawal rights if it is not settled as agreed.

15

Directors and management

As the daily management of corporate joint ventures resides at the board of director level, each party will wish to see that its interests are properly represented on the board. The most significant commercial matters (such as approving contracts or loans to the company) will not manifest themselves for shareholder consideration unless the parties' director representatives are properly appraised of the matters and the board conducts regular and open meetings.

Therefore, if a balance of power is to be created to protect the foreign party's position, this needs to be achieved at board level. Most territories will permit flexibility in the drafting of these clauses, subject to requirements in the Articles of Association or company law.

1 BOARD STRUCTURE

UK law will permit a wide degree of choice on the management structure of a company, allowing many areas of business to be delegated to committees or individual managers. The routine running of the business may be delegated to a single managing director or to a series of divisional managers. The main requirements for directors are that they keep informed of the major aspects of the company's business, meet on a regular basis and take responsibility for the various business matters not delegated to the shareholders.

In some countries a two-tier management structure is required, with a secondary board of management reporting to the board of directors which handles routine business. In their turn the board of directors will be primarily responsible for the strategic aspects of the business. This senior board may be given the title of 'Board of Supervisors' or a similar term. If such a two-tier structure is imposed, the parties should structure the management so that one of the two management boards is clearly the *de facto* decision-making body at which representatives of the JV parties will meet and deliberate on major business matters. The standard and the two-tier management structures are illustrated in Fig. 15.1.

In order to preserve the balance of power of the joint venture, provision should be made in relation to who will act as chairman of the board. It will often be desirable for the foreign party to appoint the chairman, in particular as the local party usually has the right to appoint the managing director. In certain cases the parties may prefer that the position of chairman should rotate between them from year to year. It will be sensible to specify that the chairman will not have an additional or casting vote in respect of actions at board meetings.

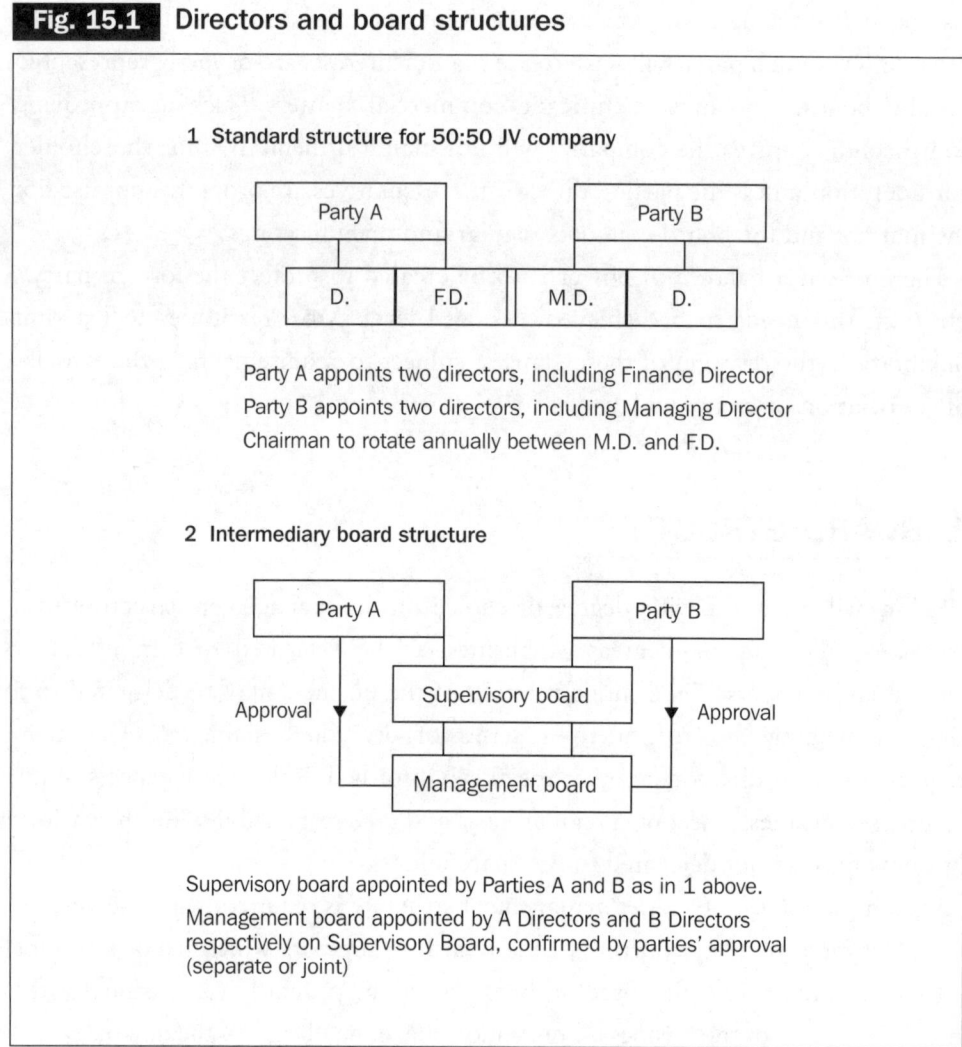

Fig. 15.1 Directors and board structures

1 Standard structure for 50:50 JV company

Party A   Party B

D. | F.D. | M.D. | D.

Party A appoints two directors, including Finance Director
Party B appoints two directors, including Managing Director
Chairman to rotate annually between M.D. and F.D.

2 Intermediary board structure

Party A   Party B

Approval   Supervisory board   Approval

Management board

Supervisory board appointed by Parties A and B as in 1 above.
Management board appointed by A Directors and B Directors
respectively on Supervisory Board, confirmed by parties' approval
(separate or joint)

The Joint Venture Agreement should also provide that the directors will act on a non-remunerative basis, so that if either party wishes to pay a salary, fees or expenses to its own directors, that is a matter entirely for its discretion.

2 BOARD PROCEEDINGS

The sections of the board provisions governing proceedings of the board, meetings and decisions are of particular importance to the structure of the JV company.

2.1 Location of board meetings

It is important to specify where meetings will habitually be held, as the foreign party in particular will need to know that its director can attend them. It is also useful to clarify the company's residence for tax purposes. A UK-resident shareholder will be prudent to specify that the board meetings will normally be held in the JV territory, or at least outside the UK, to avoid tax residency problems.

2.2 Frequency of meetings

The parties will want to provide that meetings are held at regular intervals, which will depend on the nature of the company's business and the strategic decisions to be made on finance and other matters. Regular convening of the full board will be favourable to the foreign party's interests. Normally the chairman of the board will convene these meetings, but a power should be given in the agreement for any director or shareholder to convene a board meeting to discuss any particular issue.

2.3 Notice provisions

The local companies law will provide for the minimum notice required to be given to shareholders, but the parties should anyway agree a minimum notice period. The foreign party's directors will certainly require a longer period of notice to attend board meetings held in the JV territory, and it is important to make sure that service of a notice will be by reliable means, either by courier, facsimile transmission or at least by registered airmail delivery. Notices should never be deemed to have been received by a director, and the onus must fall on the company to serve notices by an efficient method.

2.4 Quorum for a meeting

The minimum quorum for a board meeting, without which no valid decisions may be taken, should be clearly set out. With a board of four directors, it is probably necessary to provide for a quorum of two directors (one from each party), but although that is the minimum position, it may not always be sufficiently protective of either party. Care should be taken to ensure that a quorum is required to be present throughout a board meeting.

2.5 Alternate directors

It is advisable to provide that each director has the power to appoint an alternate director to attend board meetings in the event that she/he is unable to do so, upon giving written notice to the company. The agreement should provide for a maximum duration of any such appointment. The shareholders will usually seek to clear with directors in advance who the alternates may be, and the parties can provide that a temporary appointment should be made by notice from the appointing shareholder itself.

2.6 Video or telephone meetings

Parties should consider whether they wish to specify that meetings may be held by live telephone conference or video conference link-up, provided that all participants will be able to participate fully at all times and the meeting is entirely on the record.

2.7 Written resolutions of directors

It is usually desirable to provide that board action can be taken by circulating the proposed resolutions to all the directors for their written approval. Such a provision should specify that the written resolution requires the consent of all the appointed directors, and not merely the quorum or voting majority required for full board meetings.

2.8 Board decisions – Reserved Matters or weighted voting

In relation to normal business matters, voting will be on a one director–one vote basis. However, the Joint Venture Agreement will provide that certain listed matters can be actioned only by the unanimous approval of all the directors, or all the shareholders. Alternatively, this may specify a weighted majority which is required to action certain matters, or provide that one party shall have increased voting rights on certain issues.

The Reserved Matters will determine that the listed matters cannot be approved on the basis of a simple majority vote. The benefits of this for the shareholders are that:

(a) the important business matters cannot be deliberated by the managing director and local staff, but will revert to the full board for resolution;

(b) a shareholder will not be sidelined in the relevant business matters so long as it supervises its own directors adequately; and

(c) the matters which must be formally resolved will be brought to the shareholders' attention, and may subsequently also be required to be submitted for the shareholders' unanimous approval.

Where it is desired to implement Reserved Matters, it is important that proper notices will ensure that full information is provided to enable the directors to pass an informed vote.

3 DIRECTORS' FIDUCIARY DUTIES

The boards of joint venture companies are composed of directors nominated by the principal shareholders and are usually employees of the investing group. Alternatively, some nominee directors may be trusted local business contacts in the JV territory.

Where nominee directors are acting on behalf of a significant corporate shareholder, they will inevitably be concerned as to their legal position, and in particular their fiduciary duties as directors to act at all times in the best interests of the company. These duties include accounting to the company for all profits or financial benefits which are due to it, providing the board of directors with full information about any matters under the director's responsibility and avoiding conflicts of interest between the joint venture and their other business dealings.

The directors' duties to the company also include the requirement that each of them will exercise his/her discretion and take voting decisions in the best interests of the company. The question is frequently asked whether nominee directors may thus be put in a difficult position where the nominating shareholder has expressed the view that certain actions are necessary (or not desired) for the company's business and that action should be taken accordingly at board level. In the majority of cases it is suggested that the directors should not be put in a difficult position, because the existence of nominee directors is an integral part of the recognised structure of joint venture transactions and it is understood that the directors will be permitted to represent their shareholders' interests in a 'partisan' manner.

However, there will be strict limits to the application of this principle. Both shareholder and director should avoid initiating any action which could lead to a breach of the director's fiduciary duties, or in any way mislead the other shareholder(s) in any matter affecting the business of the company. It should be noted also that some recent decisions have indeed extended the fiduciary principles to include obligations to other shareholders. See Chapter 16, Section 4, Minority shareholder provisions.

In practical terms, it is suggested that a director of the JV company should in no circumstances implement actions or vote for any matters which she/he believes to be contrary to the interests of the company. It is suggested, further, that the shareholder in such a case should never put direct pressure on a director to vote for or against a stated matter, but instead should exercise his/her discretion at the shareholder level under the Joint Venture Agreement. On the other hand, mandates or general policy statements may be discussed and agreed upon by all the responsible executives of the shareholder group, in respect of the financial and business interests of the joint venture. Furthermore, the directors will be generally expected to comply with corporate resolutions or decisions which are agreed by all the shareholders.

Checklist 15 Matters for JV directors to consider

1 Understand the business and the Business Plan.

2 Availability for board meetings and other commitments.

3 Areas of delegated responsibility, e.g. finance, sales.

4 Any conflicts of interest with the JV business?

Shareholders and shares

1 SHARE CAPITAL

The provisions relating to share capital for corporate joint ventures may be determined by a number of factors. Prior to obtaining required regulatory approvals in the JV territory, the parties should ascertain the minimal share capital requirement prescribed for the company under the laws of the JV territory. They should confirm also that the initial share capital will be refundable in the event that any regulatory consents are not forthcoming. Having determined the initial share capital amount, it will then be prudent to take legal and tax advice on whether subsequent contributions should be in the form of further issues of shares or in the form of shareholder loans.

Having determined the initial level of share capital, the Joint Venture Agreement should clarify that the definition of shares for the purposes of the JV company means exclusively 'equity voting shares' in the company. The parties may consider dividing the share capital into separate classes, such as 'A' shares and 'B' shares. This may be desirable in cases where one party has special rights, or has advanced loans or a unique asset contribution. The consequence of such a division will be that the rights of each class shareholder cannot be altered or varied except by means of a 75 per cent vote of the relevant class, i.e. that shareholder acting alone. This system will be protective of minority shareholders holding 25 per cent or less.

The share capital provisions should also make clear the existence of a pre-emptive right to the effect that for the duration of the Joint Venture Agreement all further issues of shares will be made to all the shareholders in the same proportions as their initial subscriptions (or in the agreed 'Shareholder Proportion'). Frequently the JV parties will desire to include a provision that either party has the right, at its own option, to have its shares allotted instead to a nominated affiliate company, coupled with the right for either party to transfer its shares to any affiliate at a later date if the party desires to do so. The reasons to do this will depend on legal and taxation considerations affecting the party (usually the foreign party) and so it is advisable that the right should be absolute and unfettered.

In cases where the consideration for the issue of shares in the JV company is to be paid entirely in cash, there is little doubt that the parties intend the cash to be an appropriate valuation for the initial shareholding in the company. However, in cases where the capital contribution is (wholly or partly) to be made in the form of assets, equipment or know-how, additional provisions will need to be included relating to the manner of providing the capital contribution to the company, and where necessary of valuing the assets.

In some cases the contribution of capital assets, and in particular issues of valuation and legal transfer of the assets, will need to be addressed in more detail. This is sometimes done by drafting a separate Contribution Agreement, which may provide for later revaluations of certain future assets of the parties such as contract rights. See Chapter 29.

The alternative types of shareholding structure are shown in Fig. 16.1.

Fig. 16.1 Shareholding structures

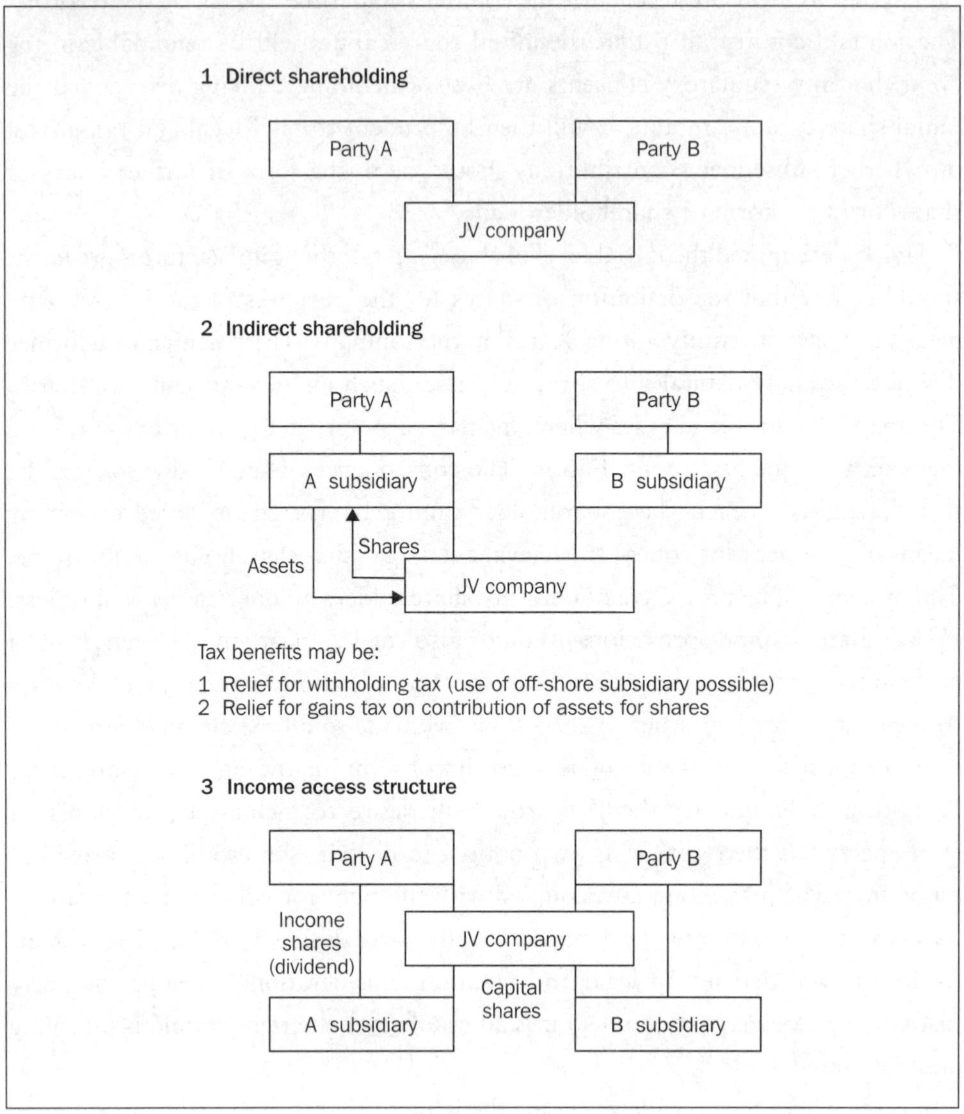
1 Direct shareholding
Party A
Party B
JV company
2 Indirect shareholding
Party A
Party B
A subsidiary
B subsidiary
Shares
Assets
JV company
Tax benefits may be:
1 Relief for withholding tax (use of off-shore subsidiary possible)
2 Relief for gains tax on contribution of assets for shares
3 Income access structure
Party A
Party B
Income shares (dividend)
JV company
Capital shares
A subsidiary
B subsidiary

2 SHARE TRANSFERS

The systems for permitting joint venture share transfers can sometimes be made too complex. The use of speculative put and call options often fails to serve the commercial needs of the joint venture. Efforts should be made to address these issues from a commercial perspective, so that if an option or transfer mechanism is used, it should be calculated to produce the result which both parties intend, and have some value as an effective deterrent.

Share transfer provisions may have varying degrees of complexity but will generally fall into three categories or tiers, starting with the most general type of provision used in joint venture arrangements.

2.1 First-tier restrictions

The first tier of transfer restrictions is the blanket ban on all share transfers by any shareholder. An absolute ban should be the first approach for almost all JV parties, since it preserves the integrity of their investment and their relationship with the joint venture partner, and removes the fear that they may end up carrying on the joint venture with an unknown partner.

However, from this starting-point the parties may move to the view that the blanket ban is only appropriate for a limited period of time. At a minimum the period should be for the initial phase of the joint venture, during which time its business will be established. This period is likely to be at least three years. On the other hand, the parties may prefer that an absolute prohibition should endure until a substantial part of the JV business has been discharged. This will often be a period of ten years or more.

Where the blanket prohibition is implemented, it is usually advisable, especially for the foreign party, to retain the exemption which will permit any transfer of a JV party's shares to an affiliate of that party.

2.2 Second-tier restrictions

The second tier of transfer rights consists of 'pre-emption rights' or 'rights of first refusal' pursuant to which a party which intends to dispose of its shares must first offer those shares to the other party (or parties) *pro rata* to its (or their) existing shareholdings in the JV company. The principle is fairly simple and at the basic level follows the lines of standard Articles of Association. However, complications will usually arise in the area of share valuation and pricing, that is to say in determining at what price the other shareholders will have the right to buy the shares.

Provisions governing the pricing of shares can cause technical and commercial difficulties, and regard has to be had to the potential outside marketability of the shares in the company in the context in which it operates. With a UK joint venture a market may exist in the shares, but with a joint venture in a developing country there is unlikely to be a real market for the shares.

In the case of international joint ventures it is not advisable that a JV party should be required to sell its shares to the other parties at the same price as that offered by a third-party bidder. Accordingly a mechanism will need to be established for the shares to be valued based on the JV company's net worth and other agreed principles. Inevitably disputes may arise as to whether the appropriate basis of valuation should be the underlying net asset value (excluding goodwill and intangible assets) or a more rounded 'fair value' reflecting the goodwill, trading prospects and other contributions made by the JV parties (see under 'Fair value' in Chapter 13).

2.3 Third-tier restrictions

This last category includes complex transfer provisions such as mandatory 'put' and 'call' options and similar arrangements triggered by specified events. These options may be permissive in nature (a right to require the sale during a specified period), or they may provide for a mandatory sale whereby one party or parties must buy out another party at a fixed price.

The necessity for put or call options to buy or sell a party's shares will usually arise in the context of termination of the joint venture, and in particular the default clauses such as contractual default, insolvency or a 'change of control' affecting one or other party (see Chapter 17).

In this situation the debate between the parties will frequently be over who will be given the right to buy the shares, and whether in fact the right of the non-defaulting party should be a right to sell and to exit from the joint venture, or to buy the other out. In general, if the joint venture is projected to perform well, the non-defaulting party will want the right to purchase the shares, obviously at the best possible price, but in this context it will not be unreasonable for the parties to agree that a 'fair price' should be determined.

If the foreign party is granted option rights, it will usually prefer a put option to sell all its shares to the local party at the determined valuation price. There may be important reasons to have such a right, including political and economic factors, or the existence of prohibitive shareholding laws. If there are such reasons, the foreign party should insist on the inclusion in the agreement of a unilateral option for it to sell its shares in the event of default. One practical difficulty may consist in agreeing the purchase price for the option, since the local party may not have available convertible currency to pay the purchase price.

There are various other complex types of option right designed to deal with the position where either party may wish to buy the shares. For example:

(a) The 'Pendulum' or 'Russian roulette'. One party makes an offer to buy the shares of the other at a price which it believes to be fair. If the other party does not believe it fair, it may itself offer to buy them at the same price, and the original bidder must accept.

(b) The 'Texas shootout'. This arrangement is designed for the situation where both parties wish to buy or both wish to sell. Each party will then make a bid and the highest bid will win the right to buy the shares, provided it exceeds the price of a prior auditors' valuation. The auction process is usually held under a 'sealed envelope' procedure, although it is possible for open bids to be exchanged.

(c) 'Bring along'/'tag along' rights. These rights have particular relevance to joint ventures with several minority shareholders, and they consist essentially of the right for a party which wishes to sell its interest to: procure that other shareholders will join the sale of shares; or be included in a (majority) shareholders' offer to buy the shares.

These mechanisms can be useful in a situation where both parties will be competing for the right to buy or sell their shares. However, it is suggested that their complexity does not always result in workable solutions to the joint venture dispute, and may not foster good planning or trust between the JV parties if they can be catapulted at any time into an untidy share auction process, by a notice from the other party.

3 MEETINGS AND VOTING

Although the shareholders exercise a large degree of control over strategic issues in joint ventures, the exercise of control on the routine business matters resides with the board of directors. If necessary, the representative directors can be authorised to act as the corporate representatives of the parties at shareholder meetings, so that a general meeting may be convened during a recess in the board meeting to pass any resolutions which require shareholder approval.

The matters which are not part of routine management and which require shareholder approval will usually be dealt with by written resolutions circulated among the shareholders. Perhaps the most important provision in the shareholder procedural section is the power to pass written resolutions of all the shareholders. The JV parties and in particular the foreign party will be well advised to set up their own internal controls so that their appointed directors are not also authorised to approve shareholder action in respect of the important Reserved Matters. Otherwise the director who is empowered to deal with the reserved matters may be subjected to significant pressure at board meetings to agree to changes.

Each JV party should decide whether to provide its board nominees with written mandates governing their conduct and voting, and the parameters of their authorisation on strategic matters. In a case where the director is the representative of the shareholder for general meetings, the mandate should clarify whether the director is permitted to convey consent on behalf of the shareholder.

In issuing any such mandates, care should be taken not to include instructions to vote for or against any specific proposed resolution. The mandate should also refrain from fettering in any respect the discretion of the director to vote as she/he thinks fit, or take any other necessary actions in respect of their office as director. From the director's viewpoint, the concern here is that of being held in breach of his/her fiduciary duties as director in respect of the company.

4 MINORITY SHAREHOLDER PROVISIONS

In certain joint venture structures, one shareholder holds a significantly smaller shareholding, but also has certain vital interests of its own to protect in the joint venture. Such minority investors are not usually expected to take a major role in the strategic and financial direction of the JV company.

The most commonly seen minority protection device is the requirement for Unanimous Approval of stated business matters. However, if the intention is to protect the smaller shareholders from abuse, the list of Reserved Matters will be aimed specifically at protecting the minority shareholders – dealing, for example, with issues of shares, or demands for further funding – and ensuring their inclusion in these votes. With a joint venture which is held 50:50, the Reserved Matters will seek to set out a consensus basis for all important matters of business strategy, including acquisition and disposals of other businesses, issues of new shares or securities, or taking new loans or finance for the company.

The shareholders may wish to establish (instead or in addition to) a list of business matters which require a 75 per cent (or similar) vote to action. Where a less than unanimous vote is thus required, the smaller shareholders will begin to suffer exclusion. They should be aware of this risk when negotiating the Joint Venture Agreement, and should insist on the unanimity device on the important legal protections including prohibitions (or pre-emption rights) on the issue of new share capital, or on calls for loans from the JV parties (see Appendix E).

The minority shareholder may be able to achieve for itself a better level of protection by means of the division of shares into classes with special rights. The division of shares into classes will automatically mean that the essential rights attaching to those shares (as defined in the Articles or Corporate Charter) will be protected from alteration. Generally, class rights cannot be altered without the vote of 75 per cent of the shareholders of that class.

Certain joint ventures may implement more complex minority shareholder provisions such as weighted voting rights whereby the vote of one named shareholder may count for two or three votes on certain issues. The use of put options can also be a valuable protection which can enable the minority shareholder to exit the joint venture upon specified events. Minority holders will also be prudent to negotiate 'tag-along' rights in the event that another shareholder wants to sell its shareholding to another principal investor or to a third party.

Another legal problem potentially faced by minority shareholders is the effect of the established common law principle of *Foss* v *Harbottle*, providing that for any legal proceedings in respect of an abuse committed by a majority shareholder, the company itself is the proper plaintiff. This is one of the principal reasons why the minority shareholder will be well advised to seek protections in the Joint Venture Agreement. A minority shareholder may be able to found an action against the majority shareholder under the doctrine of 'fraud on the minority'. A line of cases has developed this doctrine. In the leading case of *Prudential Assurance Co Ltd* v. *Newman Industries Ltd (No 2)* (1980) [2 All ER.841], it was held that fraud (in connection with a sale of assets to the company) consisted in the misuse of voting power by the majority coupled with deceptive conduct; however the existence of voting control by the majority was held not pre-requisite for an action to arise.

Section 459 of the English Companies Act 1985 has introduced a statutory remedy where a company's affairs are being or have been conducted in a manner which is unfairly prejudicial to the interests of its members generally or some part of its members.

Note, however, that where a Joint Venture Agreement provides for binding arbitration, the position of the minority shareholder is stronger in seeking remedy for any abuses, on a commercial basis and without establishing the existence of fraud. Furthermore, the ultimate remedy under English law is that a minority shareholder may apply to the court to have an English company wound up under the ground that a winding up is 'just and equitable' (Section 122(1) (g) Insolvency Act 1986).

Checklist 16 **Matters concerning shareholders**

1   What shareholding proportion is appropriate? Consider minority protection.

2   Will special class or special rights be appropriate?

3   Will special voting provisions be appropriate?

Duration and termination

Most joint ventures are intended to be long-term projects. Those relating to infrastructure, engineering or power generation may be active for a period of 15 to 20 years. One approach to these joint ventures is to avoid specifying a set duration, leaving the matter to be dealt with by express termination provisions. Another approach is to provide that the agreement will endure for a fixed term, subject to termination options and the opportunity at the end of that period to renew the agreement. Alternatively the Joint Venture Agreement may, where relevant, be expressed to endure for the duration of the commercial contract.

For all parties to a joint venture the possibilities for exit will be important. The Joint Venture Agreement will need to set out clearly the provisions governing early termination. These may include specified events which will give rise to automatic termination of the joint venture. The basic provisions will also entitle either JV party to terminate early, by giving written notice to the other party, in the event of a breach of contract or another specified event of default. The various types of termination provision are illustrated in Fig. 17.1.

Fig. 17.1 Types of termination provision

Model A Project JV

| Fixed term – 15 years | Termination of project contract |

| Automatic termination |

| No optional termination | Force majeure Object impossible |

Model B Manufacturing JV

| Notional fixed term – 10 years |

| Optional termination | Breach of contract Insolvency Change of control etc. |

| Automatic termination | Force majeure End of IP licence |

Model C Sales co-operation JV

| No fixed term | Three or six months' notice |

| Optional termination | Breach of agreement |

| No automatic termination | Insolvency and Change of control |

1 AUTOMATIC TERMINATION

A party may consider that, in the circumstances, it has an overriding interest in providing that certain events or certain breaches by the other party invoke a need for immediate termination, for example, where one JV party is providing technology or know-how to the joint venture, and the other JV party infringes its rights and damages the interests of the first party. Another ground might be, as stated, the early termination of an important commercial contract relating to the JV business, or frustration of the venture due to political turmoil.

2 TERMINATION ON NOTICE

Joint Venture Agreements will usually contain a standard range of default provisions which will entitle one JV party to terminate early upon service of written notice to the other JV party. These common provisions include the following.

2.1 Material breach

This refers to a material breach of the Joint Venture Agreement by the other JV party. If a breach of contract will result in a right of termination, it should be required to be material or else to have a 'substantial adverse effect' on the business of the joint venture. In practice, most breaches of the Joint Venture Agreement itself do not have such an adverse effect and can be resolved by other methods of dispute resolution, while those matters which more often cause commercial disputes do not usually arise out of the Joint Venture Agreement.

Two types of default are generally mentioned in the agreement. The first type is where the breach is capable of being cured by some achievable action, and in this event the defaulting party may be given a period of 30 days (or other appropriate time) to remedy the default. The second type involves a breach not capable of cure which leads to termination upon expiry of the notice period.

2.2 Insolvency

Under this heading fall insolvency, liquidation, receivership or bankruptcy of one JV party (in accordance with the laws of its own state of incorporation) such that it is no longer a suitable joint venture partner and the other party therefore wishes to terminate the joint venture. This type of clause will refer to a list of several different kinds of insolvency status, including liquidation or receivership, being subject to bankruptcy (US) or administration orders (UK), or making compositions or schemes of arrangement with the party's creditors. A reference to insolvency could usefully specify that the term 'insolvent' means 'unable to pay its debts as they fall due' (which has some currency both within and outside the UK).

Great care will need to be taken that the insolvency sub-clause adequately takes account of the legal system of the principal JV parties, or any other joint venture party to whom it may need to be applied in the future, and the legal advisers should be asked to satisfy themselves on this point.

2.3 *Force majeure*

Each JV party should have a right to terminate where *force majeure* events, usually including war, strike, unrest, political (or economic) turmoil or natural disasters (formerly referred to as 'acts of God'), interrupt and render impossible the activities of the joint venture or the performance of the Joint Venture Agreement. With an international joint venture, the appropriate remedy for events of *force majeure* is to allow the termination right to arise after a specified period (e.g. 6 or 12 months, possibly more) but *not* in the interim to suspend the operation of the Joint Venture Agreement. *Force majeure* is an important issue in the international context, since in some developing countries there is a risk of business interruptions on the production or supply side. The concept of a significant business interruption needs to be distinguished from general inefficiency in achieving production and supply targets or efficiencies in transport or communications. However, it is useful, in the event of a genuine interruption resulting from a strike, war or internal strife, if the parties know how long they would have to wait before either party has a right to terminate the Joint Venture Agreement.

2.4 Change of control

The parties may want to include provisions which will entitle one JV party to terminate the agreement in the event that the other JV party undergoes a 'change of control', in the sense that control of the other party is acquired by a new company or group whose interest had not been anticipated and with whom the first party does not wish to participate in the joint venture.

Usually the foreign party will have most concern about a possible change of control, since it will have selected the local party because of its commercial suitability to the joint venture, its business connections and possibly its regulatory status. The foreign party is therefore more likely to be threatened by a change of control, although it may wish to elect in the event whether or not to terminate.

The change-of-control mechanism, running both ways as it inevitably will, could prejudice the foreign party where it is part of a large corporate group. The parent or ultimate parent of such party may at some time change, perhaps as a result of internal reorganisation, disposal or corporate takeover, but this will not of necessity affect the joint venture. In weighing up these factors, the foreign investor may decide that a change-of-control provision is best not included in the Joint Venture Agreement.

2.5 Diminution of shareholding

Termination should be allowed if one party no longer holds shares in the company (or holds less than 10 per cent or other specified shareholding). The parties may consider that one or both parties could be given a right to terminate the Joint Venture Agreement in the event of one shareholder ceasing to hold shares. However, care should be taken in framing such a provision, as it is not usually advisable to give the outgoing shareholder a gratuitous release from the obligations of the agreement.

The Joint Venture Agreement should also provide for what happens after termination in respect of various undertakings of the JV parties, following the withdrawal of one shareholder or the termination of the enterprise. The parties should consider the following points.

1 The exiting JV party will require a release from any guarantees or indemnities given by it in favour of the company of the other shareholder(s). This is normally achieved by the existing or the new shareholder entering into a Deed of Assumption taking on the liability.

2 Loans outstanding from the outgoing shareholder will need to be repaid, or more usually the obligations will be novated to the existing or the new shareholder.

3 IP licences, any trademark licences etc. granted by the JV party to the joint venture should be terminated, and possibly any permissions given to use the party's corporate or trading name.

4 Provisions mist be put in place to initiate the liquidation of the JV company (see Appendix E, Clause 17).

Checklist 17 What grounds of termination are required?

1 Is there a logical fixed term for the JV?

2 Are there any grounds for automatic termination? For example, termination of IP licences.

3 What grounds are there for a party's optional termination? Consider if breach of contract or change of control will give a right to terminate.

18

Financial and accounting provisions

1 FINANCE FOR THE JV COMPANY

The financial provisions of the Joint Venture Agreement will aim to set out the understanding of all the JV parties regarding the preferred methods for financing the company, the obligations on the parties in respect of finance and, most important, the limits of those obligations.

For the foreign investor a crucial aspect of this is the preparation and approval of the Business Plan for the JV company. The main provision will clearly state that any proposed business matters or transactions outside the scope of the plan are not permitted without the approval of both parties. Both JV parties should have the same understanding as to the financial and lending requirements, and should attempt to conclude the first annual Business Plan before the execution of the Joint Venture Agreement and to schedule it to the agreement. Provision should thereafter be made for renewing the Business Plan in advance of each financial year.

The provisions will also address the funding obligations of the JV parties, and it should be made clear that a shareholder will be required to contribute to the funding of the company in strict proportion to its equity shares in the company (defined as its 'shareholder proportion'). The agreement should also set out the terms on which any loans will be made and recite the agreement that loans will be made on an equal basis between the shareholders. If one shareholder is to provide loans to a greater amount or on different terms, this should be expressly provided for. With joint ventures that require considerable working capital, the parties may agree to implement a revolving loan facility so that loans committed by the parties can be drawn down at the discretion of the management or by agreement of the JV parties.

The parties may decide, due to commercial circumstances in the JV territory, that it is appropriate for one shareholder to take a greater share of responsibility for negotiating loans from banks or third parties, possibly providing collateral or security where necessary.

Another important protection is that which provides that no shareholder will be required to give guarantees in respect of its participation in the JV company without its express written consent. In addition to this broad veto power on guarantees, the parties may want to provide that in the event that guarantees are to be given on behalf of the JV company, they should be negotiated strictly in accordance with a prescribed set of conditions.

A summary of the various financial issues and the potential division of the parties' responsibilities in a joint venture is given in Fig. 18.1.

Fig. 18.1 Financial issues and the parties' responsibilities

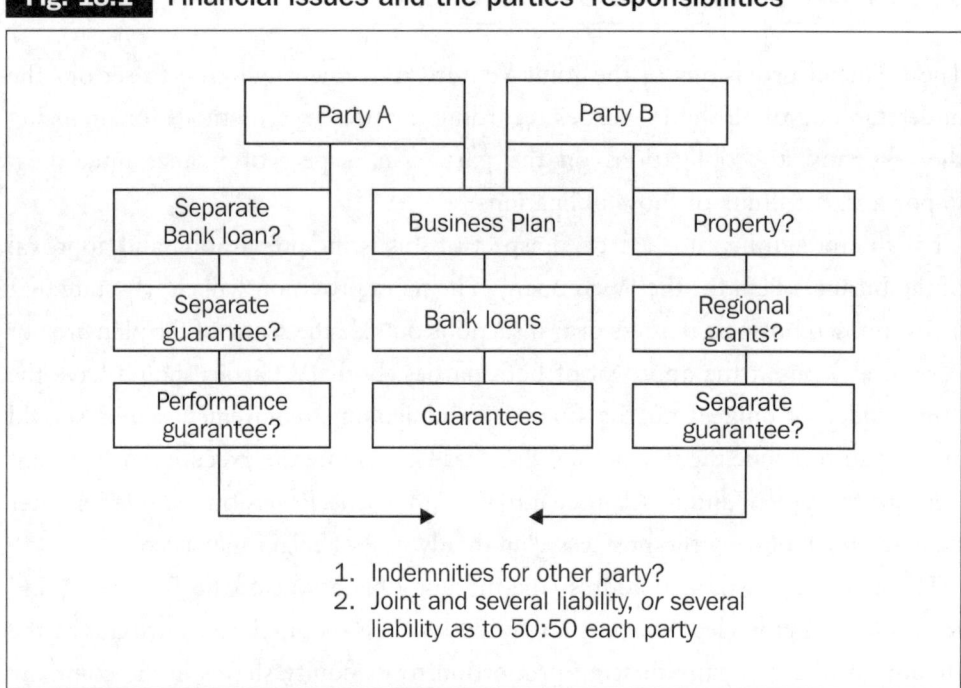

1. Indemnities for other party?
2. Joint and several liability, *or* several liability as to 50:50 each party

2 ACCOUNTS AND FINANCIAL INFORMATION

Various standard provisions will set out the official financial year of the company for fiscal purposes and who the auditors of the JV company will be. It is prudent to provide that the agreed financial year and firm of auditors will not be changed without unanimous shareholder approval. In practice the parties will agree who the auditors will initially be. It is always firmly in the interests of the foreign party to ensure that it writes into the agreement a provision that the auditors must always be a firm with an international affiliation, as well as being authorised to practise in the JV territory.

The accounting provisions will also specify which accounting requirements will apply to the auditing of the joint venture's accounts, both under local laws and, so far as possible, imposing compliance with international generally accepted accounting principles.

The JV parties will also want rights to review the accounting and business records of the JV company. The shareholders may also want to review interim budgets and unaudited financial statements on a quarterly basis. The Joint Venture Agreement should also require the board of directors to prepare management accounts which will assist the shareholders in the management of the JV company and keep them informed of developments in the business. The agreement could in this regard stipulate that the management accounts should comply with the local accounting principles so as to ensure that standards of accuracy are maintained in compiling the management accounts.

Part IV

The Joint Venture Agreement – commercial issues

19

Intellectual property issues

149

Intellectual property (IP) issues will be highly significant to the majority of joint venture projects, especially in relation to the JV parties' 'upstream' activities for the joint venture including research and development.

The first issue to address is what kind of IP rights the joint venture requires in order to undertake its manufacturing or other contract activities. At the formation stage it is unlikely that the joint venture will possess any intellectual property of its own, and a principal concern will be the terms upon which the JV parties are expected to provide technology rights to it. Although there may sometimes be commercial or regulatory reasons to transfer technology rights to the joint venture, and retain a licence as necessary, an outright transfer will reduce the party's control over the joint venture, and may result in loss of market presence.

Where the JV parties' activities do overlap with the joint venture, various competition law issues will arise out of the provision of technology rights to the joint venture (see Chapter 9 above).

Models for licensing the IP generated by production and R&D joint ventures are shown in Fig. 19.1.

Fig. 19.1 **Intellectual property licensing**

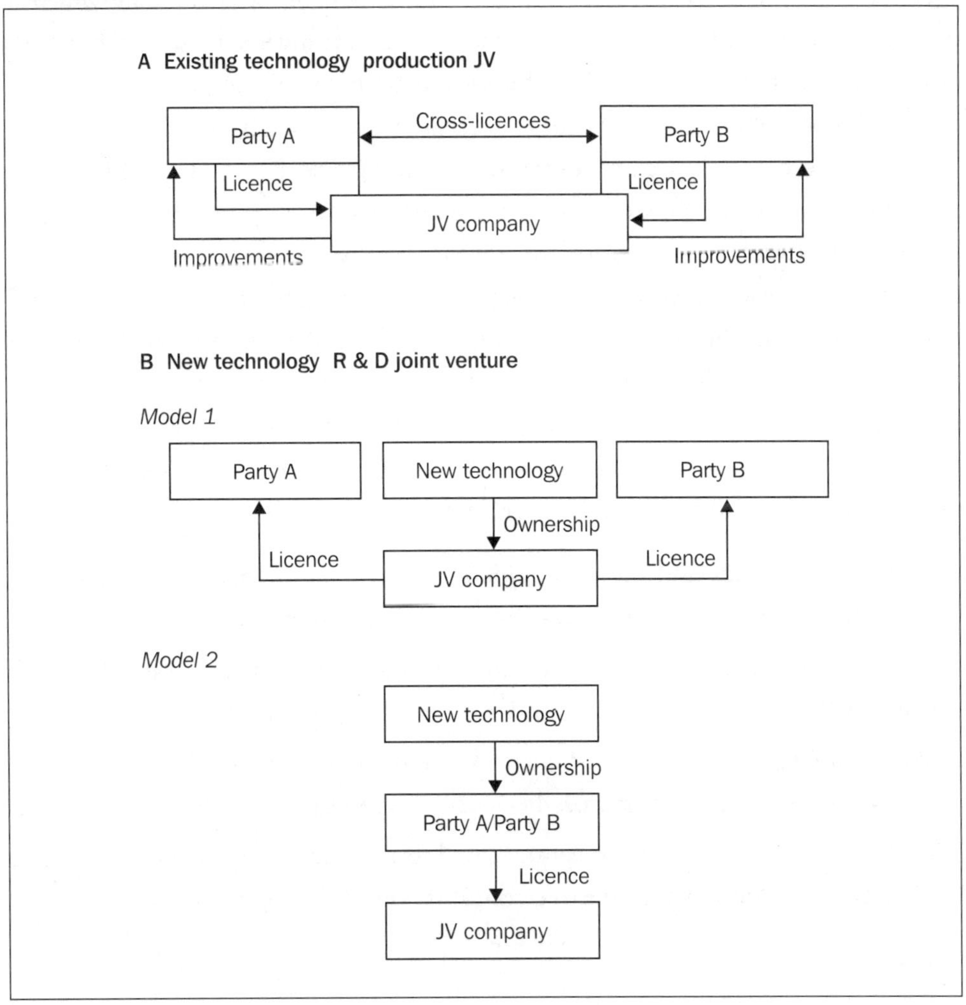

A Existing technology production JV

B New technology R & D joint venture

Model 1

Model 2

1 RESEARCH AND DEVELOPMENT JOINT VENTURES

Joint ventures often involve collaborative arrangements at the cutting edge of technological innovation which generate IP of substantial commercial value. Difficulties can arise where the results of collaborative research are required for the activities of the JV parties and the joint venture. Furthermore, questions of competition law will arise, if exclusive licence or assignment of the IP rights is likely to involve reducing the competitive activities of the parent in the field of exploitation, or foreclosing the competitive opportunities for third parties (see Chapter 9).

R&D joint ventures often involve collaboration by a number of parties, each of whom owns a specialised aspect of know-how or technology which needs to be combined with other aspects in order to be developed to a further stage of progress. In combining technologies in this manner, the parties may or may not agree to extend their co-operation into joint product development through the joint venture.

Where the co-operation of the parties remains purely in the R&D *development* field, they will usually license the joint technology back to each of the parties on equal terms. Sometimes, each party will retain ownership of technology which it principally has generated. These R&D joint venture arrangements should not have any tangible impact on the degree of competition between the parties, providing each is able to obtain the benefits of the research. Accordingly, such arrangements will generally be able to claim exemption from Article 81(1) of the EU Treaty pursuant to the Notice on Co-operation Agreements (see Chapter 9 above).

Where the R&D co-operation of the JV parties extends further into the *exploitation* phase, the arrangements will generally be more complex and interdependent. In the case of joint ventures which involve combined R&D and production activity, there will be a variety of difficult commercial questions to resolve, and it is advisable to address them in the Joint Venture Agreement rather than to have an inextricable mixture of IP rights to be resolved by the arbitrators of the courts. The parties should therefore consider the following.

1 Will the JV parties and the JV company be involved in competitive activities such that the technology arrangements can affect competition?

2 Will new technology be owned by the company and made available to the original JV parties, and if so, upon what commercial terms?

3 Will rights remain with the original JV party? On what terms will rights be licensed to the company or cross-licensed between the JV parties?

4 Upon termination of the joint venture, will termination of any exclusive licence arrangements prevent the effective continuation of the joint venture?

With regard to the potential anti-competitive effect of R&D co-operation within the EU area, the JV parties should structure the arrangement so as to fall within the R&D block exemption (Regulation 418/85) which may apply to joint exploitation also (see Chapter 9). Co-operation which is purely in the R&D sphere is not usually regarded as anti-competitive. For joint ventures involving combined R&D and industrial production, the block exemption will apply only to agreements where the aggregate market shares of all parties involved (the JV parties and the JV company) does not exceed 20 per cent (or 10 per cent if the joint venture is also undertaking direct distribution of the products).

Further, the joint production must be either protected by registered patent or similar IP rights, or else constitute know-how which will contribute to technical or economic progress. The know-how used in manufacturing the products must also be the direct result of the R&D collaboration of the parties.

2 LICENSING TO THE JOINT VENTURE

JV parties will generally wish to grant a non-exclusive and non-transferable licence to the joint venture, leaving the parents freedom in their existing activities. However, an exclusive licence of technology may be appropriate in a case where IP is dedicated for the use of the joint venture, or where the JV company is offering a newly developed product. This will give each of the JV parties mutual assurance of independence from the other JV parties.

Whatever the form of the licence, it will usually need to be on reasonable commercial terms. The duration of the licences must be for the full term of the joint venture. In the case of a licence having effect in the EU area it must comply with the EU block exemption on technology transfer agreements (Regulation 240/96. See Chapter 9 above). Any obligation to provide improvements should run both ways.

The question of whether the licence will include a substantial royalty element is principally a commercial issue to be agreed, but if a party wishes to receive royalties in respect of its technology, this will usually be in lieu of other income to be received from the JV company. The feasibility of this will depend on whether a percentage royalty can easily be implemented in respect of each product to be sold, and whether the parties can mutually agree the commercial impact on the structure of the JV company, including rights to receive dividends. The taxation implications of paying royalties to each party as against distributing the residual post-tax profits will need to be considered in some detail, and royalties should be on reasonable terms and not 'excessive' if they are expected to qualify for withholding tax exemptions under a relevant double tax treaty.

The issue of the assignability of the IP rights is of fundamental commercial importance to the parties. In theory, any exclusive rights licensed to the joint venture should permit the full commercial exploitation of those rights, including, where necessary, a decision to sub-contract manufacturing or sell part of a business. However, the JV parties will often prefer that the licences should be non-assignable in order to maintain their control over the exploitation of the rights.

Termination of the licence will also be an important issue. A party may reserve the right to terminate the licence in the event of its withdrawal from the joint venture. However, the joint venture will retain a 'paid-up licence' in respect of its existing use of the technology, and the Joint Venture Agreement should permit continued exploitation to the extent that it has paid all royalties which are due to the licensor.

Where one party is in breach of contract or terminates prematurely, the licences should usually continue in favour of the joint venture.

In the event of final termination of the joint venture it will also be necessary to consider how to split the rights in any jointly owned IP or in IP rights registered in the JV company's name. In the absence of any specific provision, an equal and joint right to registration will usually be assumed, but an agreement is preferable.

Some contractual joint ventures will not involve licensing to the joint venture but will involve the JV parties as principal contractors, each taking IP cross-licences from the other party if necessary to the business of the joint venture. However, in the case of any new IP rights generated by the parties, they may wish to provide for joint registration of the new rights for future exploitation by each party.

3 FOREGROUND AND BACKGROUND IP

In any joint venture where the JV parties are collaborating on technology, there will be various categories of existing intellectual property belonging to each party, which may be of greater or lesser importance to the JV business.

In relation to the JV parties, it is usually useful in this regard to distinguish what is sometimes referred to as 'Foreground IP', which will include all those IP rights (including research results) developed in connection with the JV business and 'Background IP', which are those rights related to the separate activities of each JV party, but which the joint venture must have access to. Foreground IP may often be licensed to the JV company (and/or other JV parties) on an exclusive basis, and with an obligation on the licensor to maintain in force full IP protection. Background IP will normally be licensed to the JV company on a non-exclusive basis. In the case of a contractual joint venture, joint registration rights will frequently be agreed upon in respect of Foreground IP cross-licensed to all the parties. However, all residual rights in respect of Background IP will be retained by the parties. See the suggested definitions in Appendix E, Clause 19.

4 NEWLY DEVELOPED IP

For many joint ventures in the research and technology field, and especially in the case of corporate joint ventures, the parties will need to establish clearly the ownership and use rights in relation to IP developed by the JV company and/or pursuant to the JV business, and the Joint Venture Agreement should attempt to provide for this. The usual policy would be for such rights to be regarded as belonging to the JV company, and for the rights to be licensed back to each shareholder on a non-exclusive and royalty-free basis, usually upon terms that the shareholders will not compete with the joint venture in the particular area of exploitation during the operative period of the joint venture.

However, in certain situations one or more of the JV parties may regard the underlying IP rights as highly sensitive and proprietary, and would prefer that the future rights should revert to the JV party from whose underlying intellectual property they were generated. As an alternative, the JV party may be granted a first option to acquire the rights from the JV company.

In the case of contractual joint ventures the usual policy is for each individual generator to own and register its own developed IP. In the event that a JV company is the registered holder of new IP developments, it will normally assign them to the shareholders jointly (or as otherwise agreed) at the end of the joint venture. The JV parties may instead prefer to provide for joint ownership and registration of the rights, with a licence to go back to the JV company. However, it is suggested that this arrangement may prevent each JV party from fully exploiting the rights individually, since any assignment, sub-licence or re-registration of rights will require the other party's express consent.

5 LIABILITY FOR IP BETWEEN THE JV PARTIES

The JV parties will seek to ensure that the Joint Venture Agreement clarifies questions of liability relating to licensed IP. For a corporate joint venture, the parties may wish to exclude any liability on their behalf for use or exploitation of IP belonging to the JV company, and further to clarify that no warranties are given by them in respect of the licensed IP rights, (including warranties as to infringement or claims by third parties). The parties may seek to impose an indemnity on the JV company in respect of loss by, or claims against, arising from the company's use. Notwithstanding the above, it is reasonable for each shareholder to retain the responsibility for registering and maintaining its own IP rights which are licensed to the JV company, including the prosecution and defence of any third-party claims relating to the underlying rights.

Warranties may be required, however, in relation to IP rights licensed under joint ventures, especially for contractual joint ventures. The JV parties will be concerned as to their co-parties' ownership rights to the IP licensed to the joint venture, in particular any 'Foreground IP'. The parties may seek to obtain a warranty that the existence of all information that may constitute Background or Foreground IP has been disclosed. They may be concerned also to know of any third-party infringements so as to avoid competitors reducing the commercial value of the joint venture's products.

Checklist 19 How can we protect our IP and know-how rights?

1 Will the parent be using the same IP in its business? If so, ensure non-exclusive licences are given to the JV.

2 Will parties grant IP rights to each other?

3 Will newly developed IP belong to the parties or to the JV?

4 Will licensing be on arm's-length terms as to royalties etc.?

5 Ensure termination provisions protect the parties' IP rights.

20

Non-competition covenants

In certain situations the JV parties will enter into non-competition covenants (or non-compete clauses) by which they will undertake not to be involved in any direct competitive activity in relation to the JV business. The question of whether such covenants will be given, and whether they will be given by all the parties or by some parties only, will frequently be a sensitive political issue between the JV parties.

1 INDICATIONS FOR INCLUSION

While it may seem inequitable for one JV party to be bound by a non-compete clause and not the other, the considerations affecting a local party will be different from those affecting the foreign party in a cross-border joint venture. Where the local party is contributing its principal assets to the business, including contracts, goodwill and customer lists, it will usually be expected that it should not continue with directly competitive activities in the JV territory in respect of the same or similar products or services. However, in the case of a foreign party which has joint ventures in a number of territories, and where joint venture activity represents a territorial expansion of its main business activities, there will be more problems in signing up to non-competition covenants.

2 INDICATIONS FOR OMISSION

In view of the various competition law and regulatory issues mentioned above, and also the practical difficulties of agreeing the scope of the non-compete clauses, the parties may be well advised to leave specific binding non-competition covenants out of the main Joint Venture Agreement, even in a situation where they envisage that the parties will not compete with the JV company. The parties may both intend that the nature of the new product range to be manufactured by the company, coupled with its exclusivity in the JV territory, should minimise the incidence of direct competition by or with the JV parties in their own markets. Another legitimate approach which can be adopted is to record in the Joint Venture Agreement their mutual understanding that the JV company will sell products within the JV territory and in so doing will not be competing directly with either of the parties.

Another approach is for each JV party to be granted an exclusive distribution agreement for its own respective territory or sales area, such that it will not be competing directly with the joint venture in the JV territory. Care must be taken to comply with the applicable EU regulations (see Chapter 9 above).

3 SCOPE OF COVENANTS

If it is decided that one or more parties should enter into non-competition covenants, such provisions should be precisely worded to ensure that they have the exact scope intended. In this regard the following considerations will apply.

(a) The covenantor, and the foreign party in particular, should ensure that the covenants do not operate to restrict the commercial activity of other companies or divisions of its corporate group. However, the local party may exert pressure to include the wider restriction to forestall competing parent activity in the JV territory.

(b) The JV parties should consider whether the restrictions will apply to all aspects of the production process, upstream and downstream. Further, the parties should ensure that the product or the product ranges that are subject to the non-competition restrictions are precisely described, possibly by reference to a schedule categorising the product.

(c) Either JV party may wish to exclude from the scope of the restrictions certain cases where it holds a percentage of shares (say 15 per cent) in another public company for the purposes of an investment only, or a situation where it acquires a business which has as an ancillary part of that business a range of products which competes with those of the joint venture. Such an acquisition may be exempted from the covenant, and this is sometimes done on the understanding that the covenantor must attempt to resell the competitive business activity provided that it can obtain a reasonable commercial price, or a similar type of provision.

Confidentiality issues

The establishment and operation of the joint venture will involve the exchange of much sensitive information, of both a commercial and technical nature. This exchange of information is likely to begin at the earlier stages of the project and to continue into the operational stages.

1 NEED FOR DISCLOSURE

While attempts to withhold any information necessary for successful co-operation in the JV business would be undiplomatic, it will be firmly against the interests of any JV party to provide technical information which is not necessary for the operation of the JV business, and where undue disclosure could significantly prejudice its own business. Furthermore, unwarranted disclosure between the parties might also be regarded as extending the scope of the parties' co-operation pursuant to applicable competition laws, resulting in a 'spillover' effect in the parent's domestic markets. Each party should consider carefully the need for such an affirmative clause, bearing in mind that it will be difficult to enforce and may penalise the more co-operative participant.

Subject to the above, the confidentiality provisions that should be contained in the Joint Venture Agreement are principally standard ones which would apply to confidential information under most commercial agreements. The principal obligations undertaken will be:

(a) to maintain the confidentiality of the released information;

(b) not to disclose the information without the prior written consent of the releasing party; and

(c) not to use the information for any purpose other than for the purposes of the receiving party's own performance under the Joint Venture Agreement, for evaluating the JV company's performance or for otherwise assisting the JV business.

In addition to binding itself, each party will normally be made responsible for procuring the observance of the clause by its own appointee directors, and possibly for procuring performance by the JV company.

An obligation of confidentiality may also be imposed on the JV company itself, which can be a sufficiently important safeguard against disclosure when a party becomes less involved in the joint venture. In cases where the company is intended to be a party to the Joint Venture Agreement (although in many cases it will not, for legal reasons in the JV territory) the parties should consider imposing the confidentiality obligation directly upon the company also.

2 EXCEPTIONS

For the sake of organisational efficiency, certain exceptions to the confidentiality obligations will generally permit the JV parties to disclose confidential information to their own employees (or their affiliates' employees), and possibly also to their independent contractors and professional advisers. If such disclosures are excepted, the responsibility should be imposed on the JV party to ensure that each relevant employee or contractor is made aware of the obligations of confidentiality under the agreement. In some cases the disclosee may be required to sign a similar confidentiality agreement, although it is suggested that this will in fact be difficult to enforce.

Other standard exemptions are frequently made to the confidentiality undertakings. The standard clauses usually include an exemption in the event that the party receiving the information is under a legal obligation to disclose part of it in some form (this may be pursuant to the rules of its stock exchange or similar regulatory authority). An exemption may also apply if the party has independently developed the confidential information, or if it can prove that it otherwise knew and had access to the information prior to its disclosure under the joint venture. Another standard exemption applies in a case where the information has become publicly known due to an external occurrence and not as a result of the JV party breaching its confidentiality obligation (or other obligation) under the Joint Venture Agreement (see Appendix E, Clause 21).

Employee issues

For many joint ventures involved in production or industrial activities, there will be a transfer of all or part of the business operated by one party (generally the local party) to the JV company. The usual scenario is that the local party will transfer its factory site to the new company (see Chapter 23) together with its related contractual rights. Contractual rights under personal employment contracts are not assignable under English law unless there are express assignment or mobility clauses in such contracts. However, certain territories may permit the direct transfer of such employment rights in the context of joint ventures or sale of a business enterprise.

1 TRANSFER OF EMPLOYMENT CONTRACTS

It is in the interests of the joint venture that effective transfer of the employment contracts is achieved, at least in respect of the main body of workers. The transfer agreements dealing with the sale of the business assets of the local party will also deal with any proposed transfers or novations of employee contracts to the JV company (see Fig. 22.1). However, neither the transfer itself nor the identity of the employees will be sufficiently clear without further attempts to clarify which employees are to be transferred. In this regard the parties may attempt, near the outset of the venture, to agree upon a schedule of existing employees who will be transferred. This will help to ascertain whether the business needs to recruit new staff either at the skilled level of management, or at the labour-intensive level.

Fig. 22.1 Structure for provision of employees

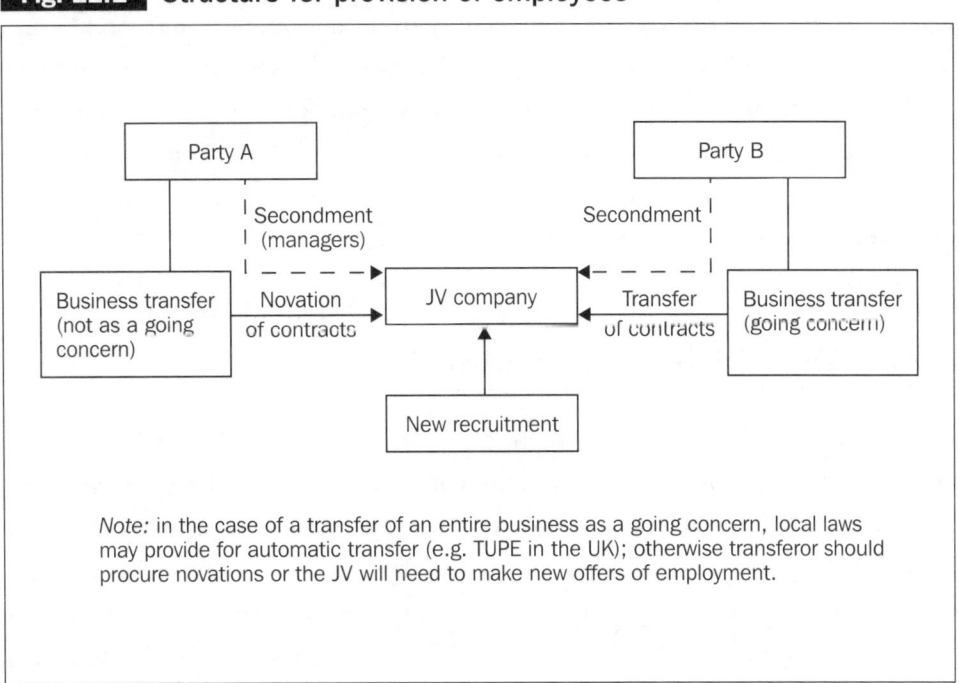

Note: in the case of a transfer of an entire business as a going concern, local laws may provide for automatic transfer (e.g. TUPE in the UK); otherwise transferor should procure novations or the JV will need to make new offers of employment.

Where a direct transfer of employment contracts is not possible, either by means of an express transfer clause in their contracts or as part of the sale of the site and plant, the parties will instead need to rely on novations of the contracts (or re-employment offers) to achieve the transfers. Since the employees will be in effect discharged from their contracts (and free to leave immediately without 'notice'), a suitable set of terms will need to be offered to the employees in order to induce them, or any negotiators acting on their behalf, to accept the employment terms.

The ability to retain the staff will depend much on prevailing labour market forces and on local trade union strength in the JV territory. If there are alternative employers, the JV parties will need to consider offering attractive terms. If there is a labour abundance in that sector, the existing terms may be offered to the employees. In fact, there is an advantage for both JV parties in rationalising the employment terms, especially where the employees come from more than one source or from several JV parties, since this can contribute to the long-term efficiency of the joint venture.

2 SECONDMENT OF EMPLOYEES

Certain skilled employees, including consultants or technicians, will often be loaned or seconded temporarily to the JV company. The parties should agree in advance between themselves the bases and time periods on which these persons will be seconded, including the basis for charging the joint venture for their services and the number of man-hours available per month or year. The JV party will frequently expect to receive an indemnity from the company in respect of any liability incurred while working exclusively on the business of the joint venture.

Where secondment is used to provide employees for the joint venture, the parties will need to agree who has responsibility for arranging immigration visas, work permits (if outside the EU territories) or similar documents. The co-operation of the local party will almost certainly be required for these formalities.

3 TRANSFERS OF UNDERTAKINGS

In the United Kingdom, where there is a transfer of an existing business or undertaking *as a going concern*, the employment of contracts of the business will be automatically transferred and their terms and conditions of employment will be assumed by the transferee without the need for consent or legal documentation. This is done on the terms of the Transfer of Undertakings (Protection of Employment) Regulations 1982 (TUPE) in respect of all employees whose employment contracts are (on the transfer date) principally performed in the United Kingdom, and will usually apply where a UK-resident company is transferring an *entire* UK business to a joint venture operation situated in the UK or in another territory (being one where the principle of employee mobility is provided for). However, most transfers from a JV party to a JV company will not give rise to a transfer of the business as a going concern but merely a transfer or secondment of employees to the new location of the joint venture. Legal advice will generally be required on the implications of employee relocations.

Most of the EU territories have a similar system which operates in the case of business transfers within or between EU territories, under the EU Acquired Rights Directive (1980) upon which the UK TUPE regulations are effectively based.

In most territories outside the EU there is no statutory regime for employment transfers. The JV parties will need to agree between themselves what regime they intend to implement for the transfer, secondment or loan of employees to the joint venture. Where they intend that part or all of a business is transferred they should specify this and clarify between themselves whether any further consequences will arise, including whether any liabilities falling on the JV company are expected to be indemnified. Sometimes the parties may give the JV company the right to terminate the contracts of certain employees on the grounds of redundancy where their transfer to the joint venture will be superfluous to the requirements of the business, in which event the JV parties would be expected to take responsibility for the costs thereof.

Generally, it will not be possible to deal fully in the Joint Venture Agreement with all aspects of employee transfers and secondments. The Joint Venture Agreement should set out the basic principles by which employees will be transferred or seconded by the JV parties to the JV company, and should shelve more detailed issues of logistics to be dealt with in a subsequent agreement between the parties at the production stage of the joint venture, which will no doubt need to be revised periodically with a view to the requirements of the JV business.

Checklist 22 **Employee matters to consider**

1   Have the manpower needs of the JV been assessed, and allocated to the parties?

2   Will secondment or transfer of your employees be appropriate?

3   Will the JV recruit new employees?

4   What are the JV's contractual and statutory obligations – trade unions, social funds, pensions etc.?

Property issues

1 PROVIDING THE JOINT VENTURE SITE

The acquisition of a suitable property site to serve as its centre of operations will often be a prime concern for an overseas joint venture, in particular for a venture based on manufacturing or assembly activities.

The most common situation for overseas manufacturing joint ventures will be the transfer of an existing factory site owned by the local party into the name of the JV company. However, for some projects involving new technology the joint venture will instead be expected to acquire a new 'green-field' site from which to operate, and the joint venture may need to be capitalised by both parties up to the level necessary for it to acquire or to lease the new site. The division of responsibilities typically made for provision of the site is shown in Fig. 23.1.

Fig. 23.1 Responsibilities for provision of the site

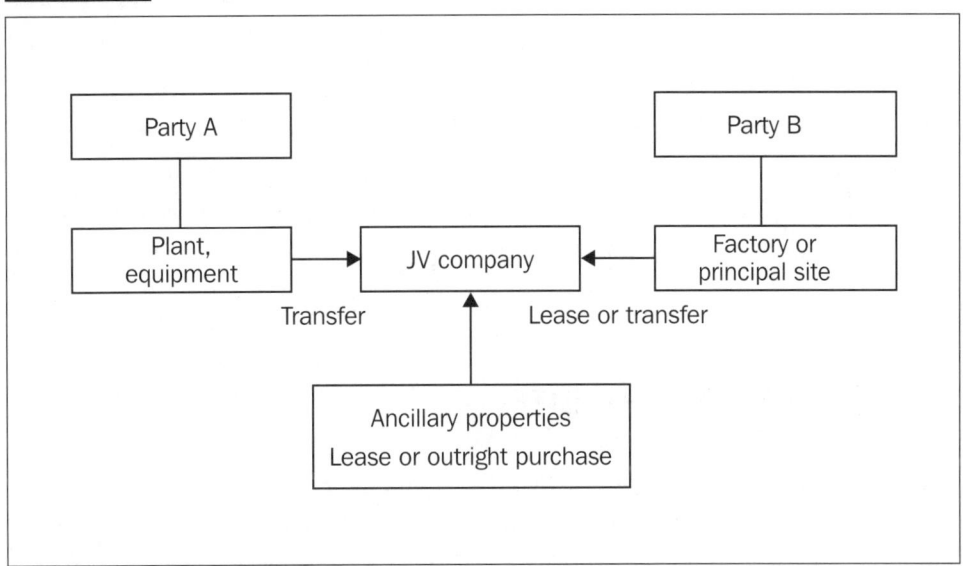

The following are some alternative routes for acquiring and establishing a manufacturing site or principal base for the joint venture.

1 The local party owns an existing factory site which will be transferred to the JV company as part of its capital contribution. In this event the need to establish a valuation for the property will be of special importance if the joint venture is based on 50:50 participation. When the valuation is established, the foreign party will be expected to match the value of the site with an equal contribution of assets, usually in the form of plant and machinery, intellectual property or similar benefits.

2 The local party may transfer the factory site to the JV company by way of an outright sale for a cash sum, and again this will raise the issue of what is a fair means of valuation. In such an event the initial capital contribution of both the

JV parties will need to include sufficient funds to cover the property, or the parties can loan the additional amount to the company.

3 The local party may instead lease the site to the JV company on reasonable commercial terms. The lease must be a long lease to cover the term of the joint venture and provide unrestricted use which will continue in the event of exit by the local party from the joint venture, and also be on reasonable arm's-length terms as to rent and other obligations.

4 An existing factory site or business can be taken over and bought for cash. Similar considerations would apply to financing the purchase of a new site, and the JV parties will normally need to capitalise the JV company at a sufficient level to acquire the site and to finance any construction or redevelopment required. If acquiring a new site is beyond the capital budget, the parties can consider taking a loan from one or more commercial banks. In advancing any sums, the lenders will closely examine the property valuation schedules, and will inevitably require a security interest in the property itself, generally a mortgage with standard repossession rights.

5 A new 'green-field' site may be acquired for the use of the JV company. This may entitle the joint venture to receive certain regional development incentives. The parties should check that the location of the site and the transport facilities are adequate for the development of the business.

2 VALUATION OF THE SITE

Where the local party is providing the factory site, the JV parties will need to agree on the appropriate manner of valuing the property. Here the parties will have opposing interests and there will be an issue to negotiate unless a readily identifiable price has been established. If alternative purchasers are forthcoming, the local party will wish to be paid something close to an open-market value in order to induce it to transfer the site, but this should normally be discounted by the fact that the JV parties intend to make profits by applying the site to the JV business. Any agreed discount is in reality a goodwill gesture which should be matched by equal flexibility in pricing the foreign party's assets.

The logical way to obtain a valuation is to appoint an appropriate local independent valuer with expertise in industrial real property, and to appoint an independent surveyor to conduct a site survey in order to provide information on the condition of the site. Other considerations such as improvements and modifications that the JV company will need to make can be applied in order to arrive at the valuation. The existence of other purchasers and alternative uses for the site must also be considered.

If an actual valuation amount for the property is not agreed at the time the Joint Venture Agreement is signed, it will be advisable to include a description of the valuation procedure and mechanics, including the identity of any expert and the considerations to be taken into account.

3 WARRANTIES IN RELATION TO THE SITE

One area where the parties will need to give each other warranties will be the title and condition of the site. These warranties will cover local planning and development matters such as the right to use the site for the manufacturing activities contemplated, good standing with the regulatory authorities, the condition of the site and the absence of liabilities affecting the site. Many of these concerns will be especially centred on the issue of environmental laws and regulation (see Chapter 24 below).

We have not attempted to suggest any specific sets of warranties to act as a universal guide for the acquisition of a site for a JV company. Standard property-related warranties will require adaptations for legal issues arising in the JV territory.

Checklist 23 Options for provision of site

1 JV party to sell site for shares or cash.

2 JV party to lease site.

3 Site to be acquired from existing operator.

4 Green-field site to be acquired – consider regional incentives.

Environmental issues

Participants in overseas joint ventures now show greater attention toward the increasing level of environmental regulation. In particular, environmental regimes are being strengthened in the CIS and Eastern European territories where past practice has been loose, and where the potential for hidden liabilities is fairly strong. The foreign party to an overseas joint venture may incur liabilities for environmental matters either directly or indirectly. Normally the principal risks exist at the level of the JV company, but some jurisdictions may in addition impose liability on a participant, in particular where the JV party is closely involved in the management.

It is advisable for any foreign party to a joint venture to require that the JV company should implement and carry out a policy of strict compliance with all environmental laws and regulations of the JV territory. This would include a requirement to provide to each party full information on any environmental problems and the solutions proposed to deal with them, including all dealings with the regulating authorities. It would also include a requirement to expend all appropriate sums on adapting the site for compliance.

1 IDENTIFICATION OF ENVIRONMENTAL PROBLEMS

Where real environmental problems are likely to exist, the foreign party should consider the implications at the early stage of the transaction, and weigh up the dangers of its incurring environmental liabilities or costs before deciding to proceed. The party should commission its own independent site survey, to be carried out by experienced independent consultants. Commonly this will be done in a number of stages according to the degree of commitment to the venture. A Phase 1 survey will involve a survey of the regulatory history of the site including discussions with management, employees and relevant officials. Phase 2 would involve a more detailed site assessment and the taking of sample materials, and a Phase 3 survey could be undertaken in order more precisely to assess the extent of the problems.

The environmental problems to be identified could include (without limitation) any of the following: methods of treating waste by-products, pollution of soil and water, exposure to hazardous chemicals, use of leaking underground storage tanks or pipes, poor health and safety procedures, or a general history of non-compliance. The potential liabilities may consist of fines due to the regulatory authorities or liability for a clean-up or remedial action, in addition to any civil or other liabilities to third parties. While heavy industrial activities on the site will present a greater risk, potential liabilities can be incurred in respect of dangerous waste by-products or spillages from lighter processes (e.g. chlorinated solvents).

2 POTENTIAL SOLUTIONS

A foreign party to the joint venture which is taking on an existing site formerly operated by the local party will want to impose specific provisions in the Joint Venture Agreement, making the major environmental liabilities a principal responsibility of the local party. By this means (it is hoped) the local party will be induced to investigate and identify the major potential risks at the site prior to signature of the Joint Venture Agreement. The agreement should also contain warranties in respect of compliance with the local environmental laws and regulations, and general good practice, as well as any appropriate negative warranties regarding emissions, waste disposal, air and water pollution, hazardous chemicals, where relevant, and similar matters. The warranties should be backed up by a full indemnity in favour of the foreign party.

Certain other solutions can be found in cases where the existing site proposed for the joint venture operations is, for environmental purposes, a 'dead loss'. The parties can consider abandoning the site and opting instead for a green-field development at which a facility could be built to the required environmental standards. In this respect it would be better to design the facility to comply with the updated EU environmental standards to take account of further regulatory development, and ensure that the site is equipped to handle adequately all waste processing, storage, discharge or emissions to the required standards under local laws or under the EU regulations.

Checklist 24 **Assessing environmental problems**

1 Do you know if the site has an environmental history?

2 Which party is responsible for remedying any problems?

3 Should the JV make alternative plans for its site?

R&D JV between UK and US medical companies

Case study 5

R&D JV between UK and US medical companies

Sheffield Medical Equipment Co. (Sheffield) is a UK company engaged in the manufacture of all types of advanced medical diagnosis equipment, including the latest generation of MRI and C-SCAN technologies. The company has started discussions with the senior professors and staff of the Medical Faculty of the University of Montana (the Faculty), with whom they already have an informal co-operation and sponsorship arrangement, regarding the establishment of a formal joint venture to combine the advanced technical progress of Sheffield in the equipment field with certain unique advances made by the team at Montana, with the intention of developing a new state-of-the-art MRI scanner for use in early cancer detection.

The intention is to form a new joint venture company which will conduct the combined programme of R&D research on the basis of technology licensed to it from both parties. Initially the company will be held as to 75 per cent by Sheffield and as to 25 per cent by the Faculty and its members (acting through their own independent company). However, there will be provision, in the event that the product development is successful, for the combined shareholding of the Faculty and/or its members to be increased to 50 per cent, and for a possible flotation of the company to be launched. As regards the R&D proposals, Sheffield will be required to fund the R&D by its share contribution and by loans at minimum annual levels provided the project achieves its stated milestones.

The parties are to license relevant technology to each other on an initially non-exclusive basis for the purpose of R&D, and each party will individually carry out their specified parts of the research programme on the company's behalf. The joint venture company will conduct limited research activities and collate the two parties' results, using a limited staff of seconded employees at a small site on the Montana campus. The JV company will none the less own all the newly developed technology discovered by both parties. However, it is agreed that each party will be granted exclusive licences of company technology in certain specified areas after the five-year period of the joint venture research programme. In addition, Sheffield is to have an option to be granted the exclusive manufacturing rights, on a commercial royalty basis, for the new generation equipment which will be derived from the R&D research.

The JV company's board of directors is to consist of four directors, of which one is to be nominated by the Faculty to represent its interests, with this number to be increased to two in the event that the product development moves into production phase. The duration of the joint venture will be unlimited, but shall be a minimum of seven years to take it into the production phase, unless terminated earlier for specified reasons, including breach of contract of because the R&D programme has failed to achieve its minimum milestone targets.

The two parties have started to negotiate the Joint Venture Agreement, with Sheffield preparing the first draft of the document.

Sheffield's first draft agreement contains the following proposals.

■ The University is to be solely responsible for providing the site and the back-up research facilities, including appropriate improvements for the company's use.

- Certain aspects of the Faculty's intellectual property and research, including patent and design specifications, need to be permanently assigned to the JV.
- Existing work programmes performed by the Faculty will be transferred, as will all laboratory personnel engaged on these.
- The Faculty is to be solely responsible for procuring all relevant US Department of Health approvals for the research programme and other required regulatory approvals.

The Faculty responds with the following counter-proposals.

- The company must pay for and procure the site for the research facility.
- The patent and design specifications provided by Sheffield must also be permanently assigned to the JV.
- Sheffield will procure finance or loan facilities on fair and agreed terms to ensure the continuation of the R&D programme, and if necessary will guarantee them.
- The Faculty will not agree to transfer the work programmes as requested by Sheffield.
- Sheffield will provide all necessary assistance with the regulatory approvals.

The Faculty adds the following provisions:

- Sheffield must also provide essential items of test equipment and tooling, and be prepared to service the same at cost.
- A number of specified matters in the Joint Venture Agreement should require the consent of both shareholders, these matters to include major changes in the scope of the research programme, issues of new shares in the company and other constitutional changes, and borrowings not included in the Business Plan.

Problem

- You are a negotiator on the Sheffield team. Consider how you would handle the contentious negotiating issues raised above.
- You are now a negotiator on the Faculty's team. Consider the same issues.

Part V

Issues of law and dispute resolution

25

Governing law and jurisdiction

1 GOVERNING LAW

The choice of which system of laws should govern the Joint Venture Agreement is of considerable importance and will affect the construction of the agreement and the parties' commercial interests in the joint venture.

The foreign party will often want to provide that its own system of laws will govern all substantive issues under the agreements. In particular, the application of English law can help to clarify the resolution of contractual disputes. The choice of English law also brings with it the general principles of English contract law which form the basis of international trade. For this reason English law is widely adopted for international commercial agreements.

In many territories the establishment of a joint venture will require the principal agreement to adopt the law of the territory itself. The restriction is most evident in those territories which have their own detailed Joint Venture Statutes. Typically in such territories the Joint Venture Agreement must state that it is governed by the laws of the territory in order for it to obtain approval from the foreign investment authorities.

In cases where a JV company is to be incorporated, the JV territory's domestic and company laws in relation to all matters concerning company administration, share capital, share issues, accounting, liquidation and similar matters must be applied to the JV company on grounds of public policy.

With certain types of commercial dispute, however, especially those where the joint venture project involves a high degree of industrial or infrastructure activity, any court proceedings surrounding conduct of disputes or enforcement of remedies will inevitably be governed by the law of the underlying commercial contracts or activities. These contracts, which may often be coupled with 'back-to-back' sub-contracts, will in most cases be governed by the laws of the JV territory.

Taking the example of China to illustrate the above principles, where corporate joint ventures are governed by the Chinese Joint Venture Law, all territorially based corporate joint ventures will be required to resolve their disputes through litigation or arbitration subject to Chinese law (see Chapter 26 below). By contrast, a 'contractual' joint venture between a UK party and a Chinese party will not be subject to the Joint Venture Law. However, because it is likely that the contractual *locus in quo* (place of substantial performance) will be the Republic of China, the Chinese authorities will not recognise the application of English law to any contractual issues litigated.

It is important to realise that there is a strong potential for confusion to arise in company law matters between two different legal systems. It is suggested that a balance can be struck by providing that the laws of the overseas territory will apply *prima facie* to the Joint Venture Agreement, subject to an exception relating to various matters of local company law and administration, and also to insolvency and liquidation matters. A suggested clause (to be discussed with local legal advisers) would run as follows:

> This Agreement shall be governed by and construed in accordance with [English law] except to the extent of any inconsistency with the companies laws of [JV territory] as they apply to the incorporation or the constitution of the JV company including matters of share capital, share rights, company administration, insolvency and liquidation procedures involving the JV company.

Whenever a foreign party must sign agreements governed by the laws of the JV territory, it should consult local legal advisers to ensure that it at least understands its likely exposure.

Another important point to keep in mind is that, whatever the chosen laws of the Joint Venture Agreement, the Articles of Association or Statutes of the JV company will always be effectively governed by the local law. The parties should ensure that an effective 'twin-track' approach is adopted in drafting the separate documents, to enable all rights arising under the Joint Venture Agreement to stand alone. The Joint Venture Agreement should also include an appropriate clause providing that it prevails over the Articles to the extent permissible under law (see Appendix E).

The following are a number of advantages and disadvantages in specifying the foreign party's own legal system to apply to the Joint Venture Agreement. First the advantages.

1 The foreign party will be better able to plan its own commercial activities.

2 Arbitrators will generally be more familiar with principles of English law.

3 The JV territory's laws may be detrimental, or its legal system inefficient or corrupt.

Some of the disadvantages of choosing the foreign law system to apply may be as follows.

1 The JV territory's courts may not recognise the parties' contractual choice of law.

2 Government authorities and other parties with whom the joint venture is customarily dealing may not be comfortable with the choice of foreign law.

3 If the local courts in the JV territory refuse to enforce a foreign judgment, the overseas party may need to litigate the issues on the merits in the JV territory.

If the parties agree that the laws of the JV territory will apply to the Joint Venture Agreement or (possibly) the ancillary agreements, the foreign party must request its own local legal advisers to provide it with written opinions as to whether any provisions of the local law could prejudice its commercial interests when applied to the joint venture.

2 JURISDICTION

The question of which courts have jurisdiction to hear cases involving the joint venture and its assets is a separate issue from that of which system of laws governs the agreements. The courts of either party's home state will usually possess 'personal jurisdiction' to hear contractual disputes involving that party. Alternatively, the courts may assume what is termed 'subject-matter jurisdiction' in cases where a contract has been made or is to be substantially performed in that territory.

The JV parties can make an understanding on the subject of jurisdiction. This may involve exclusion of the jurisdiction of the courts of a particular territory, or provision that only one national system of courts should adjudicate all contractual disputes. This may be the system of the JV territory or it may be the system of one or more of the JV parties.

Submission to jurisdiction clauses can be used, in which the parties expressly submit to the jurisdiction of the courts of the JV territory for the purpose of proceedings brought under the Joint Venture Agreement (but not for any other purposes). It is also possible to agree that the local party submits to the foreign party's territory.

For the foreign party to the joint venture, there is an obvious interest in avoiding an express submission to the jurisdiction, especially if arbitration is to be held in a neutral territory under an established arbitration forum. However, where arbitration is not provided for, or where arbitration is expressed to be non-binding, it will be difficult to avoid the presumption that the parties intend any litigation of contractual disputes to take place in the JV territory. In this regard, the foreign party may need to bring enforcement proceedings against the local party in the JV territory, and in this event the courts in the JV territory may take an unfavourable view if the foreign party has not itself submitted to the court's jurisdiction.

A joint venture party may be able to rely on the Brussels or Lugano Conventions relating to the enforcement of foreign judgments, principally in respect of enforcement against defendants resident in states which are part of the European Free Trade Association (EFTA) grouping, or in the alternative to rely on bilateral agreements between its own state and another.

3 A WORD ON LANGUAGE

In general, overseas businesses and their executives will not be sympathetic to English-speaking executives who believe that all business discourse must be conducted exclusively in the English language. However, in practice, discussions will almost certainly need to go forward with an understanding that the Joint Venture Agreement, and most other documents concerning the transaction will be written principally in the (English or European) language of the foreign party, and that the negotiations and discussions surrounding the transaction will be conducted principally in that language.

The foreign party should protect itself against language misunderstandings, usually by including a clause to the effect that the English/European-language version of the Joint Venture Agreement (and other agreements) will be the prevailing version. Another should provide that Company Minutes, official documents and other required information should be provided to each of the foreign parties in its own language and in legible form.

26

Dispute resolution and arbitration

1 DISPUTES IN GENERAL

The question of how to resolve potential disputes between the parties to a joint venture should be given due consideration in the formation stages and before the Joint Venture Agreement is concluded.

In drafting the Joint Venture Agreements the parties will need to consider striking a balance between informal methods of mediating disputes, which may be flexible but not always effective, and more formal procedures of arbitration or litigation which are intended to be binding. Often the formal procedures may be too drastic to resolve the commercial disputes which arise between the partners, and frequently their eventual use signifies the end of the co-operative phase of a joint venture.

Disputes can usually be divided into two categories: first, the predominantly commercial type, where the parties may have different ideas on how to achieve a commercial or marketing objective; second, the essentially legal type. The latter often concern rights of the joint venture parties (and possibly third parties also) under the Joint Venture Agreement or related agreements, including rights over share capital, assets, IP rights or similar matters. With this type of dispute, both sides will inevitably have to adopt quite formal positions, based on their legal rights and on the financial impact of the matters on their own groups.

In commercial disputes the parties will generally use sound business sense and a spirit of compromise to seek an accord on the issues in the interests of the joint venture. If certain commercial issues are liable to cause disputes, the Joint Venture Agreement should attempt to provide practical solutions in advance. However, if during the negotiation of the Joint Venture Agreement some areas of commercial disagreement have been shelved, the parties will be aware that these matters are likely to surface in the future as issues of contention.

2 ARBITRATION PROCEDURE

2.1 Arbitration in principle

As international transactions become more global in nature, parties to joint ventures will have a considerable interest in minimising the uncertainty involved in adjudicating disputes in the JV territory. The inclusion of a standard arbitration clause will facilitate a more reliable manner of dealing with the dispute. Furthermore, the parties can take some comfort from the fact that arbitration will take place in a neutral territory and under the established procedural rules of an appropriate arbitration organisation.

There are a number of reasons why it is more practical to agree on the substantive features of the arbitration procedure in advance. These include:

(a) when the nature of the dispute is known, the parties may not be able to agree upon matters such as the forum and venue;

(b) the arbitration forum which the parties choose should be compatible with the JV territory, as should its rules of procedure;

(c) there is always likely to be one party in a dispute who is less agreeable to arbitration and more content to resort to the local courts.

A basic outline of arbitration procedure is provided in Fig. 26.1.

Fig. 26.1 Outline of arbitration procedure

Select forum	Which arbitration organisation?
Select venue	Where is arbitration to be held?
Specify language of proceedings	(English usually preferable for multinational JVs)
Outline panel composition	Ensure equal or fair representation. Odd number of panelists, usually increased by one independent expert
Binding status	Is recourse to the courts excluded?
Choice of law	English law, venue law, *lex mercatoria*?

2.2 Arbitration clauses

The following are the issues which should be dealt with in a well-drafted arbitration clause.

2.2.1 Forum

The parties can specify which arbitration forum is to supervise the proceedings. This could be any competent national or international institution, but in the case of international commercial transactions the participants frequently opt for the

International Chamber of Commerce (ICC) as the supervisory body, and will therefore choose the ICC's Rules of Conciliation and Arbitration as the procedural rules for administering the proceedings. Other popular forums for international transactions (including, for example, international supply and distribution agreements) are the London Court of International Arbitration and the Stockholm Chamber of Commerce (in the latter case especially for shipping or maritime disputes). The consent of the institution to arbitrate is necessary.

In China the arbitration of disputes under Joint Venture Agreements is mandatory and the Joint Venture Law stipulates that all disputes involving foreign joint venture parties must be submitted to arbitration under the China International Economic and Trade Arbitration Commission (CIETAC), whose decision is final. The 'independent' party on the arbitration panel will be required to be a Chinese national unless the Joint Venture Agreement stipulates that it may instead be a foreign national.

Another option for the parties is to provide in the Joint Venture Agreement that the arbitration will be conducted under a specified set of rules without specifying what institution (if any) will oversee the proceedings. This will allow an *ad hoc* arbitration panel to be selected for a dispute which will have a clear set of rules for its guidance, and will help to initiate the proceedings in an orderly manner. A commonly chosen set of rules is that of UNCITRAL (the United Nations Commission on International Trade Law).

2.2.2 Venue

It is generally useful to decide the venue or 'seat' of the arbitration in advance. Each party will feel more comfortable if arbitration proceedings are to be held in a neutral territory. Such provision will give each party a better chance to present its case and control its costs. Political and cultural issues will also be relevant, as proceedings will be free of any prejudice or influence exerted in either party's territory. The arbitration panel should also be able more easily to apply the law of the Joint Venture Agreement (which might be the same substantive law as the venue territory) without too much conflict with the JV territory laws. The parties may none the less have certain rights to interlocutory relief under their own local system of law or the law of the JV territory.

In choosing the venue, the parties should ensure that both the venue state and the JV territory are signatories to the New York Convention on the Enforcement of Arbitration Awards, 1958, which provides for the mutual recognition of arbitration awards made *ex territoria*. See Appendix H for a list of states which are currently party to the New York Convention.

2.2.3 Language

It is prudent to provide that the arbitration proceedings will be conducted exclusively, or at least substantially, in the English language (or other European language such as French). Provision would also be made for proceedings and evidence in the native language to be translated. An arbitration forum which prohibits this policy of conducting proceedings in English should be viewed with scepticism and avoided if possible.

If the foreign party wishes to use its own legal representatives in the arbitration proceedings, the choice of language will also be important. There must in any event be a predominant (i.e. governing) language applicable to the arbitration which will have precedence, since in the event of conflicts or inconsistencies of language the parties' significant commercial rights may be affected. See suggested drafting in Clause 29 of Appendix E.

2.2.4 Panel composition

The parties may be quite comfortable with the use of a single arbitrator, especially for highly technical types of argument where it is believed that one individual is predominantly competent to arbitrate the dispute fairly.

More commonly in international agreements, the panel will be composed of three arbitrators. The principal arbitrator and chairman is effectively neutral, and is usually selected by the arbitral institution. Alternatively, the principal may be agreed upon by the parties, or selected by an appropriate professional, trade or mercantile body. The second and third arbitrators on such a panel will be nominated by each of the two parties. In the event that the joint venture has three or more parties, an appropriate modification may be made to extend the arbitration panel to five or seven members.

2.2.5 Final and binding status

If the arbitration procedure is to be effective it will generally be given a binding status as between the parties. This means in effect that the courts of the JV territory (or any territory) are excluded by the parties' agreement from hearing any arguments on the merits of the legal or commercial dispute. This takes us again to the issue of the enforcement of the arbitration ruling or award.

2.2.6 Choice of law for arbitration

Subject to the rules of the forum, the substantive laws that will govern the arbitration proceedings and the factual or legal issues will be those chosen under the Joint Venture Agreement. An exception consists of those cases where the arbitration venue itself applies its own laws to any proceedings in its own territory.

In certain cases the parties may in any event decide that a different system of laws should specifically apply to the arbitration procedure, and in this regard two principal possibilities may be considered:

(a) Law of the arbitration venue. Adopting the venue laws may greatly assist the arbitration panel in its responsibilities, especially those relating to the hearing of evidence and witnesses, discovery of documents, and the clarity of any award or judgment. In any event the venue laws will in effect provide the legal back-up for resolving any issues of substance or procedure which were not adequately addressed under the contractual law or the rules.

(b) *Lex mercatoria* – international trade law. The other possibility for the parties is to avoid the choice of a national system of laws altogether. If this is desired, a commonly chosen option for international trade agreements would be the adoption of *lex mercatoria* which is essentially a set of international trading principles understood in both the developed and developing worlds. They have not been codified into written principles and remain flexible. Many arbitration awards have been given in accordance with these principles and upheld in various national courts where enforcement proceedings have been sought.

There is an obvious advantage in choosing this system of law, since the parties are seeking to reach a fair commercial solution rather than a legal one. Another advantage is that this method will avoid any risk of a maverick ruling based on an unusual legal provision under the proper law of the arbitration. However, a disadvantage is insufficient clarity in the proceedings, and the parties and their lawyers may spend months embroiled in legal arguments and interpretations.

2.3 Enforcement of an arbitration award

If arbitration awards are intended to be final, this should be clearly agreed. It is helpful to combine the arbitration clause with a jurisdiction limitation clause which excludes hearing arguments in the national courts 'on the merits' of the dispute (including any rights of appeal), effectively limiting the court's jurisdiction to the conduct of enforcement proceedings in the JV territory.

It is important for the parties to confirm that the JV territory has acceded to the New York Convention, as without this there will be no guarantee that any arbitration procedure provided for in the agreement can be effectively implemented in the JV territory, bearing in mind the likely recourse of the local party to the protection of its own national courts.

It is surprising that some prominent territories have not acceded or have reserved their accession to the Convention, for reasons based on their perception of national interest.

The foreign party should nevertheless keep in mind that even if the JV territory is a signatory to the New York Convention, there remains the possibility that the arbitration ruling or award could be denied recognition or enforcement, since:

(a) the New York Convention allows for non-recognition in the enforcing state where there are public policy grounds for this, or where a procedural irregularity has been identified in the venue state;

(b) an issue of conflict of law may render the effective enforcement of the award impractical or unfair – for example, if the company or insolvency laws of the JV territory do not allow for a distribution of company assets in accordance with an arbitration award, the conflict of law is fatal to the enforcement;

(c) the enforcement of an arbitration award may in practice have a significant effect on third parties whose rights could be compromised. To avoid such third party enforcement problems, the arbitration rules and procedures should allow for the possibility of third party claims to be adjudicated under the arbitration. However, it is generally not possible to bring the third party within the jurisdiction of the arbitration forum without its prior agreement.

Checklist 26 **Questions about dispute resolution**

1 What type of commercial disputes are likely to arise?

2 Is there any requirement for arbitration in the JV territory?

3 What territory would be appropriate for arbitration?

4 What form of arbitration or resolution is appropriate?

27

Mediation and alternative dispute resolution mechanisms

1 ALTERNATIVE DISPUTE RESOLUTION PROCEDURES

In order to avoid every commercial debate between the parties resulting in an expensive arbitration procedure, many joint venture agreements will contain mechanisms for informal resolution of the dispute before invoking the arbitration process (see Fig. 27.1). The range of informal alternative dispute resolution (ADR) mechanisms has grown apace in recent years with the ingenuity of lawyers involved in the joint venture field.

Fig. 27.1 Mediation and ADR mechanisms v. arbitration

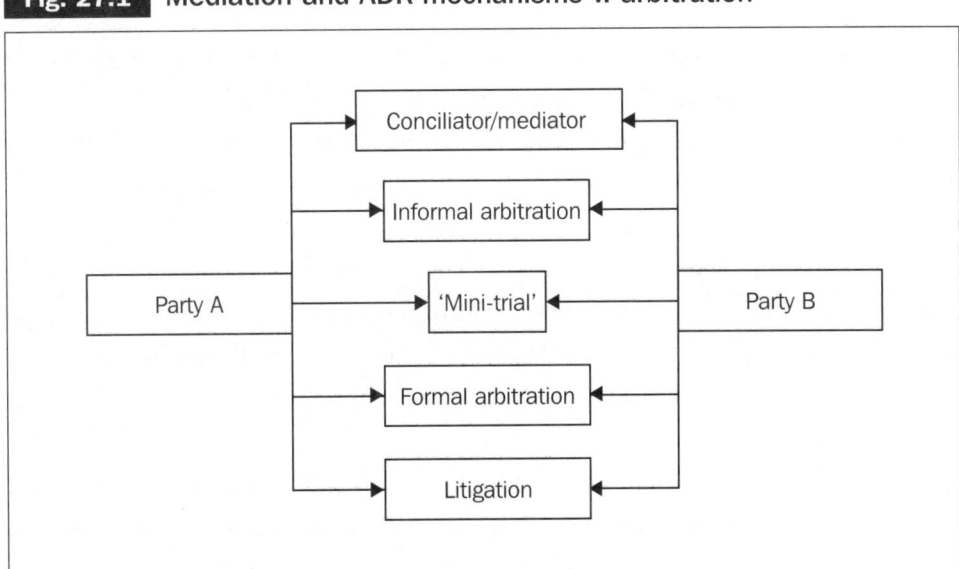

The following is a summary of the most widely used alternative dispute resolution procedures.

1.1 Mediation

This involves the mutual nomination of an independent person, panel or firm to be the mediator. The mediator may or may not have particular expertise in the technical area under dispute. The mediator will be given some discretion as to how he/she attempts to broker a compromise, whether by informal discussion or by means of a more formal set of representations. He/she may preside over the discussions, or instead choose to correspond with or talk to the parties individually.

The mediator will not generally be given the power to force any solution or action on any of the parties. Instead he/she will make recommendations to the parties on what he/she believes to be a fair and sensible resolution of the dispute.

1.2 Non-binding arbitration

This process is a more formal and legalised structure for dispute resolution. It involves the parties making written and/or oral submissions, the hearing of witnesses and the consideration of other formal evidence, under normal rules of arbitration or others agreed by the parties. The arbitrator or panel will then deliver a formal ruling or award, based on what it believes to be fair and reasonable on the facts, but this will not be legally binding on the parties.

1.3 Negotiated settlement

These settlements take one of two forms. The first would be an informal procedure intended to bring forward a commercial compromise. Initially the commercial executives will negotiate the dispute in good faith. If no agreement is reached, the matter will be referred to the chief executive of each group in the hope that this will focus on the more essential business issues at stake.

The second type of procedure is the formal negotiated settlement. The parties can appoint a time for a meeting or a series of meetings to achieve a settlement in the shortest possible time. At such a meeting each party will usually be able to attend with commercial principals and several appointed legal and financial representatives.

This procedure is sometimes referred to as a 'mini-trial'. A formal structure may be allocated to it, under which each party will make initial submissions and presentations, will examine the other party's principals if it deems it necessary, and in a final submission will summarise its own position.

Of course, additional variations for a negotiated settlement are possible. If the dispute is of an essentially legal or technical nature, the parties may (in extreme situations) wish to leave it exclusively to lawyers or possibly technicians to argue out a settlement – preferably with a limit on time and costs.

2 ALTERNATIVE DISPUTE RESOLUTION AS A SOLUTION

We should consider in the round the advantages and disadvantages of employing informal ADR procedures. Addressing the negative side first, the problem is one of flexibility. Some of the detailed step-by-step mediation processes are often not sufficiently flexible and do not take account of commercial events or of the overriding common sense of commercial parties in the interests of the business. The use of fixed procedures involving notices and counter-notices can often result in unintended consequences, where a developing matter is prematurely forced to a head in order for a party to comply with its notice obligations or so as to reserve the rights of that party. Thus, for certain issues, silence in the Joint Venture

Agreement may be the best policy. The absence of an express mediation mechanism will not prevent the parties from implementing a formal mediation procedure if a dispute arises, it is hoped in a manner which is suited to the dispute in question.

On the other side, the advantages of implementing an informal dispute resolution process include the following.

(a) It provides a means for the parties to raise commercial concerns in a civilised manner without resorting to drastic legal means.

(b) It avoids adverse publicity for the JV business, including preservation of sensitive relationships with regulatory and investment authorities.

(c) It helps to preserve the confidentiality and commercial secrets.

(d) It helps to keep costs lower.

(e) It keeps discussion to resolve the dispute on a commercial basis.

(f) It avoids a situation where one party's claims are defeated entirely.

On balance, it is suggested that in most cases the use of an informal mediation clause will be the most flexible approach for an international joint venture, and such a clause will often provide for a negotiated settlement to be concluded between senior executives from each JV party. In many cases, the parties would in fact want to discover the nature of the underlying dispute before deciding on the best means to resolve it informally.

Checklist 27 Why use an ADR mechanism?

1 To have a mediator with technical expertise.

2 To maintain confidentiality.

3 To maintain informality – a non-adversarial procedure.

4 To keep costs lower.

Avoiding misunderstandings

We have already noted that with overseas joint ventures an understanding of the national and business culture of the parties with whom one is dealing is of prime importance. It often helps in negotiating a satisfactory agreement, and subsequently in the running of the joint venture, if the personnel from the foreign party's group include personnel with an understanding of the culture and (possibly) the language of the local party.

1 STRATEGIES FOR CO-OPERATION

The art of being co-operative and friendly can go some way towards oiling the wheels of the joint venture. However, it will not be the only factor involved in preventing disputes between the JV parties. Other strategies for successful co-operation include the following.

(a) Each party should provide a clear and detailed response to pertinent due diligence enquiries, and state whether any matters have to be withheld on grounds of confidentiality. The same consideration applies to information required to be provided during the operative phase of the joint venture.

(b) In discussing commercial matters of the JV business, the parties should be open and honest about matters which concern them, including situations where the foreign party disagrees with the decision of a managing director.

(c) Full board meetings should be held regularly but not excessively often. Three to six months is suggested to be a sensible interval, but this will depend on the nature of the JV business.

(d) The respective directors or other personnel of the JV parties should be encouraged to develop regular channels of communication, including personal meetings, so that disputes on small matters do not suddenly emerge as significant.

(e) Any written information or material to be exchanged by the JV parties should be provided and returned without delay.

(f) Divisions of costs. Where sums of money need to be expended by either JV party in connection with forming the JV company or conducting its business, the parties should seek to agree in advance how the costs will be allocated.

Clearly each party is expected to pay its own costs of taking legal, financial or accounting advice. Conversely, the costs of forming the JV company and preparing business audits or marketing surveys will be joint venture costs to be reimbursed by the company, as will costs of valuing property or assets for the mutual benefit of the parties.

Conduct which is considerate and business-like should, in conjunction with well-drafted provisions in the Joint Venture Agreement, help to ensure that matters suited to commercial resolution do not escalate into full-scale litigation or arbitration.

2 DEADLOCK PROVISIONS

Deadlock provisions will usually be invoked in a late attempt to resolve an impasse between the JV parties which is threatening to damage the joint venture. The full operation of the deadlock provisions will usually be designed to lead to an exit mechanism, for one or both JV parties, if a fundamental issue has frustrated the operation of the joint venture.

A deadlock provision in a Joint Venture Agreement will contain a procedure for informal resolution of the deadlocked matter, which frequently involves negotiations between senior or chief executives of the JV parties, and then, if the deadlock persists, a procedure for one or other of the JV parties to have an option to exit, usually by selling its shareholding to the other party at an agreed valuation price.

It is recommended that it is generally prudent not to include formal deadlock provisions in the Joint Venture Agreement, especially as they may sometimes force the parties into a premature dispute. However, if they are provided, they should be drafted in such a manner as to encourage the resolution of the matter under dispute, and a reasonable time period such as six months should be is provided for, to allow for events to change or for either party to modify its initial position in the dispute. Special care should be taken if the deadlock will have the effect of triggering the parties' buy–sell options at a predetermined valuation price, which may provide an unduly tempting incentive for one JV party to terminate, and may not produce a desirable solution for either party.

Joint venture between UK and Singapore electronic systems companies

Joint venture between UK and Singapore electronic systems companies

Cardiff Electronic Systems (Cardiff) is a UK company which specialises in furnishing residential and retail buildings with electrical and lighting systems and is also a distributor for various electrical appliances which form part of these systems. Sentosa Lighting Equipment Pte Ltd (Sentosa) is a Singapore company which carries on a similar electrical business with a speciality in fitting out leisure complexes. The parties propose to combine their resources in order to tender and contract for electrical installation work in Singapore and for the China and other Pacific Region markets.

They have signed a Joint Venture Agreement to operate the business as a 50:50 joint venture company based at the premises of Sentosa in Singapore. It is structured as an equal joint venture in most respects, including the shareholding, management structure and the obligations as to funding and guarantees. Each party has contributed US$2 000 000 as initial share capital, and the parties share the responsibility of providing an additional $15 million in working capital loans. Each party is also providing technology and know-how according to agreed licensing provisions, and the capital assets which Cardiff has provided are more or less balanced by the contributions of premises and employees from Sentosa.

The joint venture has been operating for a period of 18 months and has begun to go into profit, but recently management differences between the parties have begun to manifest themselves. These differences include the following matters of disagreement.

- Both parties are claiming that the other has not provided technology and information to the specifications agreed in the JV and licence agreements.

- Sentosa argues that certain assets and equipment provided by Cardiff are defective and that its technicians have failed to remedy or replace them as required, and that accordingly under the terms of the Shareholders' Agreement it is entitled to an adjustment of the parties' shareholdings.

- Cardiff maintains that some of the technical staff that Sentosa has seconded to the JV have failed to implement the combined technology properly, and that this has caused work schedules and prices not to accord with quotations made to customers.

- Cardiff and Sentosa have a strong disagreement on whether to pursue two major contract opportunities in China.

The Joint Venture Agreement includes the following provisions.

- An arbitration clause providing for disputes to be resolved by binding arbitration under the auspices of the ICC in Paris.

- Provision for matters of dispute to be initially submitted to a mediation procedure which will involve:

  (a) an attempt at negotiated settlement between two teams of the parties, each to include three appropriate commercial people and one appointed lawyer; and

  (b) submission of the matter to the parties' deputy chief executive officers.

- Termination provisions providing for an expected duration to ten years, but subject to early termination in the events of:

  (a) breach of contract having a substantial adverse effect on the business;

  (b) liquidation, insolvency or change of control of a party; or

  (c) termination or substantial breach of a technology licence agreement.

- Following termination at its own option for a breach of contract, Cardiff may exercise a put option to sell its shares to Sentosa at an auditors' fair valuation.

- A deadlock clause which provides that in the event of an impasse between the parties on a business matter (not being a breach of contract) one party may serve a deadlock notice, and be prepared either to buy the other party's shares or sell its own shares at a fair valuation price.

- The JV agreements are all governed by English law.

Problem: The Cardiff board wishes to sort out the problems of the JV at minimum cost to itself. You are an executive of Cardiff reporting to the board on the options available to Cardiff. Consider whether you would advise one of the following:

- use of one of the mediation procedures;

- immediate recourse to arbitration;

- use of the deadlock clause to enable one party to take control of the JV business, and which may result in Cardiff being obliged to buy the shares;

- termination of the joint venture, with an election for liquidation of the JV business or the sale of it to Sentosa.

Ancillary agreements

Contribution Agreement

In most joint venture projects the parties will contribute their initial share capital of the JV company by a cash payment. The initial share capital should be sufficient to cover the initial working-capital requirements and start-up costs of the company. The JV parties will want to avoid committing excessive capital. For reasons of prudence, as well as tax planning, it may be preferable to provide capital in the form of shareholder loans.

1 VALUING ASSETS

Where the consideration for the issue of shares is to be capital assets, the principal questions will be the identity of the assets and their valuation. If one JV party is to contribute stock or components and the other JV party is to contribute equipment and know-how, they need to find a fair and equal basis for valuing the assets. Subsequently they must ascertain that the assets have been transferred to the JV company's premises in the agreed manner.

Agreeing the assets value is more important for a 50:50 JV company, since if there is a discrepancy in the asset contributions, the shortfall of one party's asset value cannot easily be made up by the issue of more shares to the other party. The parties will need to achieve a balance in the asset contributions, whether by means of a return of assets to one party, a further contribution from the other, or a mechanism for providing a cash equalisation payment between the JV parties and the company (see Fig. 29.1). If this does not achieve equalisation, it is possible to reallocate benefits or dividends to redress the imbalance.

In valuing assets, the parties will rarely accept each other's existing book values, especially where intangibles are concerned. Where the parties assign contracts to the joint venture, the value to the company will need to reflect the future revenue streams generated by the contracts. Each JV party should protect itself against the assignment of onerous or unprofitable contracts, and for this reason it is advisable that the Contribution Agreement should provide for later revaluation of contracts based on future revenue streams.

2 VALUING INTANGIBLES

A similar logic will apply to intellectual property and know-how contributions, the true value of which may not be apparent for a number of years. The future value of these benefits may be recognised by means of deferred royalty arrangements contained in the parties' Technology Licences. However, where the licence rights are incidental to the asset contribution, the parties may need to consider reviewing the value of these rights.

Fig. 29.1 Adjusting the asset contributions

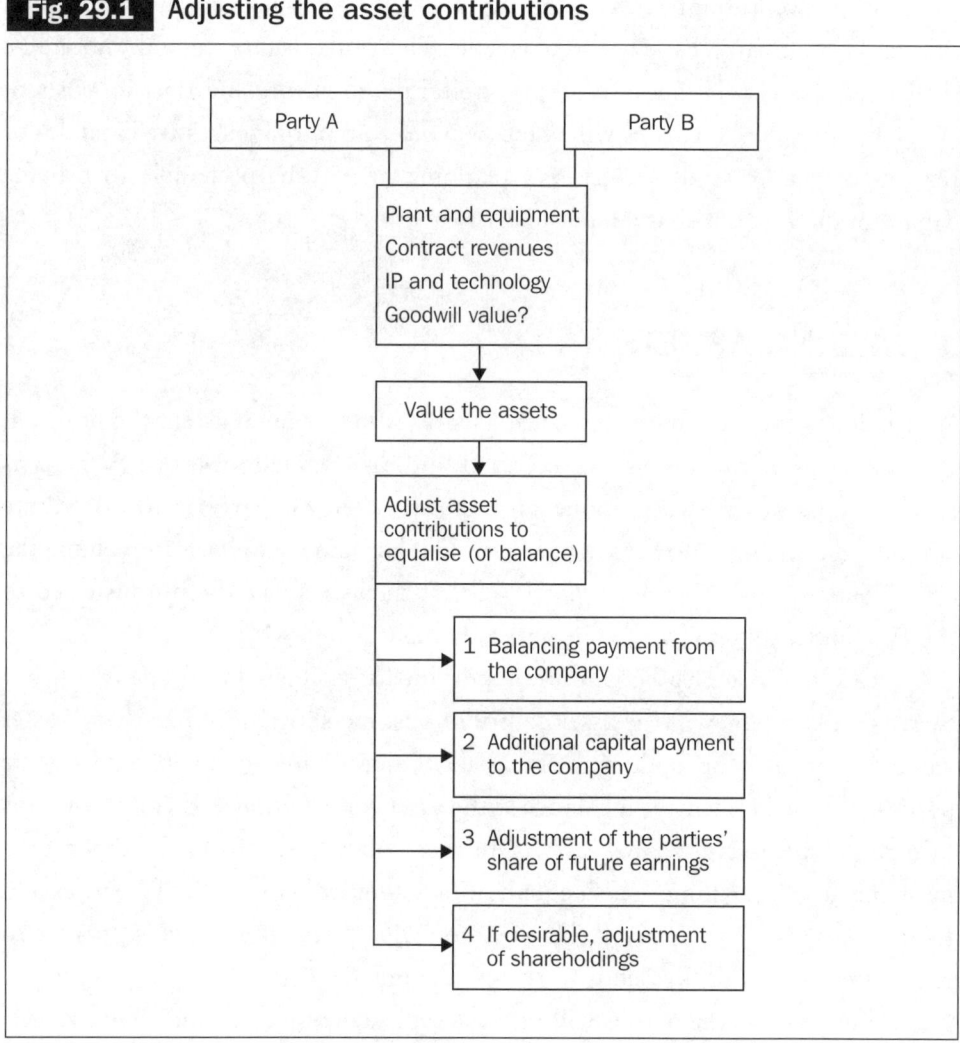

Where any of the above types of problem relating to assets valuation exist, it is recommended that a separate Contribution Agreement be executed to embody the asset transfer and valuation mechanisms. This will help to avoid confusion and provide additional detail for the revaluation of the assets. The agreement may also outline the mechanics of transfer and in effect constitute the formal document of transfer.

Where the parties transfer tangible assets such as plant and equipment, the charge to stamp duty would normally arise on the deed of transfer. However, if there is no actual deed of transfer and title is expressed in the Contribution Agreement to pass upon delivery of the assets, no stamp duty charge will arise unless the assets are fixtures to be transferred with the real property interest.

30

Technology and Trade Mark Licence Agreements

1 TECHNOLOGY LICENCE

In some joint venture projects one or both JV parties intend to transfer to the JV company technology and know-how rights over an entire area of production activity. However, in most joint ventures there will be another category of technology rights which both JV parties are actively exploiting, for which the JV company requires a licence to enable it to receive technical information and to exploit the technologies.

If both JV parties are due to contribute to the JV company technology rights of equal value, the parties may be content for each to provide a royalty-free licence to the JV company, and then extract the benefits of the technology in the form of increased profits. The draft Joint Venture Agreement in Appendix E sets out mutual IP licensing provisions (Clause 19) which create royalty-free licences to be provided by both parties to the joint venture. Fig. 30.1 illustrates the mechanics of a Technology Licence Agreement.

Fig. 30.1 **Mechanics of the Technology Licence Agreement**

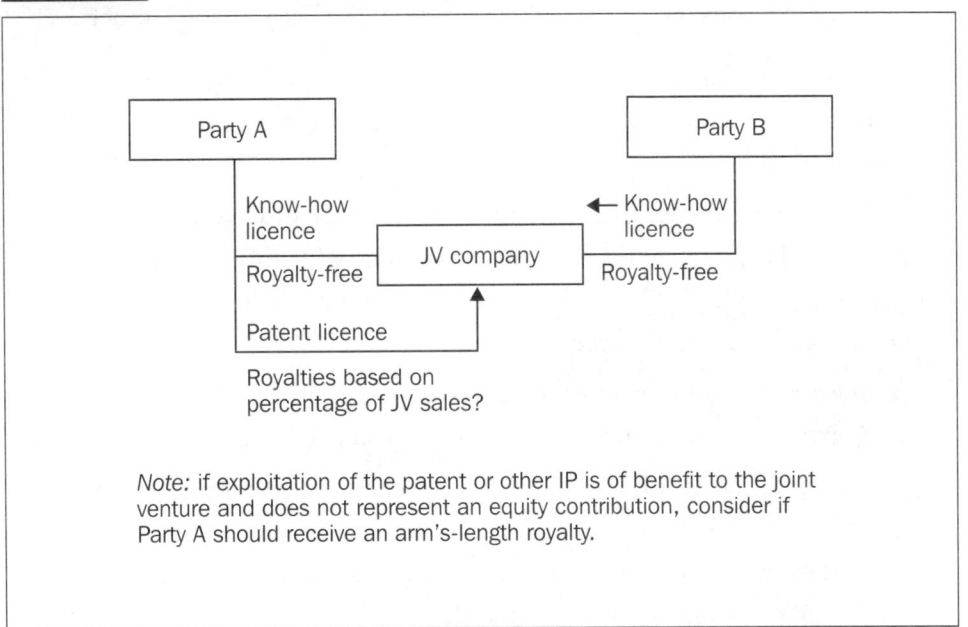

Note: if exploitation of the patent or other IP is of benefit to the joint venture and does not represent an equity contribution, consider if Party A should receive an arm's-length royalty.

Where one JV party is the main provider of know-how (frequently this is the foreign party), it may elect for commercial reasons to provide a royalty-free licence to be valued as part of its overall asset contribution to the joint venture. However, the owner should consider licensing the technology to the joint venture on an arm's-length basis and in consideration for royalty payments based on the sales achieved by the joint venture, as this is most likely to attract favourable treatment for withholding tax purposes.

The other substantial provisions of the Technology Licence relate to the terms of the licence to the company. The technical information itself will need to be properly defined, and this will usually be clarified further by reference to a schedule providing full details and a description and/or diagrams. The material provisions of the Technology Licence will deal with the conditions applying to the supply of the technical information.

It is most important from the licensor's point of view that it should itself prepare the first draft of the licence and maintain control over further drafting modifications. In this respect it is important to ensure that the law of the licensor's home state will be the operative law of the Licence Agreement, as this will help to ensure the preservation of its legal rights under the intellectual property laws of its home state.

The licensor's obligations to provide technical information and know-how should be qualified by stating that the licensor may exercise reasonable judgement as to what information is necessary for the licensee's business use. The terms of the licence will state also that the technical information is provided exclusively for use in connection with the JV business. The licensor will also want strictly to limit any third-party use of the technology.

Appendix F is a suggested form of Technology Licence Agreement. Other commercial provisions which may be contained in the Technology Licence are:

(a) a clause providing for technical assistance from the licensor, including the provision to the licensee of the services of engineers, technicians or similar support staff;

(b) a clause covering improvements to the technology discovered or developed by either JV party. A neutral way of dealing with this is to provide that neither party is obliged to provide its improvements to the other party, unless commercial terms are agreed to do so;

(c) confidentiality provisions to protect the commercial position of the licensor, with appropriate exclusions to enable the JV company to carry on its business;

(d) provisions of the EU block exemption on technology transfer agreements, for example, an obligation to provide improvements falling only on the licensee would be outside the terms of the block exemption, as would a restriction on parallel imports of products into the EU area.

Finally, among the most important commercial provisions will be the termination clauses of the licence. In particular, a clause should provide that unless it terminates earlier, the Technology Licence will terminate on the expiry or termination of the joint venture.

2 TRADE MARK LICENCE

If one JV party is licensing product know-how to the joint venture, it may be appropriate to license trade marks to help market the products. With such licences the commercial use by the licensee must be strictly limited to the particular products and to the JV business.

The licence will usually be royalty-free, non-exclusive and without rights to assign or sub-license the marks. In certain cases a sub-licence may be envisaged for the purposes of a specific sub-contract. Various conditions relating to use of the trade marks on packaging, stationery and publicity materials may be included in the licence.

The licence should also include a requirement for the licensee to notify the licensor of any adverse matters relating to the trade marks within the JV territory which come to its attention in carrying on the business, in particular:

(a) any infringements by third parties or allegations of infringement;

(b) any claims, threats or allegations made by third parties; and

(c) any other claims or attacks to which the trade marks may be subject.

In the event that any actions or proceedings are required to be taken by the licensor against any third party infringing its rights, the licensor will need to reserve the right to take action in the JV territory on its own behalf. It is advisable to apply the law of the licensor's territory to the Trade Mark Licence and to include a provision for the licence to terminate in the event of termination of the Joint Venture Agreement.

3 REGISTERED USER AGREEMENT

It is common practice to provide the licensee with a separate 'Registered User Agreement'. The purpose of this is to enable the licensee to obtain registration of its rights in the relevant territories, and it therefore needs to be governed by local law. In achieving this object it will be advisable to keep the registered user agreement to a minimal set of terms and to exclude from the final document any sensitive terms surrounding either the joint venture or the IP licensing.

Checklist 30 Issues for the Technology Licence

1 Are the parties both licensing IP? If so, should the terms be similar?

2 Does one JV party make continued use of the IP? If so, do not transfer outright, and consider the nature of improvement rights to be granted.

3 Consider whether commercial terms for royalties etc. are appropriate.

4 Trade Mark Licence – ensure strict use limits, non-exclusivity and non-assignability.

31

Distribution and Supply Agreements

1 DISTRIBUTION AGREEMENT

Where a joint venture is engaged in manufacturing, one or more of the JV parties may be given distribution rights in respect of sale of the products, or possibly the right to supply certain components for the production process. Sometimes the foreign party alone will be given exclusive rights to distribute the products in its own regional markets or possibly world-wide.

Alternatively, the JV parties may agree between themselves that each will have separate distribution rights for the products in their own sales areas. For example, in the case of a bilateral joint venture the local party may be allocated distribution rights in its domestic (or regional) sales market while the foreign party is allocated distribution rights for its own region. This division of distribution rights for the products between the domestic and overseas markets is commonly encountered in countries with a sizeable domestic market.

When distribution rights are to be given to the JV parties, the Distribution Agreement should be a 'buy/sell' supply agreement on arm's-length commercial terms, and may raise internal issues of transfer pricing. The terms may include the provision of after-sales service and repair, and also undertakings not to sell competing products of other suppliers and not to market the products under any other trade marks or brand names.

The main obligation of the company as principal will be to supply the products to the distributor upon receipt of firm written orders and on the agreed terms as to price and payment. The company usually needs to grant exclusive rights for the arrangement to work, but the distributor will probably need to appoint a network of sub-distributors to cover a large territory. An obligation for the distributor to buy minimum quantities of products will not usually be advisable, since the distributor already has an interest in selling the products and the obligation could cause a dispute.

Where the application of the agreement brings it within the scope of EU competition laws, the terms of the EU block exemption on exclusive distribution agreements prohibit any clauses which have as their effect a prohibition or restriction on the distributor (or other party) making 'parallel imports' from one EU territory to another. It is thus advisable to use the following 'white' clause which is permitted under the EU block exemption on exclusive distribution agreements:

> [The Distributor shall] not advertise or promote the Products outside the Territory or establish any branch depot or sales operation for the distribution of the Products outside the Territory. This sub-Clause shall not prevent the Distributor from responding to unsolicited enquiries or orders received from outside the Territory.

2 SUPPLY AND PURCHASING AGREEMENT

If one party is given a supply agreement to sell components or other products to the JV company, the commercial concerns will be similar to those for distribution agreements. The EU block exemption applicable to exclusive purchasing agreements is similar to that for distribution agreements, although the goods are not purchased for resale in this situation, so that the 'parallel import' provisions have less significance.

An important commercial difference in the supply agreement will be that the JV company will have a different commercial perspective. Both JV parties should agree that the company has a strong interest in protecting its sources of supply and ensuring that it has enough materials and components to continue its manufacturing operations without interruption. Therefore the JV company may need to impose obligations as to exclusivity, minimum supply quantities and a firm obligation to meet the orders placed by the company.

Therefore if one JV party has an exclusive supply agreement with the company, the supplier should be under fairly strict obligations of performance and delivery. In addition, the parties should consider whether minimum supply quantities are in the company's best interests so that the JV party can raise its own production or purchasing levels to the level required to meet the company's demand.

32

Contracts between the parties and the joint venture company

1 THE JOINT VENTURE PARTIES AS CONTRACTORS

We have seen that some joint venture projects include arrangements for one or both parties to supply goods or services to the JV company, or sometimes to each other if one of the JV parties is a prime contractor. Most joint ventures involve the sale of capital assets to the JV company and one or both JV parties will often provide ancillary services to the joint venture. These services may be technical in nature, as in the case of engineering or support services, or administrative, as where one party provides office facilities and computer support.

Contractual undertakings between JV parties are in many respects the essential ingredient of joint ventures, all the more so where the arrangements include sub-contracting of business responsibilities between the JV parties. Where the JV parties are to provide guarantees or indemnities for such contractual liabilities, a further range of contractual obligations between the parties and the JV company will arise, including provisions for:

(a) apportioning the agreed liabilities in the agreed proportions;

(b) cross-indemnifying the other parties in respect of any party assuming a greater share of liability; and

(c) exclusion clauses and liquidated damages provisions to limit the potential liability of the JV party as a sub-contractor to the joint venture.

In a joint venture that is 50:50 in structure, or is intended to be approximately equal, the existence of such commercial contracts involving the JV parties is more likely to operate in a workable and successful manner if the sub-contracting tasks and contractual benefits are shared equally. A joint venture can sometimes become ineffective where one JV party is shouldering a far greater share of the commercial activity while the other JV party assumes more the role of a passive investor and financier.

This scenario is often encountered in cross-border joint ventures where the foreign party is mainly providing cash and assets while participating in the management to a limited degree, and the local party has more involvement in the production and sales activity, and in directly supervising the staff and contractors involved in the JV business. This situation may be acceptable where the JV parties have carefully agreed upon the structure and their respective roles. However, it may be advisable in this situation to determine whether the foreign party can assume more responsibility and commercial involvement which will benefit the JV business. This may be of benefit to the joint venture itself, and can also benefit the foreign party in meeting its own responsibilities concerning the joint venture.

2 SHOULD THE JOINT VENTURE COMPANY BE A PARTY TO THE JOINT VENTURE AGREEMENT?

In some jurisdictions the authorities or investment regulators may require that the JV company is incorporated prior to, and is required to be a signatory to, the Joint Venture Agreement. In other situations there may appear to be commercial reasons why the JV company should be made a party to the main Joint Venture Agreement. This might be so that the company can derive certain benefits (such as direct licences of IP) or enter into obligations in favour of the JV parties. These may include confidentiality, the issue of shares or similar matters.

It is recommended that in most cases this is not a good idea for the joint venture. By making the company an additional party, the resultant tri-partite structure will introduce additional complexity, and may possibly afford to one party some unforeseen corporate remedies arising from its position as a (minority) shareholder. The company should not be joined to the agreement without taking proper legal advice on all the potential consequences. In common law jurisdictions the recent case of *Russell* v. *Northern Bank Development Corporation Ltd* should be kept in mind (see Chapter 7, Section 3 above).

Legal advice should be sought even where the relevant regulatory authorities insist that the company must be a party to the Joint Venture Agreement, and should similarly be sought where the JV company is expected to be a party to the other commercial agreements relating to the joint venture.

Appendices

IMPORTANT NOTES

1 These draft precedents are intended to serve as guidelines to drafting the documents for a joint venture, in conjunction with the main text of this work, and are not intended to be taken as specific legal advice. Accordingly, proper legal advice in the appropriate geographical locations should always be taken for any proposed transaction or agreement.

2 In a number of territories a separate assets transfer agreement may need to be executed which will comply with the local legal requirements.

Memorandum of Understanding (proposed joint venture)

THIS MEMORANDUM OF UNDERSTANDING is made on the   day
of   , 1999/200
BETWEEN:

1   [Local party] whose principal office is at [   ]
      (hereinafter referred to as 'Party A'); and

2   [Foreign party] whose principal office is at [   ]
      (hereinafter referred to as 'Party B')

who are referred to herein individually as a 'Party' or together as 'Parties'.

1 OBJECTIVES OF THE JOINT VENTURE

1.1   It is the intention of the Parties to establish a joint venture [for the
      production and sale of [   ] products] [to co-operate and tender
      for [   ] project contracts] within [   ] (JV Territory).

1.2   The Parties desire to form and cause to be incorporated in [   ] a
      company with limited liability to be known as [   ] Limited ('The
      JV Company').

1.3   The Parties will enter into a Shareholders' Agreement incorporating terms
      which are mutually acceptable ('Shareholders' Agreement').

1.4   The Shareholders' Agreement will contain a number of conditions to its
      validity, including the procurement of necessary governmental consents,
      investment approvals and the satisfactory completion of the Parties' due
      diligence enquiries.

1.5   The Shareholders' Agreement will include a list of matters which require the
      consent of both Parties to implement, including (*inter alia*) share capital,
      loans, finance, guarantees, acquisitions, disposals, capital expenditure and
      certain contracts.

1.6   The Parties will agree the Business Plan in advance of each Financial Year,
      with the first Business Plan to be agreed prior to incorporation of the JV
      Company.

1.7   The Financial Year of the JV Company will be the twelve month period
      ending on [31 March]. [It is intended that Messrs [   ] shall act as
      Auditors.]

1.8 The JV Company shall be located in [   ] and shall have its principal office in [   ] at [a place to be mutually agreed upon by the Parties].

2 SHARE CAPITAL OF THE JV COMPANY

2.1 The authorised share capital of the JV Company shall be [£   ] divided into [   ] ordinary shares of [£1.00] each. The initial issued and paid-up share capital of the Joint Venture Company shall be [£   ].

2.2 The shareholdings of the Parties in the JV Company shall be as follows:

Party A : [50 per cent] and

Party B : [50 per cent].

2.3 The shares of each Party shall at all times rank equal in rights, shall be identical in all respects and shall carry one vote per share. All future issues of shares shall be in proportion to the Shareholders' existing shareholdings.

2.4 For a period of [three (3)] years from the date of the Shareholders' Agreement, no transfer of shares in the JV Company shall be permitted. Thereafter transfers shall be permitted only with the prior written consent of all existing shareholders.

2.5 Notwithstanding paragraph 2.4 above, each of the Parties may transfer any or all of its shares in the JV Company to an affiliate or to its holding company. (The term 'affiliate' shall mean any company in which the Party or its ultimate holding company directly or indirectly holds 50 per cent or more of the issued share capital.)

3 PARTIES' CONTRIBUTIONS TO THE JV COMPANY

3.1 Each Party will contribute the nominal value of its initial issued shares in cash [in Sterling], and further assets in kind, including equipment and contracts required for the JV Company's business in accordance with principles agreed between the Parties.

3.2 The valuation of each Party's asset contribution to the JV Company will be undertaken by an international firm of chartered accountants agreed by the Parties, who will audit the assets on the basis of identical agreed accounting principles consistent with generally accepted international accounting standards.

4 DIRECTORS AND MANAGEMENT OF THE JV COMPANY

4.1 The Board of Directors shall comprise four (4) Directors to be nominated by the Parties as follows:

Party A : two (2) Directors [of whom one shall be nominated by Party A as the Managing Director];

Party B : two (2) Directors [of whom one shall be nominated by Party B as the Chairman of the Board of Directors].

4.2 [The Chairman of the board of Directors shall be rotated every year between the Directors nominated by the Parties.] or [The Chairman of the Board of Directors shall be elected by the Party B appointee Directors from among their number.]

4.3 The Chairman [shall] [shall not] have a casting vote in the event of a tied vote on the Board on any matter.

4.4 The overall management of the JV Company shall vest in the Board of Directors. In the first year after incorporation the Board of Directors shall meet at least monthly, and thereafter as often as necessary but in any event at least every three months.

4.5 The business of the JV Company shall be managed by a Managing Director who shall be nominated by Party A and appointed by the Board of Directors accordingly.

4.6 The Finance Director/[Chief Financial Officer] shall be nominated by Party B and appointed by the Board of Directors accordingly.

5 RELATIONSHIP BETWEEN THE PARTIES AND THE JV COMPANY

5.1 All contracts and arrangements made between the JV Company and either Party shall be approved in writing by both Parties and are expected to be on arm's-length terms.

5.2 The Parties will not be directly involved in the JV Territory in the activities mentioned in paragraph 1.1, except to pursue opportunities on behalf of the JV Company with consent of the other Party.

5.3 Separate agreements will regulate the use of all corporate names, trademarks and logos of [   ] and/or [   ], and the withdrawal of such permitted use.

6 CONFIDENTIALITY

6.1 The Parties will exchange certain information and material of a proprietary or confidential nature relating to commercial, financial, technical, marketing or other matters ('Confidential Information'). Confidential Information shall be kept confidential by the Parties and shall not be used by the receiving Party save for the purposes of the JV Company and shall not be released or disclosed to any third party.

6.2 The Parties shall also keep the existence and contents of this Memorandum of Understanding confidential and shall not disclose the same (or any part thereof) except to employees or professional advisers or as may otherwise be required by law.

6.3 The Parties shall not make any public statement, announcement or disclosure about this Memorandum of Understanding or their intended collaboration except by mutual agreement between the Parties.

6.4 Each Party shall ensure that its employees and all other persons who may be involved in these matters shall comply with this paragraph 6.

6.5 The confidentiality obligations in this paragraph 6 will survive the expiration or termination of this Memorandum of Understanding for a period of three years.

6.6 Notwithstanding anything to the contrary, the confidentiality obligations shall not apply to information:

(a) which is in the public domain or becomes public knowledge without the default of the receiving Party; or

(b) which is required to be disclosed by court order or binding legal obligation.

7 ADDITIONAL PROVISIONS

7.1 With the sole exception of paragraph 6 above, it is agreed by each Party that the provisions of this Memorandum of Understanding will not be legally binding on either Party, whether under contract, tort, statute, regulation or otherwise and are not intended to create or imply any legal relationship between the Parties with respect to the subject hereof prior to the execution of a Shareholders' Agreement.

7.2 Subject to paragraph 7.1 above, this Memorandum of Understanding shall be operative until the expiry of six months from the date hereof, or until the

Parties enter into the formal Shareholders' Agreement, whichever shall be the earlier.

7.3 Notwithstanding paragraph 7.1 above, both Parties agree not to enter discussion with any other party concerning the activities described in paragraph 1.1 during the period mentioned in paragraph 7.2.

Signed by	)	Signed by	)
	)		)
————————————)		————————————)	
	)		)
(Director)	)	(Director)	)
for and on behalf of	)	for and on behalf of	)
[ ])		[ ])	

Confidentiality Agreement (proposed joint venture)

THIS AGREEMENT is made on the   1999/200
BETWEEN:

1 [   ]
    [Address   ]; and

2 [   ]
    [Address   ].

This Agreement relates to the [Memorandum of Understanding of even date herewith] [the discussions between us] in relation to a proposed joint venture in [   ] for the assembly and sale of [   ] products (the 'Proposed Transaction').

In this Agreement 'Information' means information of any nature and in any form (oral, written or computerised) supplied to one party by the other party in connection with the Proposed Transaction.

Each party 'covenantor' hereby undertakes to and for the benefit of the other party, in consideration of the other party agreeing to supply to the 'covenantor' certain Information (which the parties each acknowledge to be of a confidential nature) and entering into discussions relating to the Proposed Transaction, as follows:

1 to keep confidential and not disclose to any person, other than as permitted under paragraph 4 below, the other party's interest in the Proposed Transaction;

2 to keep all Information confidential and not disclose the same to any person, other than as permitted under paragraph 4 below;

3 to use the Information only for evaluating and negotiating the Proposed Transaction;

4 not, without the other party's prior written consent, to disclose any Information to any person other than those senior officers and executives of the covenantor and those of its professional advisers who, in each case, need to know the Information for the purpose of evaluating, negotiating or advising on the Proposed Transaction;

5 to procure that each person to whom disclosure of Information is made by the covenantor as permitted under paragraph 4 above is made aware in advance of disclosure of the terms of this letter and to use reasonable endeavours to procure that each such person adheres to these terms;

6 [make direct contact only with those officers and employees of the other party with whom it is currently dealing or whose names and addresses are notified to it by the other party and not with any of our suppliers, customers, sub-contractors or professional advisers;]

7 if the covenantor ceases to be interested in the Proposed Transaction, and in any event upon written request of the other party, promptly to return to the other party all information without keeping any copies and hand over all notes (and any copies) prepared by the covenantor (and by any person to whom disclosure has been made as permitted under paragraph 4 above) containing any Information or relating to negotiations or discussion if the Proposed Transaction; and

8 to promptly notify the other party if any Information is required to be disclosed by law and co-operate with the other party regarding the manner of such disclosure or any action to challenge the validity of such requirement.

The above undertakings do not apply to any Information which can be demonstrated:

(a) to be in or to come into the public domain otherwise than as a result of a breach of the above undertakings; or

(b) already to be in the possession of the covenantor or to have been received by it at any time in good faith from a third party who is not bound by any obligation of confidentiality in relation thereto; or

(c) to have been independently developed by employees of the covenantor to whom no prior disclosure has been made of the Information.

Each party hereby further acknowledges and confirms for the benefit of the other party that:

(a) no representation or warranty is made or is to be implied, and no responsibility or liability is or will be accepted by either party, its subsidiaries or any of its respective directors, officers, employees, agents or advisers, as to, or in relation to, the accuracy or completeness of any Information made available to the other party or its advisers;

(b) the obligations of each party shall be deemed to be given only for the benefit of the other party;

(c) each party's obligations under this agreement shall endure for a period of three years from the date of this Agreement and shall survive the termination of any negotiations between the parties regarding the Proposed Transaction;

(d) [this agreement shall be governed by and construed in accordance with English law (and the parties hereto accept the exclusive jurisdiction of the English courts for all purposes in relation thereto)].

Signed by

═══════════════════════════

for and on behalf of
[   ]
Dated:

Signed by

═══════════════════════════

for and on behalf of
[   ]
Dated:

Information request
(proposed joint venture)

1 GENERAL

1.1 Memorandum and Articles of Association or Corporate Charter of the Company.

1.2 Chart showing the organisation and management structure of the Company.

1.3 Brochures and any printed advertising material describing the Company's business.

1.4 Registered office address and principal places of business of the Company.

1.5 Location of any overseas branch offices or affiliates of the Company.

1.6 Copies of recent Board and Shareholder Minutes and Resolutions.

1.7 Details of any consents or approvals required for the Joint Venture.

1.8 Copies of any court orders or decrees, or decisions of government or public agencies which affect the Company or could affect the Joint Venture.

1.9 Particulars of any trade associations of which the Company is a member.

1.10 Copies of audited financial statements of the Company for the last [three years].

2 ASSETS, PLANT AND EQUIPMENT

2.1 Schedules containing full details of the machinery, plant and equipment intended to be transferred to the Joint Venture, current book values and accounting bases for depreciation.

2.2 Details of significant acquisitions of fixed assets over the past three years being assets which are relevant to the business of the Joint Venture.

3 PROPERTY

3.1 Details of all properties owned or occupied by the Company which are intended to be used in the Joint Venture (with plans and short descriptions).

3.2 Valuation of any properties intended to be transferred to the Joint Venture.

3.3 Copies of any existing surveys of the properties.

3.4 Copies of any notices or court orders made in respect of the properties.

3.5 Details of any mortgages or charges to which the properties are subject.

3.6 Diagrams of factory and office layout.

3.7 Details of where the Title Deeds can be inspected.

3.8 Details of any environmental escapes, pollution, contamination or emissions.

3.9 Copies of all environmental compliance reports and all notices, correspondence or other material from governmental or other agencies.

3.10 Copies of all Health and Safety Inspection reports.

4 INTELLECTUAL PROPERTY AND KNOW-HOW

4.1 A list and copy of all patents or applications therefor to be transferred to the Joint Venture, showing ownership, country and patent number.

4.2 A list of all registered copyrights, design registrations or applications relevant to the Joint Venture showing ownership and registration number.

4.3 A list of trade marks or service marks to be transferred to the Joint Venture.

4.4 A list of any other trading names used by the Company.

4.5 Copies of any licensing agreements or arrangements relating to the above matters.

4.6 Details of any current, pending or threatened litigation or arbitration relating to the above matters.

5 LIABILITIES AND CLAIMS

[**Note** – Caution and diplomacy will be required in this area.]

5.1 Details of all indebtedness of and all guarantees or indemnities given by the Company.

5.2 Details of all product liability and product warranty claims brought or settled by the Company in the last three years.

5.3 Details of the level of expenditure on repairs/renewals of fixed assets in the last three years.

5.4 Particulars of any litigation, arbitration or other proceedings relating to the Company in the last three years.

6 EMPLOYEES

6.1 List of all employees to be transferred to the Joint Venture.

6.2 Copies of all service contracts or consultancy agreements of all directors and senior employees intended to be transferred or seconded to the Joint Venture.

6.3 Details of any disputes involving any of the above categories of employees.

6.4 Particulars of any trade unions recognised by the Company (together with a copy of the recognition agreement) and of any collective bargaining agreement or other understandings or arrangements which may affect the Joint Venture employees.

6.5 Details of any outstanding employee claims to the courts, Industrial Tribunals or their equivalent.

6.6 Particulars of any current pension, death or disability benefit scheme for directors or employees which it is intended to transfer to the Joint Venture.

7 CONTRACTS

7.1 Copies or full details of all contracts of any nature which are intended to be transferred, novated or sub-contracted to the Joint Venture Company, or which may otherwise have an impact upon the Joint Venture.

7.2 Details of any of the above agreements which are, or are required to be, registered under any unfair competition or other governmental legislation including Articles 81(1) or 82 of the European Union Treaty, or in respect of which an application or notification has been made to the Commission of the European Union.

7.3 Details of any existing or foreseeable facts or circumstances which may cause avoidance or breach of any material provision of the above agreement, whether relating to assignment or novation or any other matter.

8 CONNECTED TRANSACTIONS

8.1 Details of any contracts or arrangements involving the directors or affiliates of either party which are or may become contracts affecting or involving the Joint Venture.

9 SALES AND MARKETING

9.1 Analysis of turnover by activity/products and geographically over the last three years.

9.2 Description of products, their special features and patent or other registration details.

9.3 Size and share of market, sales organisation and principal customers.

9.4 Current level of the order book, with comparisons for each month of the last twelve months.

10 PRODUCTION AND SUPPLIES

10.1 Brief description of process of production, including details of present and future productive capacity, degree of computerisation, age of machinery.

10.2 Summaries of raw material and component purchases for the last three years, including details of discount rates and credit terms received.

10.3 Details (including costs) of all research and development work in progress.

[General note – the reference in this list to 'Company' is likely to be a reference to the joint venture partner itself, or to the division operating the joint venture business.]

Business Plan – summary (standard format)

1 GENERAL OVERVIEW

1.1 Statement of Joint Venture Company Objectives.

1.2 Summary of shareholding structure, organisation and management of Joint Venture Company.

1.3 Description of intended manufacturing and sales activities.

Product and market analyses. Competitor analysis.

Estimates of turnover in Years 1 to 5.

1.4 Corporate Development Plan – five-year period.

Strategies for growth and acquisition.

Factory, premises and asset analyses.

Employee and manpower requirements.

SWOT analysis – strengths, weaknesses, opportunities, threats.

2 SPECIFIC FINANCIAL PROJECTIONS

2.1 Opening Balance Sheet.

Parties' Asset Contributions – any deferred contributions.

Shareholder Loans at commencement.

2.2 Sales Turnover Projections – Years 1 and 2.

Capital Expenditure Projections – Years 1 and 2.

Projected Expenses of Business – Years 1 and 2.

2.3 Projected Profit and Loss Account – Year 1.

Closing Balance Sheet – End of Year 1.

Funds Flow Statement – Year 1.

2.4 Working Capital Projections – Years 1 and 2.

Liquidity Analysis for Years 1 and 2.

Required Shareholders' Loans – Years 1 and 2.

APPENDICES

1. Site description.

2. Plant and equipment.

Shareholders' Agreement relating to [Joint Venture Company]

DATED: 1999/200

(1)   PARTY A

– and –

(2)   PARTY B

INDEX

Schedules

SHAREHOLDERS' AGREEMENT

THIS AGREEMENT is made this   day of   , 1999/200
BETWEEN:

1 [Local party], a company incorporated under the laws of [   ],
  having its principal office at [   ] ('Party A'); and

2 [Foreign party], a company incorporated under the laws of [   ],
  having its principal office at [   ] ('Party B');

who are referred to in this Agreement individually as the 'Party' or together as the
'Parties'.

WHEREAS:

A [   ] is engaged, *inter alia*, in [   ];

B [   ] is engaged, *inter alia*, in [   ];

C Party A and Party B have agreed to establish a joint venture company in
  [   ] in order to undertake [the development, manufacture, sales and
  servicing of certain products as herein provided] [a contract in relation to
  [   ];

D Party A and Party B are willing to participate in (and procure the assistance of
  their Affiliates in) the aforementioned joint venture company and the
  transactions described herein upon the terms and conditions of this Agreement.

NOW IT IS HEREBY AGREED as follows:

1 DEFINITIONS

1.1 In this Agreement the following expressions and terms shall, unless the
    context otherwise requires, have the meanings respectively assigned to them:

'Affiliate'	In relation to any Party, a corporation which controls such Party, or a corporation which is directly or indirectly controlled by such Party or by a parent of the Party.
'Articles'	The Articles of Association of the Company in the form of Schedule A.
'Auditors'	The auditors of the Company appointed pursuant to this Agreement.

'Board'	The board of Directors of the Company.
'Business'	The business of the Company as provided in Clause 4.
'Business Plan'	The Business Plan of the Company in the agreed form which shall be updated for each financial year of the Company [and shall be substantially in the form of Schedule D].
'business day'	A day on which the major clearing banks are open for a full range of business in [ ].
'Company'	The [limited liability] company to be formed pursuant to Clause 3 hereof to be called [* Limited, short particulars of which are set out in Schedule 2].
'Confidential Information'	All information of a confidential nature in any form relating to any of the Shareholders or to the Company or any of their Affiliates.
['Contract']	The agreement to be entered into between the Company and [ ], as referred to in Clause 4.
['Contribution Agreement'	The agreement [of even date herewith] relating to the contribution of capital assets and contracts to the Company and the valuation thereof.]
'Control'/'control'	In respect of any corporation, the possession, directly or indirectly of: (a) a majority of the voting rights exercisable at general meetings on all, or substantially all, matters; or (b) the right to appoint or remove directors having a majority of the voting rights exercisable at meetings of the board of directors on all, or substantially all, matters.
'Director'	A director of the Company for the time being in accordance with this Agreement, including where the context admits an alternate director.
['Distribution Agreement'	The distribution agreement to be entered into between [Party A/Party B] and the Company in the form of Schedule *.]

'Financial Year'   The financial year of the Company for official fiscal purposes, determined pursuant to this Agreement.

'Group'   [in relation to either Party, that Party and its respective Affiliates].

'Intellectual Property'   All rights in intellectual property which are necessary for the conduct of the Business hereunder, whether or not registered or registrable including without limitation all rights in inventions, patents, designs, copyright, trade secrets, know-how, software, discoveries, improvements, concepts, models, drawings, secret formulas and processes and all other rights of a similar nature throughout the world including all applications for any such protection and rights to apply for any of the same [and, for the avoidance of doubt, the terms excludes trade and service marks and trade names, whether registered or not].

['Net Asset Value'   The net book value (calculated in accordance with accounting principles generally accepted in [   ]) of the Company's total assets (excluding goodwill and other intangible assets) less its total liabilities, based on the Company's financial and accounting books and records as of the end of the month immediately preceding the valuation date, with such adjustments as may be agreed in writing between the Parties.]

['Products']   [   ].

'Shares'   Equity voting shares (of any class) in the share capital of the Company at any time.

'Shareholder'   Any Party or any holder of Shares in the Company from time to time in accordance with this Agreement.

'Shareholder Proportion'	[Fifty per cent (50%)] in relation to Party A and [fifty per cent (50%)] in relation to Party B or (if different) such other proportion for each Party as equals the percentage which the nominal value of the shares beneficially owned by such Shareholder bears to the combined nominal value of the Shares owned by Party A and Party B at the relevant time.
'Site'	[ ].
'Technology Agreement'	The technology licence agreement to be entered into between [ ] and the Company in the form of Schedule *.
'Trade Mark Agreement'	The trade mark licence agreement to be entered into between [ ] and the Company in the form of Schedule *.
'Unanimous Approval'	A vote in favour of a resolution approved by all of the votes eligible to be cast (regardless of attendance) at a Board Meeting or Shareholder Meeting [or by a written resolution of all of the Directors or of all of the Shareholders] pursuant to this Agreement.

1.2 In addition the following rules of interpretation shall apply.

(a) Any reference herein to a 'corporation' is a reference to a company or body corporate incorporated in any relevant jurisdiction.

(b) Any reference herein to a 'parent' is a reference to any other corporation which directly or indirectly controls the first corporation, and any reference herein to a 'subsidiary' is a reference to any corporation(s) which is/are directly or indirectly controlled by the first corporation.

(c) Any reference herein to a Director includes where relevant a reference to an Alternate Director.

(d) Any reference herein to a statute or a statutory provision shall include a reference to it as amended or re-enacted or of which it is an amendment (but excluding any amendment or re-enactment to the extent the same has retrospective effect).

(e) The masculine gender includes the feminine and neutral gender, and (where relevant) the singular includes the plural and vice versa.

(f) The headings in this Agreement shall not affect its interpretation or construction.

(g) Each of the Schedules hereto shall constitute part of this Agreement.

(h) Any reference to [£] is a reference to [Pounds Sterling] [other currency?].

2 CONDITIONS AND GOVERNMENT APPROVALS

2.1 This Agreement shall be conditional upon, and shall not be effective until, the grant of all requisite consents, approvals and registrations by all relevant governmental authorities of [   ] to:

(a) the transactions contemplated in this Agreement;

(b) the incorporation of the Company under the laws of [   ] pursuant to this Agreement and the Articles;

(c) the investment by Party A and Party B (or Affiliates of them) in the Company;

(d) [the licensing of technical know-how by [   ] or its Affiliates to the Company;

such consents, approvals, and registrations hereafter referred to as 'Approvals'.

2.2 The Parties may by agreement in writing waive the condition in Sub-Clause 2.1 above in respect of any one or more required Approvals. Any conditions precedent which are included in the said Approvals shall be subject to written consent by both Parties.

2.3 [The Parties] [Party A] shall prepare and submit all necessary applications for the requisite Approvals. The form of the applications shall be agreed in advance. The costs and expenses of the said applications for Approvals shall be quantified and agreed in advance, and shared equally between the Parties.

2.4 [Consider any conditions relating to award or execution of commercial contract.]

3 FORMATION OF THE COMPANY

3.1 As soon as practicable after the Approvals referred to in Clause 2 above shall have been granted, [the Parties] [Party A] shall cause to be incorporated under the applicable laws of [   ], a [limited liability company], under the name of [   ]. The Parties shall, as soon as possible after incorporation of the Company, cause the following steps to be taken at Directors or Shareholders Meetings (as appropriate):

(a) the Company shall adopt its Memorandum of Association [Corporate Charter] in a manner consistent with Sub-Clause 4.1 below;

(b) the Company shall adopt its Articles in the form of Schedule A; and

(c) the Company shall have an authorised share capital of [£*] divided into [   ] 'A' Shares of £1 each and [   ] 'B' Shares of £1 each ranking equal in all respects save as otherwise provided in this Agreement.

3.2 The costs and expenses of incorporation of the Company and all related legal expenses shall when incurred be shared equally between the Parties, [and refunded by the Company after its incorporation]. Subject to the above each Party shall bear its own costs.

3.3 [Party A represents and warrants to Party B that as at the date hereof:

(a) the Company is a [limited liability/ joint stock] company duly organised and validly existing under the laws of [   ], and has the power and authority to conduct its business in any territory pursuant to this Agreement;

(b) the details of the company set out in Schedule B are true and correct;

(c) Party A is the sole legal and beneficial owner of the issued share capital of the Company of £*, which is fully paid up;

(d) the Company is not the subject of any litigation and arbitration proceedings;

(e) the Company does not own any assets as at the date hereof;

(f) the Company has not traded, entered into any contract or commitment and has not incurred any debts or other liabilities.]

4 BUSINESS OF THE COMPANY

4.1 The business of the Company will be to undertake [the development, design, assembly, manufacture, distribution, servicing and sale of [Products] OR [performance of a contract with [   ] relating to [   ]] in [   ] territory.

4.2 The Business shall at all times be conducted on sound commercial principles.

4.3 The Business will be carried on principally from the Company's factory premises at [   ]. The factory premises shall be sold to the Company by Party A as a part of its contribution of assets to the Company.

4.4 [The Company shall have the [exclusive] rights to manufacture the Products and to distribute the Products in [   ]].

4.5 The Company will undertake such other business activities as all of the Shareholder may unanimously agree in writing. [Any activities intended to be excluded.]

5 SHAREHOLDINGS IN THE COMPANY

5.1 The authorised share capital of the Company shall be [   ] consisting of [   ] Shares of [£1] each. The initial issued share capital shall be [£1 000 000] divided into 1 000 000 Shares of [£1] each, which shall initially be subscribed and held by the Parties in the following numbers and proportions:

Shareholder	Number of Shares	Percentage
Party A or its Affiliate	[500 000]	50%
Party B or its Affiliate	[500 000]	50%
Total	[1 000 000]	100%

5.2 Party A or Party B may hold shares either directly or in its own name or may designate an Affiliate to hold any of its Shares which it is required to subscribe for under Sub-Clause 5.1 above or is otherwise entitled to acquire.

5.3 In the event of an Affiliate of either Party ceasing to be such an Affiliate, the relevant Party shall ensure that any Shares held by such Affiliate shall be transferred back to the Party or to another Affiliate of such Party.

5.4 Any additional Shares issued by the Company (in excess of the initial subscription under Sub-Clause 5.1) shall be first offered to Party A and Party B simultaneously, upon equal terms and in their agreed Shareholder Proportion respectively.

6 CAPITAL CONTRIBUTIONS

6.1 The total capital contribution of [each Party] [Party A/Party B] to be paid in consideration for its Shares, shall be made partly [wholly] in cash [in Sterling] as follows:

Party	Shares	Cash Amount
Party A	[200 000]	[£200 000]
Party B	[200 000]	[£200 000]

6.2 [Each Party shall each contribute an additional capital contribution in the form of equipment, stock-in-trade, contracts, and other assets to a value of [£300 000] [and otherwise in the manner provided in the Contribution Agreement.]

6.3 All non-cash assets contributed by a Party or by an Affiliate of a Party shall count as part of such Party's capital contribution.

6.4 [Party A] shall obtain or procure at its own expense all necessary import licences, customs and value added tax clearances and similar authorisations for the shipping and transportation to the Company's premises of the assets to be contributed by [Party B].

6.5 Title to equipment, stock-in-trade and tangible assets will pass upon delivery.

7 CORPORATE MATTERS AND COMPLETION

A meeting shall be held [at such time and place as the parties may agree] not more than 30 days after all Approvals required under Clause 2 shall have been received, at which the Parties will do or procure the following:

7.1 The Parties shall subscribe for their Shares as detailed in Sub-Clause 5.1 and shall contribute their capital contributions as specified in Clause 6 above.

7.2 The Company shall allot and issue Shares to Party A and Party B respectively in accordance with Clause 5 above, their names shall be entered in the register of members of the Company and Share Certificates shall be issued to them.

7.3 Party A shall deliver to the Company the resignations of [   ] and [   ] as Directors of the Company and [   ] as Secretary of the Company, each delivering to the Company a letter acknowledging that he has no claims against the Company.

7.4 The Parties shall nominate the members of the Board as follows:

   (a) Party A shall nominate [   ] and [   ] as A Directors;

   (b) Party B shall nominate [   ] and [   ] as B Directors;

   (c) [Party B] [Both Parties] shall nominate [   ] as Chairman of the Board;

   (d) [Party A] shall nominate [   ] as Managing Director;

(e) [Party B] shall nominate [   ] as Finance Director; and

(f) [Both Parties shall nominate [   ] as Company Secretary.

7.5 The Parties shall procure that a meeting of the Board is duly held and adopts the following steps in relation to the Company:

(a) the appointment of all nominated officers referred to in Sub-Clause 7.4 above;

(b) the change of the registered office to [   ];

(c) the change of the [accounting reference date] [financial year end] to [   ];

(d) the appointment of [   ] as Auditors to the Company; and

(e) the adoption of the Business Plan in the approved form.

7.6 The Parties shall confirm the corporate actions set out in Sub-Clause 7.5 above by a resolution of the Shareholders.

7.7 [The following documents shall be executed by the Parties:

(a) the Technology Agreement; [or licences of IP pursuant to Clause 19]

(b) the Trade Mark Agreement; and

(c) the Distribution Agreement.]

[(d) the Transfer of the Site to the Company.]

7.8 Each of the Shareholders shall exercise all voting rights and other powers of control available to it in relation to the Company so as to provide that at all times the provisions hereof concerning the Company and the rights and/or obligations of each of the Shareholders or of the Company are observed and given full effect.

7.9 Each of the Shareholders shall take such steps as are within its control and as shall be necessary to enable the Company to discharge its obligations under the Contract.

8 THE BOARD OF DIRECTORS

8.1 The Board of Directors shall consist at all times of [four (4)] Directors. Party A shall be entitled to nominate two (2) Directors ('A Directors') and Party B shall be entitled to nominate two (2) Directors ('B Directors'), in each case by giving notice in writing to the Company Secretary. Each Party may in like manner remove or replace its nominee Directors.

8.2 [Party B shall have the right to nominate one of its B Directors as the Chairman of the Board and to replace such nominee.] Such nominee shall be promptly appointed as Chairman by a Board resolution.

8.3 [The Board of Directors shall, in addition to its normal function, carry out all the functions of the Board of Management of the Company under [   ] law, and may delegate ordinary business matters to a committee of the Board.]

8.4 The position of a Director of the Company will be non-remunerative. Each Shareholder shall be solely responsible for any benefits or compensation granted to its nominee Director and shall hold the Company harmless in respect thereof.

8.5 The parties shall exercise their votes as Shareholders at all times so as to give effect to the provisions of this Clause 8. Each Party will use reasonable endeavours to procure that at least one of its Directors attends each duly convened Board Meeting.

9 PROCEEDINGS OF THE BOARD

9.1 The Board of Directors may meet for the resolution of business and regulate its meetings and procedures as it thinks fit provided that a Board meeting shall be held at least once in every [three] [six] calendar months. Board Meetings shall [always] [in the usual course] be held [in * Territory] [outside the United Kingdom], at the principal office of the Company or at such other place as the Board may agree.

9.2 All business at Board Meetings shall be conducted principally in English and the official Minutes kept in the English language.

9.3 The Chairman shall convene Board Meetings pursuant to Sub-Clause 9.1 as and when he thinks fit. Any [one] [two] Director[s] may request the Chairman [Company Secretary] to convene a Board Meeting to discuss any relevant issue, or may convene such a Meeting themselves by notice to the other Directors. Such notice shall clearly indicate the matter or matters to be discussed at the Meeting.

9.4 Unless all the Directors agree in advance in writing to a shorter notice period (to be the same for all Directors), written notice of [thirty (30)] days shall be given for any Board Meeting by the [Secretary] to each Director (including each Alternative Director) at his usual (or other notified) address.

9.5 The notice shall state the date, time and venue set for the Meeting, and shall include an agenda for the Meeting setting out clearly all items to be considered, including copies of any documents to be considered. Any Director may add items to the agenda by written notice to the Chairman [Company Secretary] at least seven days prior to the Meeting. The Chairman shall then circulate the additional items to all Directors.

9.6   Any notice to a Director resident outside [   ] shall be sent by registered airmail letter with a copy by facsimile transmission (receipt confirmed) to the facsimile number provided by such Director (if any).

9.7   The presence in person of at least two Directors (or their validly appointed Alternate Directors), one nominated by Party A and one by Party B respectively, shall constitute a quorum for any Board Meeting.

9.8   If within half an hour from the time appointed for such a meeting a quorum is not present, then the Meeting shall be adjourned to the same day, time and place the following week, unless that day is a public holiday in which case the Meeting shall be held on the next day which is not a public holiday.

9.9   The Chairman shall preside over Board Meetings and oversee discussions and voting procedures, but shall not have an additional or casting vote as Chairman.

9.10   Each Director shall have the power to appoint an Alternate Director to attend and vote at Board Meetings in his place in the event that he is unable to do so. The appointment of an Alternate Director shall require a notice in writing to the Company from the appointing [Director] [Party], including the Alternate's consent to act and any time limitation applicable to the appointment, to be delivered to the Company at least seven (7) days prior to any Meeting. An Alternate Director shall have no right to remuneration but shall have all other rights of the appointing Director for the duration of his appointment. [The maximum duration of any Alternate Director appointment shall be six months.]

9.11   Board Meetings may be held by telephone or video-conference link-up provided each participant can at all times hear and speak to each other participant, and subject to all other provisions of Sub-Clauses 8, 9 and 10 hereof.

9.12   Board Meetings may be attended by such translators, advisers and professionals as each Party may consider necessary.

10 DECISIONS OF THE BOARD

10.1   Each Director present at a Board Meeting shall have one vote on any issue where he is not disqualified from voting. Except as provided in Sub-Clauses 10.2 and 10.3 below, all decisions at Board Meetings shall be taken by [a simple majority] [a two-thirds vote] of those present at a Board Meeting when a quorum is present.

10.2 Notwithstanding anything contained herein but without prejudice to sub-clause 15.8, the Parties undertake to provide at all times that no action shall be taken by or on behalf of the Company in respect of any of the following matters [in respect of any matter listed in Schedule D Part 1] except upon a valid resolution passed by a Unanimous Approval of the Board of Directors:

(a) any acquisition or disposal of assets or property at a consideration above a value of [£ *] or any acquisition or disposal of shares, securities or partnership interests in any corporation or entity;

(b) any issue, sale or assignment of (or agreement to issue, sell or assign) any securities, options or other interests in relation to the Company;

(c) any contract, or any variation to a contract, such contract having an aggregate value greater than [£ *];

(d) any change in the nature of the Business or any transaction or activity not in the ordinary course of the Business or on arm's-length terms;

(e) any agreement or arrangement with either Party [otherwise than in the ordinary course of business of the Company and on arm's-length terms];

(f) any engagement of employees, consultants or contractors at a salary or fee above [£ *] per annum;

(g) any distribution, supply, agency, manufacture or supply agreement;

(h) any borrowing or lending by or on behalf of the Company;

(i) any capital expenditure in excess of [£ *]; or

(j) any decision to commence material litigation or arbitration involving the Company or its Business.

[**Note:** this list of Reserved Matters may be added to or amended by agreement.]

10.3 A resolution in writing signed by all the Directors shall be as valid and effective as a resolution duly passed at a meeting of the Board of Directors provided it has previously been sent in draft form to all the Directors, together with any relevant papers. Such a resolution may consist of several counterpart documents in like form.

10.4 Save as provided in this Agreement the regulations regarding proceedings and conduct of Board Meetings shall be as set forth in the Articles.

11 MANAGEMENT OF THE COMPANY

11.1 The Parties shall procure that the business of the Company shall be conducted on a sound commercial basis with the object of optimising profits.

11.2 The Managing Director shall be responsible for the day-to-day management of the Business. [Party A shall appoint one of its nominee Directors as Managing Director.] OR [The Managing Director shall be appointed by Unanimous Approval of the Shareholders.]

11.3 [Party B shall appoint one of its nominee Directors as Finance Director.]

11.4 The Board may by Unanimous Approval, subject to the provisions of this Clause 11, confer upon the Managing Director such authority and responsibilities as it thinks fit.

11.5 Employees of either Shareholder or their Affiliates may from time to time be seconded to the Company for specified periods in accordance with principles mutually agreed by the Shareholders. In the event that employees are seconded to the Company such employees will continue to be employed by the Shareholder or its Affiliates and the Company shall reimburse such Shareholders or Affiliates in respect of the salary and costs of such employees in accordance with the agreed principles.

11.6 Each Shareholder (and the Company where necessary) will take appropriate action to provide insurance coverage for seconded employees for personal injury or third party liabilities.

12 FINANCE MATTERS

12.1 The Business of the Company shall be conducted strictly in accordance with the annual approved Business Plan. The first Business Plan of the Company is in the [form of Schedule D] [agreed form and initialled by each Party]. Not less than 90 days before the end of each financial year the Board shall submit for Unanimous Approval of the Shareholders the Business Plan for the following financial year.

12.2 Each Shareholder severally undertakes to provide to the Company its respective Shareholder Proportion of the funding provided for in any approved Business Plan, including share capital and/or any Shareholder loans in the Business Plan. Any additional contributions or loans not provided for in the Business Plan (including any Shareholder loans) shall be in the Shareholder Proportions and shall require the Unanimous Approval of the Shareholders.

12.3 Any Shareholder loans shall be made subject to the terms and conditions set out in Schedule E, or otherwise as approved by Unanimous Approval of the Shareholders. [All Shareholder loans shall wherever possible be advanced in [   ] currency.]

[12.4 [   ] will use its best endeavours to assist the Company in negotiating and obtaining loans from financial institutions and banks in [   ].]

12.5 Nothing in this Agreement shall require either Party to provide any security, pledge, guarantee, indemnity or similar undertaking (whether or not legal binding) in relation to the Company or the Business without its express written consent.

12.6 In the event that any guarantees or similar undertakings are required in respect of any liabilities of the Company or the performance of the Company's obligations under any contract, the terms of such guarantees shall be such that:

(a) the aggregate liability of the Party A and Party B shall not exceed the liabilities of the Company in respect of which the guarantee is to be given after the deduction of any amounts repaid by the Company;

(b) the liability of Party A and Party B respectively for any obligation shall be several and under no circumstances shall the liability of either Party exceed [50 per cent] [its Shareholder Proportion] of the guaranteed amount.

12.7 Each of Party A and Party B hereby undertakes to indemnify the other Party in respect of all amounts by which the other Party's liability exceeds the Shareholder Proportion of the other Party.

12.8 The Finance Director shall have overall control of the financial affairs of the Company and in this regard shall report directly to the Board of Directors on a regular basis. All payments or expenditure from the Company's funds and all cheques shall require the prior written approval of the Finance Director.

13 ACCOUNTING MATTERS

13.1 The Financial Year of the Company shall run from [1 January to 31 December] each year and shall not be changed except by Unanimous Approval of the Shareholders.

13.2 The Auditors of the Company shall be [   ] and shall not be changed except by Unanimous Approval of the Shareholders, provided that if one party wishes to change the Auditors the Shareholders shall decide upon a replacement firm. The Auditors shall at all times be a firm with the requisite qualifications and expertise having an international affiliation and duly authorised to practise in [   ].

13.3 The books, records and accounts of the Company shall be audited annually (or at other times agreed by the Shareholders) by the Auditors. The books, records and accounts shall be audited in accordance with [   ] statutory requirements [and shall so far as possible be consistent with [international] [United Kingdom] generally accepted accounting principles] [and in accordance with the accounting principles set out in Schedule *].

13.4 The accounting books and records and all other business records of the Company shall at all times be available for inspection of each Shareholder or its duly authorised representatives [at the Company's premises/registered office] and copies shall be supplied to any Shareholder upon request [at a reasonable administrative charge].

13.5 The Board shall cause to be prepared interim budgets and unaudited financial statements for each quarter which shall be sent to the Parties within one month of the end of the relevant quarter.

13.6 The Board of Directors shall cause to be prepared and provided to the Parties pro-forma management accounts for each calendar month in an agreed form and, upon the request of any Shareholder, such additional information, reports and/or other financial data as may be reasonably required by such Shareholder and in the form and by the dates so requested. Such other data may include (without limitation) forecasts, period and year-end accounting returns and/or cash summaries. The management accounts, reports and other such information or data shall be prepared on a basis consistent with [   ] and other agreed accounting principles, and shall be copied simultaneously to all the Shareholders regardless of which Shareholder has requested the items.

14 DIVIDEND POLICY

14.1 Unless otherwise agreed in writing by the Shareholders the Company intends to declare and pay each year dividends equal to [100 per cent] of its distributable profits determined by the Auditors and net of any applicable withholding required under [   ] law or other applicable law.

14.2 [The Board shall establish a reserve fund and shall arrange to pay into the fund such sums as may be required under [   ] law.]

15 SHAREHOLDERS' MEETINGS AND DECISIONS

15.1 The Shareholders acknowledge that the terms of this Agreement and adherence thereto are in the best interests of the Company and its Business which are intended to be conducted as a joint venture subject to the terms of this Agreement.

15.2 The Annual General Meeting of the Shareholders shall be convened once in each calendar year for the approval of the annual accounts of the Company and the appointment or re-appointment of the Auditors.

15.3 The Directors may resolve to call an Extraordinary General Meeting and, on the requisition of any of the Shareholders, shall forthwith proceed to convene an Extraordinary General Meeting for a date not later than [four weeks] [six weeks] after receipt of the requisition.

15.4 The Annual General Meeting and any Extraordinary General Meeting shall be called by at least thirty (30) days' notice in writing, given by the Chairman of the Board to each of the Shareholders, provided that an Extraordinary General Meeting may be called upon shorter notice, if agreed in writing by each of the Shareholders.

15.5 No business shall be transacted at any General Meeting except when a quorum is present. Two Shareholders present in person or by their respective nominated representatives shall constitute a quorum at any General Meeting.

15.6 Proceedings of General Meetings shall be in English, and Minutes of General Meetings shall be made and kept in English.

15.7 A resolution in writing signed or approved by letter, telex or facsimile by all the members for the time being entitled to receive notice of and attend and vote at General Meetings shall be as effective as if the same had been passed at a General Meeting of the Company, duly convened and held, and may consist of several documents in the like form each duly signed or approved.

15.8 Without prejudice to Clause 10 above, the Parties undertake to provide at all times that no action shall be taken by or on behalf of the Company in respect of any of the following matters, except upon a valid resolution passed by a Unanimous Approval of the Shareholders:

(a) any alteration to the Memorandum or the Articles of the Company;

(b) any increase, reduction or alteration to the share capital of the Company;

(c) any issue of Shares or other securities or similar rights in the Company;

(d) any borrowing, lending, credit or financing by or on behalf of the Company;

(e) any financial contributions required to be made by the Parties;

(f) any giving of any guarantee, indemnity or security by the Company;

(g) any formation or dissolution of a joint venture or partnership;

(h) any acquisition or disposal of assets at a consideration above [£ *];

(i) any contract, or variation to a contract, having a value greater than [£ *];

(j) any change in the nature of the Business, or any transaction outside the ordinary course of the Business, or any transaction outside the territory of [   ];

(k) any engagement of an employee or contractor at a salary or fee above [£ *];

(l) the appointment, removal or replacement of the Auditors; or

(m) any change to the Financial Year of the Company, terms or appointment;

(n) any commencement or settlement of material litigation or arbitration;

(o) any action for the liquidation, receivership or dissolution of the Company.

Note – this list may be added to or amended, or a longer list of Reserved Matters may be inserted as a schedule to the agreement, including specific commercial matters agreed between the Parties.

15.9 A resolution in writing shall be as valid and effective as a resolution duly passed at a Shareholders' Meeting provided it has been signed by all the Shareholders, either on original or counterpart copies.

16 TRANSFER OF SHARES

16.1 Neither Party nor its Affiliates shall (subject to Sub-Clause 16.2 below) transfer their Shares (or part thereof) to any person [for a period of [three (3)] years from the date hereof] [without the express written agreement of the other Party].

16.2 Notwithstanding Sub-Clauses 16.1 and 16.3, a Party shall be free to transfer, at any time, any or all Shares held by it to any of its Affiliates. In the event that such a transferee ceases to be an Affiliate the Party shall procure the transfer of the transferees' Shares back to the Party or to another Affiliate of the Party.

16.3 Subject to the provisions of Sub-Clauses 16.1 and 16.2:

(a) In the event that either Party or an Affiliate thereof ('Transferor') desires to transfer to a bona fide third-party purchaser all (but not less than all) of the Shares held by it, it shall first offer all its Shares ('Sale Shares') to the other Party by notice in writing, stating the number of Sale Shares proposed to be sold and the proposed third-party sale price for the Sale Shares. The other Party may accept the offer by a notice in writing to the Transferor within thirty (30) days of its receipt of the offer.

(b) The purchase price for the Sale Shares shall be the price which the proposed third-party purchaser is offering (or at which the Sale Shares are offered to it), to be stated in the notice under paragraph (a).

(c) When an offer has been accepted pursuant to paragraph (a) above, the Transferor shall execute and deliver to the other Party a valid transfer of the Sale Shares against tender of the full purchase price [in Sterling] pursuant to paragraph (b) above. The Sale Shares shall be transferred free from all liens, charges, equities or encumbrances.

(d) No sale of the Sale Shares may be made to a third Party at a price the same or lower than that offered to the other Party, and unless the provisions of this Sub-Clause 16.3 have been fully complied with and the sale is in good faith.

[**Note** – Sub-Clause 16.3 is not appropriate if an absolute prohibition on share transfer is intended, but may be used where the prohibition is to be temporary, as a fall-back. The result of the operation of this clause could be a new and unwelcome joint venture partner.]

16.4 No transfer of Shares in the Company shall be effective unless the transferee has entered into a Deed of Adherence in the form of Schedule F, or into a new agreement with the Parties hereto on identical terms to this Agreement.

17 TERMINATION

17.1 [This Agreement shall terminate automatically in the event of:

(a) failure to procure all required government consents to this Agreement prior to [   ]; or

(b) termination of the Contract in accordance with its terms.]

17.2 Either Party ('first Party') shall be entitled to terminate this Agreement by giving thirty (30) days' written notice to the other Party ('other Party'), to be served within the period of thirty (30) days following the occurrence of any of the following events:

(a) In the event that the other Party commits a material breach of any term hereof [having a substantial adverse effect on the business of the Company] which breach is not capable of remedy, or if capable of remedy in the event that the party in breach shall have failed to remedy such breach within thirty (30) days of a written notice requesting remedy having been served.

(b) In the event that the other Party becomes insolvent (meaning that it is unable to pay its debts as they fall due) or goes into liquidation [or bankruptcy] proceedings or has a receiver or administrator appointed over its assets or makes a composition or assignment for the benefit of its creditors.

(c) [In the event that the other Party suffers a change of Control.]

[(d) [In the event that due to strike, riot, act of God, fire, flood, war, political or labour unrest or similar cause, the continued operation of this Agreement or the business activities of the Company are substantially interrupted, prevented or delayed for a period exceeding [six months] [one year].]

[**Note:** – the option sale provisions in Sub-Clauses 17.3 to 17.5 need to be considered in commercial context.]

17.3 In the event that this Agreement is terminated by either Party pursuant to paragraphs (a), (b), [(c) or (d)] of Sub-Clause 17.2 above the following provisions shall apply and termination by notice shall be without prejudice to the operation thereof:

EITHER (A) – PUT OPTION:

(a) The Party serving the termination notice ('Selling Party') shall be entitled to offer to sell and to require the other party ('Buying Party') to purchase, and the Buying Party shall be obliged to purchase, all the Shares held by the Selling Party (and its Affiliates) at the valuation price to be determined in accordance with Sub-Clause 17.4 ('Valuation Price' for Clause 17 purposes).

(b) The Selling Party may serve a notice in writing to that effect on the Buying party with a copy to the Chairman within [ten (10)] business days of the original notice of termination under Sub-Clause 17.2, following which the Chairman shall forthwith instruct the Auditors to value the Selling Party's Shares in accordance with Sub-Clause 17.4. [In the event of manifest error in valuation the Buying Party may withdraw its offer to purchase the Shares.]

(c) Within [thirty (30)] business days after the Auditors' valuation has been notified to it pursuant to Sub-Clause 17.4, the Selling Party shall deliver to the Buying Party valid transfer documents for all its Shares and the Buying Party shall be obliged to tender to the Selling Party the Valuation Price in cash [in Sterling] upon delivery of valid transfer documents.

(d) The Selling Party's Shares shall be sold as beneficial owner and free of all liens, charges, equities and encumbrances.

(e) Completion of the sale shall be conditional upon the receipt of all required governmental or regulatory approvals and consents. If consents are required for the transfer of Shares, the period for completing the sale shall be extended to [120] days after the Auditors' Valuation is notified.

OR (B) – CALL OPTION:

(a) The Party serving the termination notice ('Buying Party') shall be entitled to offer to buy and require the other Party ('Selling Party') to sell, and the Selling Party shall be obliged to sell to the Buying Party [(or such other persons as the Buying Party may specify)], all the Shares held by the Selling Party (and its Affiliates) at the valuation price to be determined by the Auditors in Sub-Clause 17.4 ('Valuation Price' for Clause 17 purposes).

(b) The Buying Party may serve a notice in writing to that effect on the Selling Party with a copy to the Chairman within [ten (10)] business days of the original notice of termination under Sub-Clause 17.2, following which the Chairman shall forthwith instruct the Auditors to value the Selling Party's Shares in accordance with Sub-Clause 17.4. [In the event of manifest error in valuation the Buying Party may withdraw its offer to purchase the Shares.]

(c) Within [thirty (30)] business days after the Auditors' valuation has been notified to it pursuant to Sub-Clause 17.4, the Selling Party shall be required to accept the offer and to deliver to the Buying Party valid transfer documents for all its Shares, and the Buying Party shall pay to the Selling Party the Valuation Price in cash [in Sterling] upon delivery of valid transfer documents.

(d) The Selling Party's Shares shall be sold as beneficial owner and free of all liens, charges, equities or encumbrances.

(e) Completion of the Sale shall be conditional upon the receipt of all required governmental or regulatory approvals and consents. In the event that any consents are required the period for completing the Sale shall be extended to [120] days after the Auditors' valuation is notified.

[**Note** – the efficacy of this provision will depend on any share ownership restrictions in the JV Territory.]

17.4 [In the event of a sale under Sub-Clause 17.3, the Chairman shall instruct the Auditors to value the Shares on the basis of the [Net Asset Value] [Fair Value] of the Company, without regard to the fact (if so) that the sale represents either a controlling or a minority interest, and to promptly certify to the Chairman and to each Party the Valuation Price. The Auditors in so doing shall act as experts not as arbitrators. [Either Party may elect to refer the Valuation Price to arbitration under Clause 29, which shall be final and binding as to the sale price. In such event the Auditors' valuation shall be deemed to have been given on the date of the arbitrators decision.]

17.5 Following the completion of any sale of Share pursuant to Sub-Clause 17.3, this Agreement shall terminate forthwith with respect to the Shareholder who has as a result ceased to hold any Shares. The parties shall procure that the withdrawing Shareholder shall be released from all guarantees given by it in respect of the Company and that the Company shall repay in full any outstanding loans owed to it.

17.6 Upon termination of this Agreement howsoever arising:

(a) the Shareholders shall forthwith cease the use of any trade names or trade marks [or other intellectual property rights] belonging to the other Shareholders, and shall procure that the Company will do likewise;

(b) except where a notice is served under Sub-Clause 17.3(b), the Shareholders shall promptly pass all necessary corporate actions and resolutions to wind up the company by means of a members' voluntary winding up or its equivalent procedure, and shall do all such acts and things as shall be required to liquidate the Company in a manner fair and just to all the Shareholders.

18 DEADLOCK

[**Note** – consider carefully whether a written deadlock procedure is desirable!]

18.1 For the purpose of this Clause 18, a deadlock shall be deemed to exist when both of the following conditions have occurred:

(a) The Parties have been unable to agree on any matter requiring their agreement and one Party serves a preliminary notice on the other Party stating that it believes there exists a disagreement of fundamental importance which cannot be resolved by further negotiation between them; and

EITHER:

(b) Any matter subject to a notice under paragraph (a) above has been considered as such at two successive quorate Board Meetings or at two successive quorate General Meetings of the Company (in either case the meetings to be within [three (3)] months of each other) and has not been resolved upon with unanimity at either such meeting. Following this a Board Meeting has been duly held to reconsider the matter within [three

(3)] months after the second indecisive meeting above, and thereupon, deadlock shall be deemed to have occurred if:

(i)   unanimity in favour of such resolution is not achieved at such Board Meeting; or

(ii) the Board Meeting does not have a quorum present within one hour after the time duly appointed for such meeting.

OR:

[(b) such disagreement shall have persisted without resolution for a period of [six (6)] months after service of the notice in (a) above whereupon a deadlock shall be deemed to have occurred on the expiry thereof.]

18.2 If a deadlock is deemed to have occurred under Sub-Clause 18.1, paragraph (b) above, any Party may within thirty (30) days of the event that has given rise to deadlock serve a notice in writing (a 'Deadlock Notice') on the other Parties and the Company stating that in its view a deadlock has occurred and identifying the reason.

18.3 The Parties each undertake that following the service of a Deadlock Notice they shall forthwith refer the deadlock for resolution to the Chief Executives of the parent company of each of their Groups, and if not successful they shall use all reasonable endeavours in good faith to agree on a procedure for resolution of such dispute.

[Note – 'pendulum' share sale provisions may be used to provide for sale of one party's shares, but if they are not considered appropriate the Clause should end at Sub-Clause 18.3.]

19 INTELLECTUAL PROPERTY

[Note – these mutual IP licensing provisions apply principally where both JV Parties are providing IP rights for a collaborative joint venture. Where one party is the principal licensor the use of Appendix F may be more appropriate.]

EITHER (A) Suggested clauses for corporate joint venture agreement:-

19.1 Each Shareholder hereby grants to [the [each] other Shareholder and to] the Company a non-exclusive, royalty-free and non-transferable licence to use such Shareholders' Intellectual Property for the purpose of the Business [and to the extent necessary for the activities of the Business pursuant to this Agreement].

19.2 Within thirty (30) days after this Agreement has become unconditional each Shareholder shall disclose and make available to the Company copies of all documents and information necessary for the use of its Intellectual Property pursuant to Sub-Clause 19.1.

19.3 [Any Intellectual Property generated by or on behalf of the Company [or] pursuant to the Business, including any improvements or developments made by or on behalf of the Company, to the Intellectual Property licensed to the Company by the Shareholders ('Future IP'), shall as between the Shareholders and the Company vest in the Company. Each Shareholder shall have a non-exclusive, royalty-free and irrevocable licence to use the Future IP for any purpose not in direct competition with the Business, with the right to grant sub-licences and the Company shall provide all requisite information to each Shareholder for such purpose.]

[Note – the parties may wish to assign these rights back to one or both parties for special reasons.]

19.3 The licences shall be non-assignable but shall include the right to grant sub-licences provided such sub-licences are exclusively for the purposes of the Business.

OR (B) Suggested clauses for contractual joint venture agreement involving contracting by the JV Parties and cross-licensing of technical developments:

19.1 For the purposes of the following provisions of this Clause 19:

'Foreground IP' means any Intellectual Property developed, created or acquired by the Company or one or both of the Shareholders as a result of or in the course of carrying out work under or relating to any contract awarded to the Company [whether such work is or was carried out before or after the date of this Agreement];

'Background IP' means Intellectual Property other than Foreground IP developed, created or owned by the Company or one or both of the Shareholders and necessary for the carrying out of any work in relation to the Business.

19.2 Each Shareholder hereby grants to each other Shareholder and to the Company:

(a) an exclusive, royalty-free and non-assignable licence to use its Foreground IP for the purposes of the Business; and

(b) a non-exclusive [royalty-free and non-assignable] licence to use its Background IP for the purposes of the Business.

19.3 The Shareholders shall, where Foreground IP is jointly originated by more than one of the Company and the Shareholders, provide that one of them shall take such steps as may be agreed to obtain and maintain such protection as may be available, including patents, copyrights and the like. Such protection shall, if the joint originators so desire, be taken out in their joint names, on a basis of equal funding of related expenses including but not limited to patent upkeep and maintenance. Failing agreement on such joint protection, the party responsible for obtaining the protection shall be entitled to procure such protection in its own name. In that event the party acting as proprietor shall grant to the co-inventing party (or parties) and to the Company an irrevocable, non-exclusive and non-transferable right, free of charge, to use the Intellectual Property concerned for all purposes. Moreover the party acting as proprietor shall grant to any other party an irrevocable non-exclusive licence, free of charge, to use such Intellectual Property solely for the purposes of the Company's business. The expression 'use' where used in this Sub-Clause 19.3 shall in cases agreed to be appropriate between the Shareholders include the right to grant sub-licences.

IN BOTH CASES continue here:

19.4 Each licence granted to the Company or to either Shareholder shall continue for the duration of this Agreement.

19.5 Upon termination of the licences for whatever reason all rights granted thereunder shall cease and the Company shall assign the Future IP to the Shareholders jointly (or as otherwise agreed by them). In the event of the termination of one of the licences only the Company shall have no further right to use or exploit the Intellectual Property licensed to it pursuant to such licence but shall not be required to assign the Future IP until the termination of all other licences.

19.6 Neither Shareholder shall be liable to the Company for any use or exploitation that the Company may make of the Intellectual Property licensed to it and neither Shareholder gives any warranty that use of the Intellectual Property licensed by it to the Company will not infringe any intellectual property rights of a third party.

19.7 The Company will agree to indemnify each Shareholder for any losses, damages, costs and expenses suffered or incurred by such Shareholder as a direct result of the Company's use of the Intellectual Property licensed to it by such Shareholders.

19.8 Each Shareholder shall be responsible in its sole discretion for the maintenance, prosecution enforcement and defence of the Intellectual Property which it licenses to the Company.

20 NON-COMPETITION

[   ] undertakes for itself and on behalf of its Affiliates for the duration of this Agreement not to be engaged, directly or indirectly, in any business, company, project or entity (other than the Company) which is or may be involved in the development, design, manufacture, sale, distribution, repair or servicing of the Products or any products which are or may be [similar to] [competitive with] the Products.

[**Note** – the competition aspects of this clause must be carefully considered, especially for a joint venture where the JV Parties carry on business principally in the EU area. Limitations on the scope of the non-compete covenants may be appropriate, or a separate agreement. See Chapter 20 above.]

21 CONFIDENTIAL INFORMATION

21.1 [Subject to Clauses 19 and 22 each Shareholder shall disclose to the other Shareholder and to the Company such of its own proprietary and confidential information as is necessary for the successful operation of the Business to the extent that such Shareholder is not prohibited from doing so by law or by of any applicable regulations or contractual arrangements entered into prior to the date hereof from making such disclosure.]

[**Note** – caution is required here in creating an affirmative disclosure obligation.]

21.2 During the term of this Agreement and after the termination or expiration of this Agreement for any reason each of the Shareholders undertakes to, and shall procure that any Directors appointed by it shall [and that the Company shall]:

(a) keep all Confidential Information confidential;

(b) not disclose any Confidential Information to any other person other than with the prior written consent of the disclosing Shareholder or in accordance with Sub-Clauses 21.2 and 21.3; and

(c) not use any Confidential Information for any purpose other than for the performance of this Agreement, the evaluation of the performance of the Company or the pursuit of the Company's Business in the best interests of the Company.

21.3 During the term of this Agreement each of the Shareholders may disclose Confidential Information to its employees (and to employees of its

Affiliates) to the extent that it is necessary for the purposes of this Agreement and to its professional advisers for any purposes in connection with this Agreement.

21.4 Each of the Shareholders shall procure that any person to whom it discloses any Confidential Information pursuant to Sub-Clause 21.3 is made aware of and complies with all the obligations of confidentiality under this Agreement as if the recipient were a party to this Agreement.

21.5 The obligations and restrictions contained in Sub-Clause 21.2 shall not apply to any Confidential Information which:

(a) at the date of this Agreement is in or at any time after the date of this Agreement comes into the public domain other than through breach of this Agreement by the relevant Shareholder;

(b) can be shown by the relevant Shareholder to the reasonable satisfaction of the other to have been known to the relevant Shareholder prior to the disclosure to it;

(c) has been developed independently by the relevant Shareholder or any of its Affiliates prior to the disclosure to it; or

(d) is required by law or applicable regulation to be disclosed and then only to the extent of such requirement. [Provided that in such event prompt written shall have been given to the other Party to enable it to seek appropriate relief to prevent such disclosure.]

22 EMPLOYEES

22.1 The Parties shall by mutual agreement in writing make arrangements to transfer or second to the Company any employees required by the Joint Venture Company for the purposes of its Business [and which are not readily available on reasonable terms in the JV Territory].

[**Note** – subsequent agreements or arrangements will deal with employees in more detail – local legal advice will be required.]

22.2 [Party A and the Company will each use their best endeavours to novate to the Company all rights and benefits under the employment contracts of [those employees employed at the Site][the employees listed in Schedule *].

[**Note** – the local laws may or may not permit assignment of the employment contracts to the Company.]

22.3 [If any Shareholder or any of its Affiliates transfers to the Company an undertaking or part of an undertaking for the purposes of the Transfer of Undertakings (Protection of Employment) Regulations 1981 (as amended)

(TUPE), then the Shareholders expect that certain employees of the transferor Shareholders or Affiliates (each a 'Transferred Employee') will become employees of the Company by virtue either of an express agreement between the Company and the Transferred Employee or in its absence by the operation of TUPE.]

[**Note** – this provision is appropriate for a UK-based joint venture. A reference to the EU Acquired Rights Directive can be substituted if appropriate.]

22.4 The Parties shall co-operate and do all within their respective powers to obtain temporary immigration visas, work permits or other necessary documentation to facilitate any agreed employee transfers or secondments to the Joint Venture Company.

23 PROPERTY

23.1 Party A shall transfer to the Company full legal and beneficial ownership in its factory site at [   ] ('the Site') under the laws of [JV Territory]. The transfer shall be completed pursuant to Sub-Clause 7.7 above.

EITHER:

23.2 The consideration for the transfer under Sub-Clause 23.1 shall be the sum of [   ] [which shall represent a proportionate part of the capital contribution of Party A under Clause 6 above].

OR:

[23.2 The consideration for the transfer under Sub-Clause 23.1 shall be determined by a valuation of the Site by [   ] as independent valuers, who shall act as experts and not as arbitrators, and shall be determined on an arm's-length basis in accordance with the principles to be agreed by the Parties.]

[23.3 Party A warrants to Party B in terms of Schedule *.]

24 ENVIRONMENTAL MATTERS

24.1 The Company shall at all times operate a policy of strict compliance with environmental laws and regulations in [JV Territory].

24.2 Party A warrants to Party B:

(a) that it has complied with all applicable environmental laws and regulations (including without limitation laws relating to [   ]) in [JV Territory] in respect of its ownership and operation of the Site;

(b) that so far as it is aware all previous owners of the Site have complied with all applicable environmental laws and regulations in [JV Territory]; and

(c) that all information provided by Party A to Party B in respect of environmental matters affecting the Site was when provided complete and accurate in all respects.

24.3 Party A undertakes to indemnify and hold harmless Party B in respect of any breach of the warranties contained in Sub-Clause 24.2 above.

25 ANNOUNCEMENTS

Neither Party shall make any public statement or announcement except in a form and on a date previously agreed in writing with the other party.

26 COSTS

Save as expressly otherwise provided in this Agreement, each Party shall bear its own costs and expenses in connection with the negotiation, preparation and implementation of this Agreement.

[**Note** – any additional costs to be allocated between the JV Parties should be specified here.]

27 ASSIGNMENT OF RIGHTS

Each Party may assign the benefits of this Agreement to any of its Affiliates to whom it shall have transferred its Shares pursuant to Clause 16. In the event the assignee ceases to be an Affiliate the Party shall procure the transfer of its rights (and its Shares) back to it or to another Affiliate of the Party. In order for any assignment or transfer of Shares to be effective under this Agreement, the proposed transferor shall provide that the proposed assignee or transferee of Shares hereunder shall, prior to the assignment or transfer becoming effective, enter into a new agreement with the Parties hereto on identical terms with this

Agreement. The original Party shall remain liable for all obligations hereunder until such time as no Shares are beneficially owned by such Party or its Affiliates.

28 GENERAL PROVISIONS

28.1 The terms and provisions of this Agreement shall continue in full force and effect notwithstanding completion of the matters set out in Clause 7.

28.2 This Agreement shall constitute the entire agreement and understanding between the Parties in connection with the transactions referred to therein.

28.3 No amendment or variation to this Agreement shall be effective unless made in writing and executed by both Parties.

28.4 No waiver of any term or condition of this Agreement shall be deemed made unless such waiver is in writing and signed by the waiving Party.

28.5 This Agreement shall not be deemed to constitute a partnership between Party A and Party B nor shall it make either Party an agent for the other.

28.6 In the event of any conflict or inconsistency between this Agreement and the Articles of the Company, the terms of this Agreement shall prevail [unless the conflict would bring the Articles into non-compliance and [   ] law]. In such event the Parties shall agree substitute provisions of this Agreement to comply with [   ] law.

28.7 This Agreement may be executed in several parts being counterparts to this Agreement.

28.8 In the event that any provision or term contained in this Agreement shall be held invalid or unenforceable, the remaining provisions of this Agreement shall not be affected and shall remain in full force and effect without regard to the invalid provisions which shall be deemed severed from this Agreement.

29 ARBITRATION

29.1 In the event of any dispute arising between the Parties hereto as to their respective rights or obligations under this Agreement or as to the interpretation of any of its terms, or otherwise in relation to the Company, such dispute shall be referred to arbitration under the auspices of the [International Chamber of Commerce (ICC) in accordance with its Rules of Conciliation and Arbitration.]

29.2 The venue of the arbitration proceedings shall be [city] [or such other venue as the Parties shall mutually agree].

29.3 The arbitration panel shall be composed of three (3) arbitrators. One arbitrator shall be selected by [the President of the ICC] and shall act as Chairman of the panel, and one arbitrator shall be selected by each Party.

29.4 The arbitration shall be conducted substantially in the English language, and all documents produced in evidence or submitted to the arbitrators shall be in English or shall be accompanied by a substantially accurate English translation thereof.

29.5 The arbitration shall be final and binding on the Parties as to all matters adjudicated therein. The Parties agree that judgement on any arbitral award or order hereunder may be entered and/or enforced in any court having jurisdiction whether in [   ], the United Kingdom or other relevant territory. Subject to the foregoing, the Parties waive all rights of appeal or other recourse to any court from any arbitral award or order hereunder.

30 GOVERNING LAW

30.1 This Agreement shall be governed and construed in accordance with the laws of [   ].

[30.2 The Parties hereby irrevocably submit to the jurisdiction of the courts of [   ] in connection with any matter arising out of this Agreement or the affairs of the Company. [Appointment of an agent for service within jurisdiction.]]

31 LANGUAGE

31.1 The English language version of this Agreement shall in the case of a conflict take precedence over a foreign language version of this Agreement.

31.2 If any records of the Company (including Minutes) are kept in English and another language, the English version of such record shall be deemed to prevail.

32 NOTICES

Any notice or demand under this Agreement shall be in writing, in English and in legible form, and signed by or on behalf of the Party giving it and any notice may be served by personal delivery or by facsimile transmission (receipt confirmed) to:

Party A   Attention: Company Secretary

Address:

Fax:

Party B   Attention: Company Secretary

Address:

Fax:

Any notice or demand so served shall be deemed to have been served upon personal delivery at the address given above or in the case of facsimile transmission immediately after despatch of the facsimile transmission (with a printed confirmation of receipt).

The address or other details for notices of either Party may be altered by that Party by written notice to the other Party under the terms hereof.

IN WITNESS WHEREOF the Parties hereto have executed this Agreement on the date written above.

Signed by	)	Signed by	)
	)		)
———————————	)	———————————	)
	)		)
(Director)	)	(Director)	)
for and on behalf of	)	for and on behalf of	)
[ ]	)	[ ]	)

——————————————   ——————————————

SCHEDULE A
JOINT VENTURE COMPANY
ARTICLES OF ASSOCIATION
[OR CORPORATE CHARTER/STATUTES]

SCHEDULE B
DETAILS OF THE COMPANY

SCHEDULE C
CAPITAL CONTRIBUTIONS

PARTY	ASSETS	VALUE (£)
Party A	Cash	
	Equipment	
	Stocks	
	[Contracts]	
	[Know-how]	
		_____
	Sub-total:	_____
Party B	Cash	
	Equipment	
	Stocks	
	[Contracts]	
	[Know-how]	
		_____
	Sub-total:	_____
		_____
TOTAL ASSETS VALUE:		_____

SCHEDULE D
BUSINESS PLAN

SCHEDULE E
TERMS OF SHAREHOLDER LOANS

SCHEDULE F

DEED OF ADHERENCE

THIS DEED OF ADHERENCE is made on   , [   ]
BETWEEN:

1 [   ] whose registered office/principal place of work is at [   ] (the 'Transferee'); and

2 [   ] whose registered office is at [   ] (the 'Transferor'); and

3 [   ] whose registered office is at [   ] (the 'Other Shareholder').

WHEREAS:

The Transferor intends to transfer to the Transferee [number] ['A'/'B'] Shares in the Company, (the 'Relevant Shares').

NOW THIS DEED WITNESSETH as follows:

1 The Transferee hereby agrees to assume the benefit of the rights of the Transferor under a Shareholders' Agreement entered into between the Transferor and the Other Shareholder dated [   ] (the 'Shareholders' Agreement') and the Transferee hereby agrees to assume the burden of the Transferors' obligations under the Shareholders' Agreement to be performed on or after the date of this Deed, each with effect on and from the date of this Deed.

2 The Transferee undertakes to be bound by all the terms and conditions of the Shareholders' Agreement in all respects as if the Transferee were an original Party to the Shareholders' Agreement holding the Relevant Shares in place of the Transferor.

3 The Transferor and the Other Shareholder hereby consent and agree to the assumption by the Transferee of the benefits and burdens under the Shareholders' Agreement pursuant to paragraph 1 above.

4 The Transferor hereby agrees that it shall remain bound under all its obligations contained in the Shareholders' Agreement in respect of any breach occurring prior to the date of this Deed. Notwithstanding this the Transferor agrees for the benefit of the Other Shareholder and the Transferee that it shall have no further benefits or rights under the Shareholders' Agreement with effect on and from the date of this Deed.

5 This Deed is made for the benefit of all the parties to the Shareholders' Agreement and any other person or persons who may after the date hereof become a party to it.

[6 Provisions regarding guarantees or loans given by the Transferor. Transferee to procure release/repayment and substitution for Transferor?]

7 This Deed shall be governed by construed in accordance with the laws of [   ].

IN WITNESS WHEREOF the parties have executed this Deed on the date written above.

Technology Licence Agreement

THIS AGREEMENT is made this   day of   , 1999/200
BETWEEN:

1 [LICENSOR] a company incorporated in [   ] whose registered
   office is at [   ] (the 'Licensor') and

2 [JV COMPANY] whose registered office is at [   ] (the
   'Licensee').

WHEREAS:

A The Licensor (or its Affiliates) is the proprietor of certain technical information
   and know-how in relation to the manufacture of [   ] and related
   activities.

B Pursuant to the Shareholders' Agreement (as defined below), a subsidiary of
   the Licensor proposes to enter into a joint venture with [   ] in
   relation to [   ] [the manufacture and sale of the Products as
   hereinafter described].

C In connection with the above the Licensee has requested and the Licensor has
   agreed to license the Technical Information (as defined herein) to the Licensee
   subject to the terms herein contained.

NOW IT IS HEREBY AGREED as follows:

1 DEFINITIONS

1.1 In this Agreement the following terms and expressions shall have the
     meanings respectively assigned to them:

'Affiliate'   a corporation which is in relation to a party
                                         directly or indirectly a parent, a subsidiary or
                                         the subsidiary of a parent.

'Effective Date'   The later of the date of this Agreement and the
                                         date on which all consents or approvals of the
                                         Government of [   ] and of any
                                         other relevant bodies required under Clause 2
                                         of the Shareholders' Agreement shall first have
                                         been obtained.

['Improvements'	Any further information or know-how in relation to the Technical Information which either party shall acquire after the date hereof and during the term of this Agreement which it has full and free rights to disclose without the consent of and without accounting to others [and which if applied to any of the Products or to the processes of manufacturing the same] improve their commercial potential.]
['Net Sale Price'	In relation to Products sold by the Licensee, the actual invoice price in each case:

(a) exclusive of any import, export or customs duties or of any sales, value added and similar taxes payable on the supply of the Products in question;

(b) exclusive of transport, delivery and related insurance, packing and installation charges;

(c) less usual trade agency or quantity discounts actually allowed not exceeding in the aggregate [per cent] of such invoice price; and

(d) less the cost to the Licensee of parts or components for the Products purchased from the Licensor and incorporated therein;

but making no other deductions of any nature and provided always that in the case of any disposal otherwise than by way of a bona fide sale for full value there shall be substituted for the actual consideration (if any) an amount equal to the Net Sale Price (calculated on the foregoing basis) that could then reasonably have been expected to have been obtained on a bona fide sale for full value.]

['Products'	[ ].]
'Shareholders' Agreement'	the Shareholders' Agreement dated [ ] between the Licensor and [ ].

'Technical Information'   such designs, drawings, specifications, know-how, formulas, processes, software and other information relating to techniques, processes and methods used by the Licensor as at the date hereof in relation to [   ] which are in the Licensor's possession and control, and of which full and particular details are contained in Schedule A hereof.

2 TECHNICAL INFORMATION

2.1 The Licensor (or, at Licensor's option, any of its Affiliates) shall promptly following the Effective Date supply to the Licensee the designs, drawings, software and other documents (or extracts therefrom) comprising such Technical Information as is in the reasonable opinion of the Licensor necessary for the purposes of this Agreement.

2.2 The Licensor shall not be obliged to make any alterations (whether as respects mode of presentation, systems of measurement or otherwise howsoever) to any documents extracts or copies which it supplies hereunder as part of the Technical Information.

2.3 The Licensor warrants that it has the right in each case to disclose such Technical Information as is communicated to the Licensee pursuant hereto but gives no warranty that the use or application of the same will not infringe any patent, design, copyright or similar rights of any other person.

2.4 In the event that any inaccuracy or defect shall at any time become known to the Licensor in any Technical Information so supplied by the Licensor the Licensor will promptly use reasonable endeavours to make and supply the appropriate corrections.

2.5 The Licensor or its Affiliates shall be under no obligation or liability of any kind to the Licensee and the Licensee will indemnify and hold the Licensor and/or its Affiliates harmless against all liabilities of any kind arising directly or indirectly out of or by reason of the use by the Licensee of such Technical Information. This clause shall survive termination of this Agreement howsoever caused.

3 TECHNICAL ASSISTANCE AND VISITS

3.1 The Licensor shall upon request by the Licensee at times reasonably convenient to the Licensor and subject to payment of [its standard charges for such services from time to time in force and all other expenses reasonably incurred in connection therewith] provide to the Licensee at the Licensee's premises the services of such number of technical personnel or engineers as the Licensor shall on each occasion consider necessary for the purpose of assisting the Licensee in the manufacture and testing of the Products and with the training of the Licensee's employees for that purpose.

3.2 For the purpose of training Licensee's staff in the methods used by Licensor in relation to the manufacture of the Products the Licensee shall be entitled during the term of this Agreement on request but in each case at a time reasonably convenient to the Licensor and subject to payment of the Licensor's standard charges for such services to send suitable qualified employees of the Licensee up to [   ] in number to the Licensor's premises for visits not exceeding in the aggregate [   ] man-days per annum, the Licensee to be responsible for all its own employees' expenses.

3.3 The Licensor shall have the right at its own cost and on reasonable prior notice to inspect the premises of the Licensee and of any of the Licensee's permitted sub-contractors from time to time engaged in the manufacture of the Products.

4 IMPROVEMENTS

In the event that either party shall during the continuance of this Agreement devise or develop any Improvements (whether patented, patentable or otherwise) it shall (subject to where appropriate to a reasonable opportunity first of applying for any patent registered design or other like protection in respect of the same) promptly communicate the same to the other with all necessary supporting documentation.

5 LICENCE

5.1 The Licensor hereby grants to the Licensee, for the consideration provided in Clause 6 below, a non-exclusive licence to use the Technical Information provided by the Licensor for use exclusively in connection with the [   ] activities provided in the Shareholders' Agreement.

5.2   The Licensee shall actively promote and exploit the rights granted hereunder.

5.3   The Licensee hereby undertakes that it will not at any time during the continuance of this Agreement use the Technical Information for any purpose other than the due exercise of the rights and licences hereby agreed to be granted to it.

5.4   The Licensee hereby undertakes not to take any actions inconsistent with the Licensor's (or its Affiliate's) continuing ownership of the Technical Information, to promptly notify Licensor if it becomes aware of any infringement thereof and to defend such infringement at Licensor's request and expense.

5.5   The Licensor (and its Affiliates) reserves all rights to continue the use of the Technical Information itself for its own business.

5.6   The Licensee shall fully co-operate to achieve appropriate registration in [   ] or elsewhere in respect of all or any technology rights, patents, trademarks or similar property of the Licensor.

6 PAYMENTS

6.1   In consideration for the licence granted hereunder the Licensee shall pay to the Licensor:

(a)   the sum of [   ] payable within 30 days of the date hereof;

(b)   a royalty of [   ] per cent of the Net Sales Price in respect of each Product sold by the Licensee.

[**Note** – the parties may for taxation or commercial reasons desire to structure the arrangements as a royalty-free Licence.]

6.2   The Licensee shall:

(a)   maintain complete and accurate books and records in sufficient detail to enable the royalties payable hereunder properly to be determined and shall permit the Licensor or any independent firm of chartered accountants appointed by the Licensor access thereto for the purpose and to the extent necessary for examination and audit of the same.

(b)   not later than one month in each case after:

(i)   31 March and 30 September in each year, and

(ii)   the date of expiration or termination of this Agreement,

render to the Licensor a statement of the royalties due in respect of such preceding six-month period certified (if the Licensor shall so require) by the Licensee's auditors together with payment of the sum due in respect thereof.

6.3 In respect of any payments hereunder:-

(a) payments shall be paid to the Licensor in Sterling in London so such account as it shall from time to time nominate free of all taxes (other than such as are required by the laws of [   ] to be deducted therefrom) and free of all bank and other charges of whatsoever nature;

(b) royalties shall be converted into Sterling at the open market exchange rate in [   ] for transfers of Sterling to London on the date of payment;

(c) the Licensee will afford the Licensor all assistance reasonably requested for the purpose of ensuring that (so far as lawful) all sums payable hereunder are payable free of tax or at any reduced rate applicable and will (to the extent that the Licensee is nevertheless required by law to deduct tax from any payment due under this Agreement) promptly furnish to the Licensor such certificates or other evidence of deduction and payment thereof as the Licensor may properly require.

7 CONFIDENTIALITY

7.1 The Licensee undertakes that it will at all times keep confidential the Technical Information and will not without the prior written consent of the Licensor disclose the same to any other person provided always that such undertaking shall not extend to any information which:

(a) is already in the Licensee's possession at the date of first communication by the Licensor; or

(b) is now or (otherwise than by reason of any breach of such contract or undertaking) becomes public knowledge;

(c) is received without restriction by the Licensee from any other person having the right to disclose such information; or

(d) is communicated solely to the extent required by court order.

7.2 Without prejudice to the provisions of Clause 7.1 above (breach of which by any sub-contractor shall be deemed to be a breach by the Licensee) the Licensee may communicate to sub-contractors such Technical Information as may be reasonably necessary to enable the Licence or such sub-contractor (as the case may be) to perform its respective obligations, provided that it obtains undertakings of confidence from such sub-contractors, similar to these provisions, and provides a copy of such undertakings to the Licensor upon request.

8 ASSIGNMENT

This Licence Agreement is personal to the Licensee and the Licensee shall not assign, charge, sub-licence or otherwise deal with or dispose of any of its rights or obligations hereunder without the prior written consent of the Licensor.

9 FORCE MAJEURE

Either party may terminate this Agreement with immediate effect by giving written notice to the other party within six months following the occurrence of either of the following events.

9.1 In the event that due to strike, insurrection, riot, act of God, fire, flood, war, political or labour unrest, act of any government or any other cause similar thereto, the continued operation of this Agreement or the business activities of the Licensee are interrupted, prevented or delayed for a period exceeding [six months].

9.2 In the event that any law, regulation, order or directive of any competent governmental body, agency or department having jurisdiction over the Licensor or the Licensee makes the continued operation of this Agreement unduly burdensome or impossible for either party.

10 TERM AND TERMINATION

10.1 Subject to the following provisions of this Clause this Agreement shall continue in force for the duration of the Shareholders' Agreement.

10.2 In the event that at any time the term of this Agreement:

(a) the Licensee is in breach of its obligations hereunder where such breach is irremediable or (if capable of remedy) is not remedied within 30 days of a written notice from the Licensor requiring its remedy; or

(b) the Licensee is or become insolvent or make any composition with its creditors or has a receiver, administrator or manager appointed over the whole or any part of its undertaking or assets or enters liquidation or bankruptcy proceedings or ceases to carry on business in its then current manner; or

(c) the Licensor owns no shares in the capital of the Licensee;

then and in any such event the Licensor may at any time within six months following the relevant event by notice in writing terminate this Agreement with immediate effect together with the rights and licences hereby granted or agreed to be granted by the Licensor.

10.3 This Agreement shall terminate forthwith upon termination of the Shareholders' Agreement for whatever reason.

10.4 Upon Termination the Licensee shall promptly on request by the Licensor return to the Licensor or (at the election of the Licensor) destroy all copies of any documents or extracts (including those in electronic storage) comprising or containing the Technical Information, including all such documents and extracts which have been supplied to sub-contractors.

10.5 The obligations of the Licensee pursuant to Clause 7 above and this Clause 10 shall survive the termination of this Agreement howsoever arising.

11 GENERAL PROVISIONS

11.1 All information relating to this Agreement or its negotiation shall be kept confidential between the parties and their Affiliates, and all information provided to employees or third parties shall be kept to a minimum and imparted on a confidential basis. Provided that this shall not apply to information which is already in the public domain (otherwise than by a breach of any obligation of the Licensee) or to information required to be disclosed under any binding legal obligation in a relevant jurisdiction.

11.2 No waiver of any term or condition of this Agreement shall be deemed made unless such waiver is in writing and signed by the waiving party, and any such waiver shall not constitute a waiver of any other provision of this Agreement. Either party may subsequently withdraw a waiver by notice in writing to that effect.

11.3 No amendment or variation to this Agreement shall be effective unless made in writing and executed by both the parties.

11.4 This Agreement may be executed in several parts being counterparts.

11.5 The clause headings in this Agreement are for reference only and shall not affect its interpretation. Schedule A hereto shall constitute part of this Agreement.

11.6 If any provision of this Agreement shall be held invalid or unenforceable in any relevant jurisdiction the remaining provisions shall remain valid and enforceable in all respects, and the parties will attempt in good faith to agree upon a legally valid substitute provision for the original.

12 ARBITRATION

12.1 In the event of any dispute between the parties in relation to this Agreement or incidental thereto, such dispute or difference shall be referred to arbitration under the auspices of the International Chamber of Commerce in accordance with its Rules. The arbitration shall be final and binding on the parties as to all matters deliberated therein.

[**Note:** – Clause 29 of the Shareholders' Agreement may be substituted here.]

13 GOVERNING LAW

13.1 This Agreement shall be governed by and construed in accordance with the laws of [England].

13.2 Subject to Clause 12 above, the parties hereby irrevocably submit to the exclusive jurisdiction of the courts of [England].

14 LANGUAGE

14.1 The English language version of the Agreement shall take precedence over any foreign language version of this Agreement.

15 NOTICES

15.1 Any notice or demand under this Agreement shall be in writing, in English and in legible form, and signed by or on behalf of the party giving it and any notice may be served by personal delivery to the addresses of the parties as given above (or as otherwise notified) or by facsimile transmission (with a printed confirmation of receipt), to the following fax numbers:

IN WITNESS WHEREOF the parties hereto have executed this Agreement on the date written above.

Signed by   )   Signed by   )

)   )

_____)   _____)

)   )

(Director)   )   (Director)   )

for and on behalf of)   for and on behalf of)

[   ])   [   ])

_____   _____

SCHEDULE A
TECHNICAL INFORMATION

Article from *The Economist,* 6 April 1996

MANAGEMENT BRIEF

Keeping cool in China

Many a company sees the vast Chinese market as its best hope for growth. The third in our series of case studies looks at how Fedders, an American maker of air-conditioners, found its way in

IN THE summer of 1995, as the temperature began to soar in Beijing, representatives from more than 200 of the world's air-conditioner companies rolled up at one of the city's many trade fairs. Everybody loved the steamy weather, especially as lots of Chinese seemed happy to fork out around 5,000 yuan ($600), a sum equivalent to several months' wages, for an air-conditioning unit for their homes. It was clear that a combination of China's climate and its growing economy was creating an enormous new market for keeping people cool.

One American company, Fedders, was already hard at work trying to crack this market. Based in Liberty Corner, New Jersey, the firm had got its start in the heat-transfer business by building radiators for America's earliest cars and aeroplanes. It then used that technology to pioneer air-conditioners, especially compact ones that could be slotted into a window or a hole in the wall, and run off household electricity. Fedders is now America's biggest manufacturer of room air-conditioners, employing 2,000 people.

However, the firm faces constraints in its domestic market. Although its sales have grown steadily for the past three years (to $316m in 1995), making room air-conditioners is its only business. It is, moreover, a seasonal business in America, with a huge peak in demand during the spring and summer, followed by a slack time when sales do not even cover fixed costs.

So another line of revenue would be useful. Growth prospects in America are also limited. Although a warm summer can stimulate demand, the American market is largely a mature one in which most customers are buying replacement units. Any big increase in sales would have to be wrung out of a rival's market share—but those rivals are formidable consumer-electronics giants, such as America's Whirlpool or Japan's Matsushita. Three years ago, Fedders therefore decided that the best way to grow was to venture abroad.

The company had already built some overseas expertise by using a global sourcing unit to seek out high-quality, low-cost components. But it was a huge

© David Simonds, 1996

step from that to investing in production facilities of its own in another country.

Fedders decided that Asia, with its steamy climate and expanding middle class, was the best place to go. But where in Asia? The candidates were the three most populous markets: China, India and Indonesia. The company had already been testing the waters carefully, establishing some limited production agreements with firms in China, India and Taiwan, and setting up a small Asian headquarters in Singapore.

Like many other companies, Fedders concluded that, at least for the present, China was the best option. Annual sales of room air-conditioners in China, barely 500,000 five years ago, had risen to over 4m by 1995, making it as big as the American market, but one that is still grow-

ing. On some estimates, only about 12% of homes in the main Chinese cities, such as Beijing, Shanghai and Guangzhou, have an air-conditioner. In Hong Kong, it is hard to find a home that has not got one or more.

Yet entering the Chinese market is never easy. Many foreign investors have had nightmarish experiences of getting burned at the hands of grasping local officials and wily business partners. Promises fail to materialise, rules change mysteriously, and contracts do not seem to mean very much. The problem for Fedders was to feel its way into China while avoiding these pitfalls.

Into the Middle Kingdom

Fedders decided to ask the Chinese for help. One of the first things the company did was also one of its wisest. It hired about 20 people who could speak Mandarin, the official language. Its plan was to employ at least one of them in each of the firm's functional areas. Many of those it hired were American citizens who had been born and educated in China. Some had also been through an American business school.

From the start, it was clear that Fedders needed a local partner. It compiled a list of about 120 air-conditioning producers in China. However, most were

small and weak, so the list was eventually whittled down. By September 1994 one of Fedders's Chinese employees, mainland-born Zhong Liu, was travelling in China with a colleague checking out the remaining firms on the shortlist. They eventually reached Ningbo, an industrial city on the eastern seaboard.

The firm Mr Liu had come to see was the Ningbo General Air Conditioner Factory. His luck was in. Ningbo, which reported to the regional government, had begun producing room air-conditioners in 1978, but still had only a tiny output. The factory's boss, Cai Kang Qian, had been transferred from the local government in 1989 to shake things up. This firm was also in the throes of change, and in the market for a partner.

Mr Cai had taken advantage of China's economic reforms by forming some limited agreements with foreign firms to assemble imported products. In 1991 the firm moved to a new factory in an economic zone just outside Ningbo and increased its output to about 40,000 units a year. It also opened sales offices in the main Chinese cities, set up a network of repair and service centres and established a brand name, Xinle.

But in spite of its booming home market, the Ningbo General Air Conditioner Factory was, like Fedders, worried about its future. It was facing mounting competition, both from local companies, such as Chunlan, a big mainland producer of electrical goods, which is backed by Hong Kong investors, and from a growing number of formidable-looking joint ventures with Japanese, South Korean and American firms, such as Carrier, part of United Technologies Corp. Mr Cai decided that his factory, too, needed a joint-venture partner, but he had not been impressed by any of the potential suitors—except Fedders.

Mr Liu also liked what he saw. Ningbo was a good location from which to export (a vital part of the American company's strategy). The Chinese firm's workforce numbered about 500, which was reasonable compared to the bloated payrolls of many firms in China. The firm's facilities were good, and—unlike so many Chinese firms—it was not hobbled by debts to other Chinese companies.

Having got a good report

MANAGEMENT BRIEF

from Mr Liu, the Ningbo General Air Conditioner Factory made it on to Fedders's final shortlist of three. Another team from Fedders visited China in January 1995. This group included Sal Giordano, Fedders's chief executive, Bob Laurent, executive vice-president of finance and administration and Gary Nahai, the president of the firm's international division.

They too were impressed. There was a "good feeling" about the people, says Mr Laurent. "They were business people and running the company to make a profit," he says. "Naturally we wanted to make some changes, but there was not nearly the learning curve required by other factories we saw."

The two sides thereupon reached a preliminary agreement on a capital structure for a joint venture. The goal was to boost Ningbo's production to 500,000 units within three years, half of which would be exported. The joint venture would be responsible for sales inside China, while Fedders would handle all the exports.

How to make friends

Having got the outline of a deal, months of due diligence then followed. During this time Fedders sent more teams to China. They were drawn from all parts of the American company, from finance to engineering, and each included a Mandarin-speaking employee. Managers from Ningbo also visited Fedders's operations in America.

This, say the participants, proved to be a sharp but valuable learning process. Sometimes things that neither side expected to be a problem would be. Often it was simply a matter of interpretation, such as translating the title of chief financial officer into Chinese. Why, some of the Chinese wondered, should an accountant have to be an "officer"? This left Mr Laurent sure of one thing: "If we didn't have our Chinese employees with us, I don't think we would have ever got to the bottom of things."

The effort made by Fedders to understand their partner greatly impressed Ningbo's Mr Cai. He says that both sides recognised how badly they needed one another. When problems did crop up, they were usually solved in the traditional Chinese manner: over dinner.

The embryonic joint venture

also gained the support of the regional government. This was essential not only for legal reasons but also to lubricate wider relationships. When finance from a Chinese bank seemed to have been blocked, the difficulty was explained (again, over dinner) to the vice mayor. A week later, the problem was solved.

Along with other foreign investors in China, Fedders had to take on some social obligations. It did not, like some firms, find the cost of schools, sports stadiums or police stations appearing on the balance sheet. But it did have to agree to take responsibility for all existing employees and to provide them with housing if required. It says it accepted this as part of the price of entering China, and well worth paying.

© David Simonds, 1996

Many western countries forget something rather significant when they enter a developing market: the quality of the product itself. This can be a fatal mistake. Fedders says that from the start it had planned to make its most up-to-date air conditioners in China. It quickly discovered that even that was not going to be good enough. The reason was that many Chinese buyers wanted a more sophisticated product than the standard air-conditioner sold in the United States.

Why? In America, an air-conditioner is little more than a box that keeps the room cool as cheaply and as efficiently as possible. In China, it is a major consumer purchase, and therefore frequently a status symbol. Chinese customers will spend about as much time fussing over which make of air-conditioner to buy as

Americans would over choosing a new car or an expensive hi-fi.

Many Chinese also prefer so-called split-type air-conditioning units. These machines have the unit containing the fan inside the room and the heat-exchanger mounted on a wall outside. As very few split-type units are sold in America, Fedders did not produce them. To enter China, it would have to. This meant a new product had to be designed. The result was a stylish split-type air-conditioner that is lightweight, energy-efficient and packed with features, such as remote control and an automatic air-sweeping mechanism.

In July 1995 Fedders and the Ningbo General Air Conditioner Factory at last signed a contract establishing their joint venture.

The new company, called Fedders Xinle, was capitalised at $24m. The American partner put in $8.4m and a Chinese bank provided an 86m yuan ($10.4m) long-term loan. For its part, the Chinese side provided its existing business and all its assets. Fedders owns 60% of the joint venture, and can appoint three of the five board members. Mr Cai became president, Mr Laurent chairman and Mr Liu, a senior vice-president.

Fedders Xinle's grand opening was held in November the same year. It was quite a party, not least because, despite all the difficulties, this had been one of the fastest joint-venture deals ever to be put together in China. But the story is far from over. The most urgent task facing Fedders Xinle is to ramp up its production this year to 200,000 units, launch its new high-tech prod-

uct, and then hit its target of 500,000 units two years later.

Meanwhile, it also has to make some money. Mr Laurent says he is confident of receiving a quick return on his investment. His optimism stems partly from the sales potential in China, and partly from exports to other parts of Asia, to Japan and (with its new product) to America itself.

There is, though, another way for the joint-venture to return its investment. Entering China has created an entirely new group of potential suppliers for the parent company: companies that used to supply the Chinese partner. Provided these firms can meet the right quality standards, they will also be able to supply parts to Fedders's two factories back home. If just one of those Chinese suppliers can shave $1 off the cost of an air-conditioner in America, Fedders will save up to $1.5m a year, and the Chinese suppliers will have found a huge new market.

Holding out such carrots should help keep the attention of Fedders's new business associates in China. So will the possibility that the joint venture could help drive Fedders into other Asian markets. In Indonesia, for instance, hefty duties are imposed on imported air-conditioners. Those assembled in Indonesia from imported parts attract much lower tariffs. The Chinese factory could be used to supply the parts for an assembly operation in Indonesia.

Securing the supply of enough components to meet all this expected demand has become critical. Last December Fedders announced plans to acquire NYCOR, a New Jersey-based producer of heating and cooling components. One of NYCOR's subsidiaries, Rotorex, makes compressors. These are a vital part of an air-conditioner, but are in short supply. Rotorex is a big supplier to Fedders, and in January 1996 announced that it too was establishing a joint venture in Ningbo.

Hot stuff, indeed. Yet there is plenty of hard work ahead before Fedders Xinle proves itself. There will be many more problems, and lots more dinners needed to sort them out. Still, if Fedders had simply stayed home in New Jersey it would not now be feeling its toes tingle as it takes its first steps in the world's most thrilling new market.

Signatories to the New York Convention (as at 1 August 1999)

Algeria
American Samoa
Antigua and Barbuda
Argentina
Armenia
Australia
Austria
Bahrain
Bangladesh
Barbados
Belarus
Belgium
Belize
Benin
Bermuda
Bolivia
Bosnia and Herzegovina
Botswana
Brunei
Bulgaria
Burkina Faso
Cambodia
Cameroon
Canada
Cayman Islands
Central African Republic
Chile
China
Colombia
Costa Rica
Côte D'Ivoire
Croatia
Cuba
Cyprus
Czech Republic
Denmark
Djibouti
Dominica
Ecuador
Egypt
El Salvador
Estonia
Finland
France
Georgia
Germany
Ghana
Gilbraltar
Greece
Guatemala
Guernsey
Guinea
Haiti
Hong Kong (SAR)
Hungary
India
Indonesia
Ireland
Isle of Man
Israel
Italy
Japan
Jordan

Kazakhstan
Kenya
Korea (Rep. of S.)
Kuwait
Kyrgyzstan
Laos
Latvia
Lebanon
Lesotho
Lithuania
Luxembourg
Macedonia
Malaysia
Mali
Mauritania
Mauritius
Mexico
Moldova
Monaco
Mongolia
Morocco
Mozambique
Netherlands
Netherlands Antilles
New Zealand
Niger
Nigeria
Oman
Panama
Paraguay
Peru
Philippines
Poland
Portugal
Russian Federation
San Marino
Saudi Arabia
Senegal
Singapore
Slovakia
South Africa
Spain
Sri Lanka
Sweden
Switzerland
Syrian Republic
Tanzania
Thailand
Trinidad and Tobago
Tunisia
Turkey
Uganda
Ukraine
United Kingdom
United States of America
Uruguay
Uzbekistan
Vatican
Venezuela
Vietnam
Virgin Islands
Zimbabwe